Literacy, Language and Community Publishing: Essays in Adult Education

Edited by
Jane Mace

MULTILINGUAL MATTERS LTD
Clevedon • Philadelphia • Adelaide

Library of Congress Cataloging in Publication Data

Literacy, Language and Community Publishing: Essays in Adult Education/
Edited by Jane Mace
Includes bibliographical references and index.
1. Functional literacy–Great Britain. 2. Adult education–Great Britain.
3. Publishers and publishing–Great Britain. I. Mace, Jane.
LC156.G7L58   1995
374'.012'0941–dc20   94-47982

British Library Cataloguing in Publication Data

A CIP catalogue record for this book is available from the British Library.

ISBN 1-85359-280-3 (hbk)
ISBN 1-85359-279-X (pbk)

Multilingual Matters Ltd

UK: Frankfurt Lodge, Clevedon Hall, Victoria Road, Clevedon, Avon BS21 7SJ.
USA: 1900 Frost Road, Suite 101, Bristol, PA 19007, USA.
Australia: P.O. Box 6025, 83 Gilles Street, Adelaide, SA 5000, Australia.

Cover illustration (from *The Wonderful World of American Advertisements*, Follett,
1972, originally published 1892): A perfect typewriter, best manifolder. Terms to
agents liberal. Portable, inexpensive, writes all languages. Read Mr. Howell's
opinion: 'I wish to express my very great satisfaction with the Hall Tapage
typewriter. Impressions and alignment are both more perfect than any
typewriter that I know, and it is simply a pleasure to use it. It is delightfully
manageable.' (Signed W.D. Howells.) Send for catalogues and specimens of
work. N. Typewriter Company.

Typeset by Editorial Enterprises, Torquay.
Printed and bound in Great Britain by the Cromwell Press.

Literacy, Language and Community Publishing

Multilingual Matters

Please contact us for the latest book information:
Multilingual Matters Ltd,
Frankfurt Lodge, Clevedon Hall, Victoria Road,
Clevedon, Avon BS21 7SJ, England

Contents

Notes on the Authors

Patricia Duffin is Publications and Training Coordinator with Gatehouse Books, Manchester, and author of *Then and Now: A Training Pack for Reminiscence Work*, Gatehouse Books, 1992.

Stella Fitzpatrick is Publications and Training Coordinator, Gatehouse Books, Manchester, and has contributed to M. Hamilton, D. Barton and R. Ivanic (eds) *Worlds of Literacy*, Multilingual Matters, 1993.

Roxy Harris is Senior Lecturer in English Language Teaching, Thames Valley University and co-author of *Language and Power*, Harcourt Brace Jovanovitch, 1990.

Mike Hayler is a Primary School Teacher in Brighton and an active member of the community publishing group, Queenspark Books.

Sav Kyriacou is Coordinator of the Ethnic Communities Oral History Project, London, and author of 'Cypriots in London — the Greek Cypriots' in N. Merriman (ed.) *The Peopling of London*, Museum of London, 1993.

Jane Mace is Senior Lecturer in Community Education, Goldsmiths' College; and, most recently, author of *Talking about Literacy: Principles and Practice of Adult Literacy Education*, Routledge, 1992.

Wendy Moss is Lecturer at the City Lit Training Unit, London, co-editor of the *Research and Practice in Adult Literacy Bulletin* and author of *Writing Letters*, National Extension College, 1985.

Rebecca O'Rourke is Lecturer in Adult Education at Leeds University and co-author, with Jean Milloy, of *The Woman Reader: Teaching and Learning Women's Writing*, Routledge, 1992.

Helen Sunderland is Tutor/Trainer and Adviser for ESOL (English for Speakers of Other Languages) with the Language and Literacy Unit, Southwark College, London, and co-editor of *Refugee Writings*, Literacy and Language Unit, 1992.

Sean Taylor is a former Writing Development Worker at Eastside, Tower Hamlets, worked for three years as a literacy tutor at Hackney Community College, and is currently writing and teaching in Brazil.

Alistair Thomson is Lecturer in Continuing Education Research and Development, University of Sussex, co-editor of *Oral History*, and author of *Anzac Memories: Living with the Legend*, Oxford University Press, 1994.

Judy Wallis works on a project for adults returning to education at Lewes Tertiary College, and between 1991–93 was Project Coordinator, East Sussex Adult Basic Education Writing and Publishing Project.

(Several contributors have also been longstanding members of the Federation of Worker Writers and Community Publishers.)

Introduction

Now, I will live a realistic life and I will prove to myself that I can learn to write and to describe my life as my deep and realistic sentiments hear it.

(Jean Guy Pelletier, in ITFL, 1991: 122)

I'm not being greedy or anything like that nor am I only thinking of myself; I can read and write but some of us need better education and a chance at the things that we would like to be. (Janet, in ITFL, 1991: 96)

These two extracts are from a book which appears to embody a paradox: a community publication produced from a worldwide network. It embraces a global compass of authorship and language, gathered from a decentralised process of writing and editing. Over a period of a year, the International Task Force on Literacy organised a 'book voyage' to villages, workplaces, homes and community centres, collecting texts such as these from over 40 countries, written by women and men meeting as learners in local literacy projects and classrooms. Alongside the printed texts (each one translated into Spanish, French and English) the book reproduces their handwritten originals, in many scripts and languages.

It was, the editors tell us, intended to provide a vehicle for learners to express their own feelings and realities, in the year (1990) designated as 'International Literacy Year' (ILY); and for the reader, the sense of making a voyage ourselves is evoked not only by the learning journeys described by authors like the two I have quoted here, but also by the maps, photographs and descriptions of political context which preface each section.

The resulting publication adds, among other things, to a cumulative literature of testimonials to the struggle for and the benefits of a full literacy life. Such literature is the expression of those known in our culture as illiterate: the *conscious* expression, as one writer puts it, of those who have historically been confined to a 'busy silence' (Allen, 1989: 9). (The emphasis is on 'conscious': it is not that they have no other means of expression.) The opportunity to describe a life as 'deep and realistic sentiments hear it' and to have an audience and readership for such a description is the achievement of national and local movements of participatory adult literacy education. It was out of these movements that the 'book voyage' grew. By the late 1980s it was no longer a surprise to find workshops on 'learner produced materials' featuring in international conferences of literacy educators (Gayfer, 1987). The other (still prevailing) images of shadowy illiterates, passive and victimised, gave way to what could be called a 'culture of public literacy' on the part of people previously only half-seen by others. This culture is vividly illustrated by the growth of learners' groups and networks; and by occasions such as the 1993 launch of the South African Learners Association in Durban: an event which included

> groups of learners from the various provinces presenting messages in English, Swahili and Afrikaans. *Cultural presentations were made which included the creative work of the learners themselves.* (ILSS: 1994: 7, my italics)

This 'public literacy', taking a variety of forms, has also characterised the work of literacy work in the UK. Over a period of 18 months in the late 1980s, for example, the Wales Student Writing project held four residential writing weekends, nineteen writing workshops, ten tutor training events, and a national writing festival, involving over a thousand learners and their tutors (Morris, n.d.).[1] In 1990, the ILY celebrations included (in Kent) a series of 'writing events' in prison adult basic education (ABE) programmes; newly published magazines of student work (in Lancashire, South London, Dyfed and Somerset); and exhibitions or 'writing walls' of student writing (in Havering and Bradford) (ALBSU, 1990: 23–5).

Participatory literacy education which engages learners in processes of making their reading and writing public to this extent represents a movement towards a democratisation of a previously élite medium of expression. It is in that sense that this literacy movement has converged with another, deriving from a similar democratic impulse: namely, that of community publishing — a movement which extends to constituencies of people beyond those defined as literacy learners, who nevertheless share in common with those women and men (because of other inequalities such as gender, race, disability, class or age) a similar experience of 'busy silence'. The same principles of decentralisation which guided the 'book voyage' is at the centre of the processes engaged in by groups of hitherto unpublished authors in writing and publishing autobiography, poetry and fiction in the community publishing movement.

In both of these movements, there has been one central issue in common: how and in what way to use or to challenge the particular language which happens to be the favoured or dominant one? Mixed in with this question has also been the political controversies about *standards*: both the 'standard' variety of the dominant language in question, and the 'standard' of the literacy in that language which is (or is not) produced by the system of schooling. It is in the UK, as David Corson has suggested, more than anywhere else in the English-speaking world — where non-standard varieties of language continue to be 'stigmatized or socially marked' — that the 'ideology of correctness' is most acute (Corson, 1993: 103). Irene Schwab, referring to the six years' work of the Afro-Caribbean Language and Literacy Project among hundreds of students in further and adult education in London, refers succinctly to the effects of this ideology:

> People using varieties of English other than the Standard have been taught to consider these variations as a sign of their inferiority — socially, economically, and intellectually. (Schwab, 1994: 135)

The UK, despite the 'ideology of correctness' in the English language, is also intensely multilingual (a survey of the thousands of schoolchildren in London, for instance, found that the sum of languages spoken in the homes from which those children went to English-medium school each day was no less than 184 (ILA, 1989)). It is from this context — where both language variety and the relative status of more than one language are at issue — that this book addresses the relationship between literacy education and community publishing, and the choices (or the lack of choices) between one language and language variety and another.

Drawing on 20 years' experience of community publishing and adult literacy education in this country, the essays that follow explore the answers to the following questions that persist in many countries of the world:

* What are the specific issues that face those adults who define themselves as literacy learners (that is, with 'problems' in reading and writing) when they make the choice to write for readers beyond the teacher?
* What are the motives that move other adults (not literacy students) to take part in writing groups, creative writing classes or community publishing projects, and what kind of learning do these activities entail?
* What are the language choices and constraints at issue for both these groups?
* What are the relative power relationships between learners and teachers, between writing workshop members and writing workshop convenors, between authors and editors?
* What is there that we need to know about adults as readers, of all kinds of writing, if we, as adult educators, are to make useful and creative opportunities for literacy and community publishing work?

As recent studies have suggested, literacy is alive and well in an immense range of social and cultural contexts outside that of formal education; and both children and adults face choices and dilemmas concerning their own sense of identity and power every time they decide to use writing (Hamilton *et al.*, 1994; Barton, 1994). The literature on children's reading development has always been disproportionately large in relation to that on their writing development.

However, in the last 30 years, research on the latter in this country has included two major studies: the Schools Council Project on the Written Language of 11–18 Year Olds carried out between 1966 and 1971 (Britton *et al.*, 1975; Martin, 1983) and the National Writing Project Study between 1985 and 1988 (National Writing Project, 1989). These offered powerful arguments for the value of young writers developing a 'sense of audience', and exploring poetic and expressive forms of writing beyond immediately practical ones.

What is missing is still some account of the theoretical and practical frameworks within which *adults*, disenfranchised from the dominant cultural and literary forms, can succeed in creative educational work which effectively develops their repertoires of writing and reading. Sue Gardener, one of the few British researchers in this area, relates this omission to the marginal position of adult education itself (Gardener, 1991: 180). At the same time, in recent years, there has been a strong feeling among adult educators that the times we are now living in — despite the evidence of the 'public literacy' referred to earlier — do not favour creative approaches to exploratory writing.

Certainly, in policy development of arts funding for the promotion of literature, there has been some reason to feel encouragement: 'Everyone should have the opportunity to express themselves in imaginative language, and continually improve their skills in doing so' (Niven, 1991: 5). Writing workshops and community publishing groups, whose work had at one time been regarded as 'of little, if any, solid literary merit',[2] appeared now to have become acceptable a part of the effort to encourage a comprehensive writing opportunity for all. However, set against the powerful and apparently inexorable move towards greater measurability of 'skills' in reading and writing in the statutory funding of education settings which, since the mid-1980s, has been driving in the opposite direction, such encouragement is of little account. In these settings, a sense of entitlement to expressive writing 'in imaginative language' seems, to many educationalists, further away than it has ever been. With cuts in spending on adult and school education has come a growing central pressure to assess and limit the curriculum. As Anne Barnes, of the National Association for the Teaching of English sees it, this tendency is one with an agenda of social control:

> If you can make a series of hurdles which children have to jump over to speak and write English in an acceptable way, it is a good way to control society. Society is much more difficult to control if you make everyone articulate and fluent. (Quoted in Judd & Strickland, 1993)

Policies about the teaching of English in schools have always had implications for adults, particularly the large number of men and women whose schooling did not conform to a linear academic path. Among these are the many people who enrol for adult basic education (ABE) classes each year, declaring themselves 'no good at' reading and writing; those whose first language is not English, but another language (often with another script); and the majority of the population whose dialect does not happen to be that of Standard English. The same ideology of the marketplace which is now forcing schools to compete with league tables of exam results has had its effect on the funding of a curriculum of literacy and language education for adults.[3] What was once proposed as a choice — the opportunity for adult students of literacy or English for Speakers of Other Languages (ESOL) — to gain credits and certificates for their learning achievements — is increasingly reported by organisers of those programmes as a requirement, both on those students and their teachers. Basic funding, in the 1990s, now depends on 'performance outcomes' and evidence of attainment in employment-related reading and writing tasks.

However, since the mid-1970s, both the movement of participatory adult literacy education and that of community writing and publishing have insisted on developing an alternative view (including the 'culture of public literacy') shared by English teachers such as Anne Barnes and policy-makers in the arts such as Alastair Niven. The purpose of this collection of essays is to map out some of the landscape this view represents, not in relation to the schooling of children, but as it concerns a wide range of adult communities and individuals: women and men, young and old, monolingual and multilingual, with or without confident literacy skills. In direct opposition to imperatives to 'improve standards' within a narrow framework, the approaches discussed argue for the effectiveness of a broader and more generous view both of literacy and of literature, capable both of recognising the authenticity of students' and writers' own powers of self-expression and of grappling with the contradictions and dilemmas which this recognition entails. Complex solutions, after all, are harder to provide than simplistic answers.

The contributors bring together some theoretical and practical debates from language and literacy education with those of creative writing and community publishing work; and from a range of experience in these fields, each draws on and returns to the practical business of achieving good learning and development opportunities for the participants. Illustrated by accounts of firsthand experience, the principle common to all of them is that of *democracy*: an idea which, as several accounts suggest, may have uncomfortable lessons to teach the educators as well as the learners. After all, as Bertolt Brecht once wrote, literacy itself implies one group ceding power to another:

> You who are starving, grab hold of the book: It's a weapon.
> You must take over the leadership.[4]

It began from a series of conversations in the autumn of 1992. Rebecca O'Rourke had just finished a year's work with me researching the extent and effectiveness of student writing and publishing in adult literacy education in this country.[5] Our postal survey of some 200 literacy educators, and Rebecca's travels round a range of settings in England, Wales and Ireland to meet with and interview students and tutors had led to a number of findings. Particularly significant seemed to be two changes which Rebecca had noted in the activity since the early 1970s: on the one hand, a decline in *nationally circulated* publications and in specific student writing projects and events; and on the other, a sense that student publishing had 'become ordinary, rather than extraordinary', with small-scale, diverse forms of public literacy (suggested by the examples given earlier on activities in International Literacy Year) becoming more widespread.

Stella Fitzpatrick and Patricia Duffin in Manchester, meanwhile, had been working on an idea they wanted to publish about the approaches they used in Gatehouse Books (the only ABE publishing project in this country, which, since its establishment in 1977 has produced over 40 student publications). In East Sussex, Alistair Thomson had been having discussions with Judy Wallis about her experience as a Writing Development Worker, a post funded as a combination of creative writing and ABE work, and raising issues about both; and he and Mike Hayler had also just begun a research project to understand something of the learning reported by members of the writing workshop and community publishing they both belonged to, QueenSpark, in Brighton.

Meanwhile, the work that Wendy Moss and I had just completed, in teaching a two-year post-graduate diploma course in Literacy and Adult Learning at Goldsmiths' College in London, had given us the opportunity to develop thinking about the relationship of language studies, literacy uses and oral-literate cultures, and how these perspectives influenced the day-to-day practice of the adult education educators who were our students. During the course of discussions among another, similar group of colleagues about approaches to teaching writing in a workshop I convened that autumn, the use of poetry and poetic writing emerged as an important theme — which led Sean Taylor, one of the group, to write an article on the ideas and practices which he uses in his teaching. There seemed in all this to be the germ of an idea for a book which could focus on literacy, creative writing and community publishing. Given the multilingual and linguistically diverse contexts of all this work, I asked three other people with known reputations in the field to make contributions: Roxy Harris, Helen Sunderland and Sav Kyriacou. The result is the book in front of you.

Each chapter describes a particular context in which the reading and writing work described took place (in adult literacy or language classes, refugee groups, oral history and reminiscence projects, and community publishing and writing workshops). Each then picks out some issues which the author explores (such as blocks to writing, transitions from speech to text, control and collaboration); and each, then, asserts some of the features from these experiences which, in terms of effective and creative adult learning, seem to constitute good practice. Each of us also agreed to include something of ourselves, and of our own learning journey within their accounts. As you will see, these take different forms. Some of us have chosen to include a personal account of our own 'literacy histories' in the narrative (O'Rourke, Duffin, Fitzpatrick, Hayler and Thomson); and all of us have included critical reflections on our own practice among the case studies we have described. The book is structured as follows.

In the first section, '*Writers, Publishing and Learning*', three chapters examine the book's key themes, namely the power relationships between writer(s), editor(s) and publisher; the relationship between reading and writing; and the learning entailed in the process of developing writing for publication in a community setting. As Stella Fitzpatrick suggests in the first chapter, 'when writing is offered for someone else to read, the writer's self esteem is offered with it'. Her analysis sets out some of the difficult decisions to be made during the moves from sociable talk about feelings, ideas and experience to writing about these things; and articulates the learning to be gained both by learner-writer and by publisher-educator in the course of preparing writing for a public readership. Using examples from her work with student writers as workshop leaders, as performers of reading, as editorial groups and as individual authors, she identifies some of the risks for an author deciding to 'go public', argues for the crucial importance of creating a 'safe harbour' in which new writers can be confident of respect and trust as they move from tentative draft to public text (whether performed orally before an audience or published for a wider readership); and proposes some guidelines for good practice which embrace both community publishing and ABE.

What do people read? What are the pleasures that reading can offer? Rebecca O'Rourke, drawing on her findings from two national research studies (on literacy student writing development and on creative writing in adult education) and from her own teaching with a women's course and a prison education class suggests that much is still to be done to encourage students to extend their reading repertoire. She identifies an unevenness of attention in research and practice towards *reading* rather than *writing* development, and argues that educators could learn from the new approaches to reading adopted by librarians to help them re-think their classroom use of all sorts of reading material, including community publications.

Mike Hayler and Alistair Thomson relate the development of one of the longest-established community publishing project (QueenSpark, Brighton), of which they are both members, to that of the national movement in writing workshops and community publishing. From research which they carried out with 24 other members of the project, they analyse three kinds of learning reported by participants in this example of the movement: learning related to writing development, learning related to personal development and learning related to democratic practice. While they argue for a recognition of the learning benefits to be derived from activity, they also report that, in the community publishing project at least, participants valued their experience of it precisely because it was not seen as an educational organisation,

The second section, '*Function and Creation*', offers four perspectives on what is argued here to be a false divide between 'functional' and 'creative' writing.

Judy Wallis begins with a reminder that many adult literacy tutors, as well as their students, bring ideas and prejudices to the classroom about what 'good' writing should be like. Using interview material and examples of her own practice in ABE in Sussex, she then develops her argument that an exclusive concentration on functional literacy inhibits, rather than encourages, the achievement of the functional competence it is designed to promote. (An argument, incidentally, that would be recognised by many adult education teachers; Guy Allen, for example, found that most students reported 'striking improvements' in writing for more formal purposes as a result of the 'latent ability' which their experience on introductory courses in expressive writing had released for them (Allen, 1989: 10).) In her view, too, students stand to gain confidence rather than lose it, if their teachers are willing to reveal their own vulnerability as writers.

Secondly, Helen Sunderland, reflecting on her experience as a teacher and trainer working in ESOL, describes the significance of autobiographical writing in English for adults with a variety of first languages and a range of political and cultural backgrounds. Her account of two projects organised in South London with refugees suggests how this 'creative' writing from personal experience, far from being a diversion from the serious business of 'functional' language and literacy work in English, may actually make this easier and more meaningful — as well as providing education for a wider readership.

A key question in literacy education in any country is the question of providing relevant and dignified reading material for adults who are 'beginners' at reading. In policy debates about literacy and development internationally, the question 'Who will write the primers?' is often assumed to be answered by the employing of teachers as authors of simple fictional or instructional texts. Gatehouse Books in Manchester has been answering this question rather differently, with books written by adult students. However (as chapters by Wendy Moss and Rebecca O'Rourke suggest) not all these texts are immediately accessible to someone entirely new to reading. Patricia Duffin, here, describes two approaches to ensuring both the interest and the accessibility of their publications: first, Gatehouse's policy of publishing books called 'Beginner Readers';

and second, the key role they assign to 'readers' groups' (whose task is to offer constructively critical feedback to writers sending them texts for publication). In an analysis of the first, she sets out the delicate negotiation between publisher and student author of a 'beginner reader'; and, in an account of the second, she describes the sensitivity felt by readers in their relationship with authors whose writing struggles are only too similar to their own.

In my own chapter, based on work with three reminiscence projects with elderly people moving from oral discussion to published writing, I explore the losses and gains made between spoken conversation and written text, in the name of 'reminiscence' or 'life story'. Using the idea of *intersections* between oral and written work, the chapter offers examples of the creative moments these can provoke. From an account of changes made by two people — an interviewee/author, and me — to the transcript of her interview, I pursue some of the issues raised in earlier chapters about different (and possibly conflicting) judgements as to what kind of writing feels like *good* writing. Like other chapters (notably Fitzpatrick, Wallis and Taylor) this one points up the need for educators and editors sometimes to surrender our own versions of 'creativity' in writing in the name of ensuring the author's entitlement fully to choose her own voice.

In the third and last section, *'Language Choices and Intentions'*, four writers examine issues in the genesis of written work, and develop a theoretical framework for challenging prejudices about 'correct' writing in classroom and workshop settings raised in the last section. Roxy Harris poses the usual assumptions about 'standard' English in reverse form: why, when the majority do not speak it, is it proposed as the majority form for writing? The research and practice of the six-year Afro-Caribbean Language and Literacy Project on language and diversity in adult/further education settings for which he was the coordinator provides the foundations for a question which, he argues, has hitherto been neglected: namely, the question of how to recognise dialect forms which exist in the interstices between one variety and another — between Caribbean English and Standard English — and, having recognised these, how to make explicit for learners the nature of the language choices open to them. Using examples of writing gathered from primary, secondary, adult and further education contexts, he argues for a more conscious approach to the 'disappearing language' which occurs, often as a result of teachers' unconscious attitudes and influences, between particular varieties of speech and the speakers' written work.

Research describing the distinctive linguistic features of oral and written language informs Wendy Moss's account of the different discourses at work between adult literacy educator and student when the first is acting as a scribe for the latter's text. 'Creeping standardisation', as her chapter argues, may also occur in 'language experience' work. As her evidence suggests, with the best of intentions, tutors make subtle changes in the course of transcribing students' spoken words. From a detailed analysis of four pairs of adult learners and their tutor-scribes using this method to make learner-produced writing, she picks out the potential for mis-hearing and mis-recording when the two people involved are working to different linguistic agendas, and proposes principles by which this important approach to encouraging literacy development can live up to its claims for empowerment.

The Ethnic Communities Oral History Project, based in West London, has worked with members of a number of different language communities. As Sav Kyriacou describes, the policy of writing and publishing experience in the writer's first language, together with one which ensures that the author(s) maintains choice and power in how they express themselves on paper, implies some complex issues to be faced throughout the process: including whether or not the authors actually want their text to be published in their mother tongue or in English; the relation between transcribed speech in one language and its translation into another; and the assumption that an author published by the project should be 'representative' of the ethnic community of which they are a member.

Finally, Sean Taylor, taking up the tensions between writing intended to impress and writing as a tool of expression, discusses the meaning of 'improvement', drawing, like Roxy Harris, on examples from both children and adults. Describing three examples of his own work in East London (in an adult literacy group, a writing workshop and as a writer in residence based in a school) in which he encouraged students to experiment with poetic forms of writing, he argues for the eloquence of the 'living, chaotic powers' of language which both speech and poetry can release. His essay feels like a fitting *envoi* to the collection.

Jane Mace   September 1994

Notes

1. None of the student-writers in this project chose to express themselves in the Welsh language. As I have learned on a more recent reading of the Welsh language question, the reasons for this language choice, like every other, has political and cultural significance (Mace, 1994a).
2. Charles Osborne, Literary Director, Arts Council of Great Britain, quoted in Maguire *et al.* (1982).
3. See, for example, ALBSU (n.d.). It has also been noticeable that the theme of the 'costs to industry' of a nation's perceived level of illiteracy has been gaining currency in recent years, with 'business leaders' now adding their concern to claims that 'poor basic skills' cost them money. One figure currently favoured by the tabloid press, always used out of any other financial context seems to be '£4.8 million a year in lost

orders, mistakes and retraining' (*Daily Mail*, 22 March 1994: 'Age of the Illiterate', p. 1). A variant on this is a radio commercial being used at the time this book was going to press, inviting companies to find out more about how they could help resolve the problem on the basis that 'poor basic skills cost an average company £165,000 a year' (Classic FM radio, March 1994).

4. From Brecht's poem, 'In Praise of Learning', reprinted in Hoyles (1977).
5. Funded by the Leverhulme Trust, the research was fully reported in O'Rourke & Mace (1992); aspects of the findings were also discussed in O'Rourke *et al.*, (1993) and Mace (1994).

References

ALBSU (Adult Literacy and Basic Skills Unit) (1990) *International Literacy Year*. London.
— (n.d.) *Accrediting Basic Skills: Basic Skills and the National Curriculum*. London.
Allen, G. (ed.) (1989) *No More Masterpieces*. Toronto: Canadian Scholars' Press.
Barton, D. (1994) *Literacy: An Introduction to the Ecology of Written Language*. Oxford: Blackwell.
Britton, J. *et al.* (1975) *The Development of Writing Abilities (11–18)*. London: Macmillan.
Corson, D. (1993) *Language, Minority Education and Gender: Linking Social Justice and Power*. Clevedon: Multilingual Matters.
Gardener, S. (1991) Learning to write as an adult. In D. Barton and R. Ivanic (eds) *Writing in the Community*. London: Sage.
Gayfer, M. (ed.) (1987) *Literacy in Industrialised Countries: A Focus on Practice*. Toronto: International Council for Adult Education (*Convergence* XX (3–4).
Hamilton, M., Barton, D. and Ivanic, R. (1994) *Worlds of Literacy*. Clevedon: Multilingual Matters.
Hoyles, M. (ed.) (1977) *The Politics of Literacy*. London: Writers and Readers Publishing Cooperative.
ILEA Research and Statistics Branch (1989) *Language Census*. London: Inner London Education Authority.
ILSS (1994) *Newsletter* 9 (February). St Lucia, W.I.: International Literacy Support Service.
ITFL (1991) *Words Are What I've Got: Writings by Learners from all around the World during International Literacy Year*. Toronto: Sister Vision Press.
Judd, Judith and Strickland, Sarah (1993) Illiterate England, *Independent on Sunday*, 7 Feb.: 19.
Mace, J. (1994) Literacy interests or literacy needs? Contexts and concepts of adults reading and writing. In *Convergence* XXVII (1): 58–66.
— (1994a) Drink in every word: Learning about Welsh literature. *RaPAL Bulletin* 25, 12–20.
Maguire, Paddy *et al.* (1982) *The Republic of Letters: Working-Class Writing and Community Publishing*, p. vi. London: Co-Media.
Niven, A. (1991) Literature Discussion Document. *National Arts and Media Strategy*. London: Arts Council.
Martin, N. (1983) *Mostly About Writing: Selected Essays*. New York: Boynton Cook.
Morris, M (n.d.) *Wales Student Writing Project Report, January 1988–December 1989*. London: ALBSU/Welsh Joint Education Committee/Cyd-Bwyllgor Addysg Cymru.
National Writing Project (1989) *Becoming a Writer*. Walton-on-Thames: Nelson.

O'Rourke, R. (1993) Student publishing in adult literacy. *NALA News* (Spring): 2–5. Dublin: National Adult Literacy Agency.

O'Rourke, R. and Mace, J. (1992) *Versions and Variety: Student Publishing in Adult Literacy Education*. London: Goldsmith's College. (Available from Avanti Books, 8 Parsons Green, Bolton Road, Stevenage, Herts SG1 4QG.)

Schwab, I. (1994) Literacy, language and identity. In M. Hamilton, D. Barton and R. Ivanic *Worlds of Literacy* (pp. 134–43). Clevedon: Multilingual Matters.

Stewart, C. (1991) Literacy and community publishing. *Literacy Broadsheet* 32 (Mar.). Australia: Adult Literacy Information Office.

1   Sailing Out From Safe Harbours: Writing for Publishing in Adult Basic Education

STELLA FITZPATRICK

Talking about becoming a published writer (Tynan 1992: 7–10) Sheilagh said,

> Nobody ever my lifetime had ever picked a piece of work up of mine and said it was worth really anything. I've suffered isolation; a thirst for education; for wanting books. I've felt very vulnerable because I've felt the poor quality of my reading and writing. Now, I felt, these people are interested enough to like that piece of work I did. If someone said to me, what happened to you that year, *that* would have been it. It just blitzed me. It did something new for me.

'These people' were the Gatehouse peer readers, who selected Sheilagh's writing for publication. We'll return to them soon. What 'blitzed' her was her writing being thought good enough to be in a book.

What constitutes the particular experience of education Sheilagh was having, that freed her to make almost extravagant statements like these? What were the activities that she was taking part in, and the principles underlying them? Was she being grateful for small things, as women often are? One of the things I will argue in this chapter is that apparently 'small' differences are often highly important stepping stones for adults returning to education to build confidence in reading and writing. Unconfidence in an area identified as a childhood learning experience for most is a delicate matter to bring to adult literacy classes. It is the immediate, coveted opportunity which counts and self-esteem has to be risked and may be forfeited, for the acquisition of new skills. In this situation, a shift which recognises strength and identity is not small. It is a powerful fulcrum to lift the load of skills to be tackled. Sheilagh's comment particularises the experience of being chosen, but it is plainly about more than this. Her comment is about safety, attention and worth. When her writing was valued, *she* was valued. Her words reveal how engaging in education as an adult attracts to itself all other areas of worth and worthlessness in a person's self-consciousness. They show how writing expresses identity and because of this, the potential locked into writing is huge.

What other contexts would there have been for Sheilagh's writing, that is, her self, to be appreciated, had it/she not been selected by the 'peer readers' group? Her tutor would have read it, perhaps marked it or otherwise commented on it to her. If Sheilagh is in a group, the group might have taken up her writing about her mother and treated it with care. A class or college magazine might have included it, or maybe a creative writing group would have discussed it and thus acknowledged her effort. These are the possibilities we may cite, but to what extent are these options feasible or available in the present income-generating, functionally oriented climate? Gaye Houghton writing in the RaPAL (Research and Practice in Adult Literacy) newsletter (1993: 7) outlines her experience of having to prioritise the demands of funders in her work as a college-based coordinator for an adult training scheme, and concludes:

> The demands of funders will become all-pervasive and ... many basic skills tutors will be forced into serious professional disquiet about the way they have to deliver Basic Skills programmes, no matter how strongly they adhere to the 'traditional' ABE philosophy.

The prevailing educational mood is not about reflection on past and present experience through writing, scribed or self-written. The shift which focuses attention on the self can be overlooked or remain unperceived in an accreditation driven plan. But if this recognition is a pre-condition for internal shifts which lead to new realisations for a student, then maybe we are relinquishing a vital element. Reporting on a year spent identifying and reviewing the extent of student writing in the UK, Rebecca O'Rourke reminds us (1992: 60–70) that there is no evidence to show that developing personal writing skills prevents people from achieving job-related outcomes. On the contrary, she affirms that a widening of the curriculum to admit student writing and publishing would provide a broader base of language skills and confidence from which to move forward. Similarly, Josie Pearce and Adele Tinman and others (O'Rourke *et al.*, 1992: 10–8) identify the polarisation of accreditation-based basic skills work *versus* student writing and publishing and urge the integration of the two areas, using examples from their practice. However, hard pressed literacy tutors may struggle to find space to integrate creative-writing development work with the demands of an accreditation-based curriculum and newer tutors, influenced by the new model, may see the development and publishing of writing as an irrelevance.

Attending to the person through what they choose to reveal about themselves and their ideas in speech and writing is an underlying principle of effective adult education. This principle is doubly important to the transactions between adult literacy educators and their students, where an individual steps forward into a potentially face-threatening situation. The juxtaposition of 'threatening' and 'safe' marks the encounter from the outset. In what follows, I want to describe how the glimpses of self shared with the world through the person-centred education embedded in writing/publishing activities within adult basic education (ABE) can combine safety with danger in a dynamic and liberating way. First, I will introduce the writers whose experience and words inform this chapter, then I will discuss the idea of 'safe space' *versus* the 'dangers of autobiography'. Next, by reference to other studies of literacy and writing, I want to distinguish between the conscious decision of literacy students to develop their writing for publication and the everyday uses which women and men may (or may not) make of writing. Then I will describe two activities by which people making this conscious decision can be given the opportunity to risk public exposure from the security of the safe space and, finally, bringing in my literacy work with a single writer, I return to my central paradox, namely that public achievement from this origin also depends on public statement of previous failure, and that while this originates in the safety of the trusted group, it depends on the danger of reaction from an unknown public.

The Writers

This chapter is framed around my work with several student writers from adult basic education.

Sheilagh T is a woman in her fifties. A warm, strong and intelligent contributor to group discussions, she is both supporter and supported in her relationship with Gatehouse, a community publishing organisation, based in Manchester, UK, developing and publishing writing with people from ABE. She plays a role on the management committee of Gatehouse and her writing appears in *Telling Tales* (Tynan, 1992). Generous with her time and full of energy, Sheilagh only sags when it comes to getting words down on paper. Her visual impairment has dogged her progress through education. My relationship with her began when her writing was selected for publication in 1991, and is as an editor and collaborator.

Victor G lives on a windswept housing estate in north Manchester. Imaginative and creative in his writing, he uses colour and metaphor to show his vision of the world. He is the author and illustrator of *A Guide To The Monsters Of The Mind* (Grenko, 1991) and is also represented in *Telling Tales* (Grenko, 1992). Always questioning and interpreting, Victor is often excited by ideas.

From time to time anxiety and vulnerability overwhelm him and he suffers from mental ill-health. I met Victor first in 1988 at a writing workshop, when his cartoonist's skill was much in demand. Later, I was his editor for the development of *A Guide To The Monsters Of The Mind* and *Telling Tales*. He and I collaborated in writing about the experience of developing his colourful cartoon book (Fitzpatrick & Grenko, 1994).

Peter G is a Yorkshireman who speaks directly, offering perceptive responses to others in the writing workshops he leads with me, using his own account of his lack of literacy skills as a tool to draw out other histories. Peter's writing is thoughtful and full of imagery. I have acted as his scribe on several occasions, one of which is detailed in this chapter.

Dorothy B was born in Jamaica. Orphaned as a baby, she was brought up by aunts. She had no formal schooling until her early teens. Dorothy is a keen writer, documenting events in her life as a way of externalising and reflecting upon them. She and I have been on writing weekends together and have worked together in the 'peer readers' group, as I describe later in this chapter. I have found her to be warm, spontaneous and very conscientious in this work. I also refer to Alan, Chris, John, Jim, Pat and Victoria for whom Gatehouse is one point of contact in their otherwise busy lives, working and educating themselves.

Safe Space

Returning to education as an adult often entails a struggle. Fatigue, lack of self-esteem, material things like securing a grant or organising childcare can be difficult obstacles to overcome on the way. Once people are enrolled on a course, conflict can continue if partners feel insecure about the changes education brings. (Kath Newsham (1983: 18–20) for instance, in describing her increasing confidence, regrets her partner's dislike of her new self through education. 'He says I've changed quite a lot through coming here and he doesn't like the change.') In spite of the struggle, once inside the classroom, what many call their 'second chance of education' brings an allowance of time and space to pursue personal priorities. As educators, we undertake one half of an implicit bond, in providing for this hard won space. Within our work with groups and classes, we aim to cultivate above all a basic foundation of trust, whether we teach basic skills to adults, computer skills or a stylistic approach to English literature. This can be identified in the interest which informs the transactions between student and tutor: mutual respect for experience and point of view; the integrity which underlies suggestions for procedures and areas of work; and shared goals in pursuing the acquisition of new skills and knowledge. This sense of rootedness and safety doesn't preclude disagreement or disappointment.

Rather, it provides a basis from which to articulate this, and hopefully to deal with and accommodate it.

For example, writer Chris Curley felt that his writing had been condensed and stifled because it had been identified as a text for adult beginner-readers and therefore required to be short and succinct. This fact had to be acknowledged and negotiated as Patricia Duffin describes (this volume, p. 81–96). During the evaluation workshop for his second published work, *Telling Tales*, Victor Grenko reflected on his dismay at the length of time between writing and publication:

> By the time you get published, the sparkle's gone. When you first begin, you don't realise how long the actual process will be. You're waiting for so long, you almost give up on the work altogether. It gets done and you feel good but it's hard to explain. If you went to the shop and bought a cake and they said to you, 'You can't eat that cake for four years', this is what I'm getting at.

Both Chris and Victor are voicing their disappointment in an aspect of embarking on the process of publication. But the experience they are reviewing has also provided a richness which includes risk and challenge. At the launch of his book, *The Cardigan* (Curley, 1993), Chris read extracts from his writing before a 100 people. During 1990 Victor travelled to a conference and talked to a group of academics and professionals about the experience of documenting mental ill-health. Paradoxically, the safe space enables risks like these to be taken. Its function is to provide support so that the individual can stretch or be stretched. It is a space in which to experiment or make mistakes, rather than to be bland or cosy, where certain stifling pressures can be released and other exacting challenges presented, by the individual, or by the educational setting. The dynamic comes from this.

When the space is safe, it can be temporarily moved away from areas of danger through facing new experiences, which offer a risk of loss of face, real or imagined. In the environment of literacy publishing, people are, in effect, achieving a public attention through the medium of their weakest skill. Their strength and identity must shine out (and inwards, to themselves) or be diminished. For tentative and unpractised writers, publicly offering personal writing for others to share is an intensely risky activity. As Sheilagh put it: 'The most important thing for me was to stand up and read something in public. You don't know what that cost me. Nobody will know what that cost me.' When writing and writer go outside the safe group onto a more public platform, (as when an autobiography is sold and circulated) the experience is like making preparations, in a trusting and trusted harbour, for a voyage into the unknown. The cost of 'going public' is high, but so are the rewards if what you offer is accepted, because positive values accrue to the person through acceptance of the writing. I believe that trusting relationships which promote new endeavour are fundamental to the best forms of education.

A safe space allows people to change roles. Undertaking the initial risk meant that Victoria became a performer, experienced with audiences, with her African robes of brilliant colour and Patwa poems. Peter became a subject for television, a raiser of funds, a workshop leader of especial sensitivity because of his own history. John became an administrator, a writer, a publisher. And I have become an editor and theorist. These are a few of the roles we have undertaken, because we were provided with a safe space in which to rehearse them.

There are times, however, when the safe space doesn't provide all that is needed by participants. Listening to tapes of a series of interactions with one writer, for instance, reminds me of how out of temper that person became about the possibility of change to their writing, and how insistent that person could be, when their expected outcome was threatened or not realised. I remember how on these occasions I invented reasons for absenting myself, albeit briefly, from the talk, in order to give myself some relief, to consider what was happening and to recover my own opinions. Safe space is what educators try to provide and what we need for ourselves. It can feel risky, as a tutor, trying to create the space. It is a struggle, often with self-doubt, rather than something fostered by a super-educator, operating from a position of great internal strength.

Educators are crucial catalysts in their students' learning. The very regularity of our meetings, often held in battered old premises, is an ongoing opportunity for learning and growing, both for ourselves and for our students. In my own experience of safe space, as both receiver and provider, some things need to be constant for this learning to happen. Listening always has to go on, face to face, through writing, or by audiocassette. For example listening to a cassette tape away from the activity it has recorded, in order to transcribe an extract or check some aspect of the process, often reveals to me more about the activity than I had perceived as an absorbed participant. The listening might bring clarity about what someone actually said and meant, rather than what I thought they meant, or it might show me how I need to wait rather than rushing in to fill a silence. Through what is said (or suppressed), the power relations within the interaction are mapped out, and these do not always favour the tutor, as my example in the previous paragraph points out.

As I have already stressed, when writing is offered for someone else to read, the writer's self-esteem is offered with it. We create security in a context of writing by attentive listening (as well as contributing) to ideas, expressed in talk initially. Then, once members of the group have started writing, we need to suggest time and space to work again on the first draft. At this stage the listening, from ourselves and from the other members of the 'safe' group, becomes constructively critical. In education for literacy, group members are usually encouraged to write or dictate their words immediately in the supportive atmosphere of the workshop, rather than alone at home (though of course this happens too). In this environment there are fewer unrelated interruptions, others are also writing, spellings can be swapped, and reading and talking about each other's work can go on. It is this network of question and response, discussion and listening which recognises the worth of the message and provides a springboard for its public airing.

The Dangers of Autobiography

When a book goes out which reveals the author's lack of education there is a collision between the acclaim awarded to a published writer in our culture (as evidenced by the literary prizes and the popular signings in bookshops) with the shame of semi-literacy, a shame that other people feel that those called 'illiterate' ought to or that they do feel. It takes some courage. *Why* then should a student-writer want to agree to be published? Is the book for their family? Is it a tangible sign of their achievement, a proof, like an exam certificate or a degree? Is it a step out of the shadows into the main cultural stream, a 'normalising' of the endeavour of living and thinking, as written about? Or is it a message to the world and, in particular, to others in the world who feel themselves to be ignorant as well as 'illiterate', that there is another vision to be had of the meaning of literacy itself?

All writers feel themselves vulnerable when their words are consumed and weighed by others The edge of risk is intensified, however, when weakness or handicap is revealed through the writing. In Victor G's words,

> If you write about yourself then you strip yourself naked towards other people and they read your book and say, 'Ah, that's that person'.

The glossy quality of a book's production can strengthen a writer but the words 'adult basic education student' can sap them. The safe space of the original group is the opportunity to weigh these matters, if they loom large enough to be disturbing.

The mixed message of publishing work by authors defined in this way means that frustration and anger are inches away from feelings of satisfaction and achievement, especially in face-to-face encounters. Feeling vulnerable, since mental ill-health is a stigmatised area, Victor G decided to remain anonymous at the launch of his book. He savoured the celebration and praise, but was unable to claim it for himself in person. His achievement was underpinned by his lack of achievement.

A public signing of the book by the author is a convention adopted from mainstream practice which generally works well for community publishing too.

However, at the launch of Gatehouse's collection *Just Lately I Realise* (1985) two of the writers were at an embarrassing disadvantage because they sign their names with laboured difficulty instead of with a flourish. For them too, celebration was close to humiliation.

The sense of danger is also there in the public encounter through the book. A custom in many books of student writing is to provide a glimpse of how the writing looked in an early handwritten draft. The point of this is to reveal to other would-be writers that all of us need to scribble, cross out and adjust spellings before writing reaches its untouchable, printed stage and, in so doing, to empower them in turn, to recognise their potential as writers. Susan saw the point of it, but didn't feel strong enough to present this side of her writing. 'I've always been put down by my Dad. This is a chance to show my family what I can do.' She couldn't afford to risk her fragile self-esteem.

Vindication or Irrelevance?

Kathleen Rockill (1993: 156–75) writes of Hispanic women who are stopped from leaving the house to attend literacy classes by husbands who exercise power through sexual control. She shows that for these women the politics of literacy are exercised in terms of language, gender issues and sexual oppression. Similarly, Jennifer Horsman (1994: 169–81) in her study of a group of women in rural Nova Scotia shows that the same oppressive forces are at work disorganising their lives and frustrating their educational aims. She goes on to argue that the failure of the women she interviewed to achieve their job-related goals in attending literacy classes is because of a mismatch between their literacy goal and the reality of job opportunities in the area, and unrelated to any power of literacy acquisition itself to transform their lives. Through researched, carefully documented accounts such as these, we learn the circumstances and factors contributing to the low self-esteem of those women. These writings are a body of evidence. But many of us frequently listen to stories such as these in our professional lives. The written accounts by students of literacy which survive to publication constitute another body of evidence, particularly for readers whose lives follow similar patterns. They are, for some of these readers, the expression of their own hopes, reliefs and frustrations. They offer a proof that causes outside an individual's control can affect opportunity for learning. Each individual success means hope for their own attainment of skills and a visibility for the neglect, oppression or illness which has blocked their progress in childhood or in adulthood. For others, testimony from a fellow student does not mean vindication but serves to increase the distance between the present and attaining their own literacy goals. The tangible success of others can fix some learners all the more securely in unconfidence about their own ability.

However, those educators and professionals who say, 'Not *another* book of student writing!' or who leave the books to gather dust in the resources cupboard (O'Rourke & Mace, 1992: 51–9, O'Rourke, this volume, pp. 23–40) are contributing to the misguided notion that a curriculum influenced by a body of work controlled by learners themselves counts for little, instead of seeing the significance for many of testifying to an important experience and the cumulative persuasiveness of an accumulating body of work.

The early piece of writing completed and approved by the writer, and the discussion that springs from it in the group she is part of, are important breakthroughs to her feeling her influence on the world. When a group of people are prepared to be an audience and make space for each other's writing, the group coheres around the central activity. The individual writer is focused on and 'listened to' and has power to try out writing and potentially to discourse with unknown others. She has opportunity to retell and reconsider significant experiences while practising those basic skills she stepped forward to learn. An excitement is generated about uncovering shared areas of experience and presenting them through writing for more public consumption. For the student of literacy these can be wide-ranging, but practising recording one's own words in some form is a necessary part of achieving them. David Barton & Sarah Padmore (1991: 62–74) document the uses of writing in an in-depth study of a small group of people in Lancaster, UK. They found a surprising number of the people they interviewed wrote personal accounts sometimes to share and sometimes for themselves alone. But both they and Shirley Brice-Heath (1983), who studied the literacy practices of communities in the southern United States, note that most of their subjects decline to write unless obliged to for essential purposes like noting a date on the calendar or communication with their child's teacher. In contrast, the student of literacy has made a conscious decision to shed this position of a 'non-writer' in the determination to strengthen their grip on the written word. How we encourage them to go about this is a matter for our principles, practices, our curriculum and our strengths as teachers.

Fostering a Public Interest

So far, I have been arguing two points: first, that composition and the expression of opinion and experience through writing is central to the work of teaching literacy skills to adults; and second, that the practice of making this writing available to a wider audience in some form is an extension of this which sets up a dynamic tension between reward and risk of failure. I would now like to go on to describe three activities connected with these themes: performing or reading writing aloud to an audience; leading a writing workshop for peers; and reading and responding to the writing of peers.

'And now I'd like to introduce the writer'

Speaking your writing aloud to an audience is another telling of the message, another publication. It is the making of an *entertainment* out of the struggle to capture and express thought. It encourages appraisal, shared or unshared, of message and of writer. For the audience at least, the activity is beyond the written page. They hear the results and may catch glimpses of the hard effort. Those members of the audience who have themselves read their writing aloud to a group of people will have gathered increased awareness of their current role as participators in the event. But some audiences are not familiar with public readings as an activity. Although a sense of engagement with public address or public testimony may develop through school, church or legal courts, or more informally through 'turns' at family parties or the 'karaoke', an individual's active participation in any of these literacy events may be minimal. Consequently, uncertainty and unease may be felt about response as a member of an audience. Some talk is necessary outside of the public event about how an audience plays a part in receiving and encouraging performers and how the role of receiver/reader might be reversed. An opportunity to read aloud through sharing writing in an informal group is a good way of giving context.

For the performing writers and readers, the activity brings a mixture of apprehension and pleasure. It puts matters into their hands, for the substance of it is produced from their work, by them rather than by a tutor. This shift of mode and protagonist is liberating and alarming. Planning the entertainment, rehearsing and timing individual contributions is absorbing work. Often, the imminence of direct confrontation with an audience forces re-appraisal of the writing and last minute adjustment. Interacting in a public way with the audience may require the writing of an introduction, or ad-libbing, gesturing and joking, depending on one's confidence. How familiar the audience is to performers will increase or decrease the perceived risk, but not the struggle, for timidity and the mechanics of reading can interpose themselves between message and audience. Use of the 'safe space' to practise and anticipate is crucial. Sometimes, the writer isn't the best reader of their work. If modesty or anxiety prompts them to choose a substitute, they know where the pauses are and can advise. They know, with relief, when a reader is making their words 'sing'. But in spite of the tensions, a peculiar affinity stretches between performer and audience. Sensing the delicacy of the reader's confidence and the extent of their courage, the audience responds.

The writer as visiting speaker/workshop leader

It is always hard for new writers to organise their thoughts and find the words for writing. Few have experience of the processes, practical and intellectual, of developing first draft work to published text. As part of the strategy to explain and demystify the process of publication, we find it is important to ask our writers to find a way of talking about the experience to others. Not only does this encourage the writer to examine again the spurs, the difficulties, the process, but she must engage with an audience again and select what will summarise the experience and interest them. By telling of her journey to publication she can draw out her audience's stories of their writing journeys. Again, this needs a 'safe space' to plan and anticipate before the risk is undertaken. Sheilagh, for example, had to believe that her history as a writer was interesting to other people, and that by telling her story and drawing out those of her audience she could fulfil her aims as a visiting speaker. For her to be persuaded she needed three realisations: trust, a recognition of her achievement in successfully going through the process of being published and a model of how the session might be structured. She had to know what she had to offer before she could offer it.

Between March and July 1993, I coordinated a course developed specifically to further the idea of writers sharing their writing and publishing experience (a magazine, a book, an exhibition) with other audiences, through workshops. I worked with a group of writers, among them Chris, Dorothy, Peter and Victor, who found it interesting to look more closely at how to lead a workshop about their experience. The course was conceived within an ABE context. It began with group participation in a residential writing weekend and comprised 14 weekly sessions of three hours each. Twelve writers took part. Each session consisted of a two-hour workshop, a break and a period for evaluation and discussion. Although Gatehouse workers devised and planned the course, we were learners too, since we had not attempted to implement these ideas practically before. Over the weeks, a range of course leaders, mostly professionals and one student writer, led sessions in their particular area of specialism. The content of the course comprised a central theme of how to plan and lead a workshop, combined with the related special topics introduced by course leaders, such as 'relaxation', 'working with memories', 'using the tape recorder', working with an audience', and so on. During the sessions the leaders introduced activities and groupwork on their topic. They also explained how and why they had planned these activities and recapped on how they had carried them out as well as how each activity furthered the aims of the workshop. This process provided much material for evaluatory discussion at the end of each session. Notes from these workshops were kept and circulated to each participant, in order to build up a record of the course as a resource for later work.

As the course continued, we learned that more time should have been allowed each week for reviewing as a group that week's workshop and the direction and impact of the total course, rather than providing only for individual evaluations. There were also times during workshops when one individual dominated or monopolised group time on a repetitive theme. We had a collective strength to deal with this through discussion and through building into the course structure an opportunity to think about what promotes active participation and what destroys it.

Towards the end of the course each student-participant took part in a series of individual and small-group tutorials to enable them to reflect on those parts which were particularly interesting to them, and to plan their own personal workshop. Shortly after this, individuals tried out their planned session on the rest of the group, using aspects of their writing experience or the process of being published, or some other aspect of their personal history as the central theme. They received comments and opinions, spoken and written, to help them evaluate the effect of their workshop. The course has been followed by invitations for participants to lead workshops with other groups, wishing to share in these writers' experiences and use it as a spur to action for themselves. As well as a centre of interest, the course has provided the prospect of future 'freelance' work, paid and unpaid, for the writers involved.

Reading and responding to the writing of peers

As a grant-aided organisation in the voluntary sector of education, with income from sales of its books, Gatehouse must operate efficiently as a small business and keep the needs of its readers as well as its writers in mind if it is to continue and survive. An important element in this strategy is an awareness of what the market is interested in reading. It is partly in order to help us determine the interest of this reading public that we ask student writers from ABE and some tutors to join Gatehouse editors in choosing material for publication. Running alongside this practical purpose for a peer reader group's existence is the importance of loosening the power and control exercised by individuals over the process and content of what is selected for publication, to democratise these choices and to allow users of Gatehouse services to influence the working of the organisation.

Groups of 'peer readers' are linked to a specific publication, usually an anthology of writing, and will meet for a limited period until their task is completed, or as in the case of the *readers' group* are convened to deal with the many unsolicited manuscripts which a publisher receives, and are more ongoing and long-term. (See Patricia Duffin's account, this volume, pp. 81–96.) I shall focus on the first of these two types of group. The group given the task of reading and selecting writing for an anthology is dealing with writing on a particular theme, for an identified book: stories, short articles and scripts are whittled down to the few that are felt to be special in some way. Sometimes writers who have contributed these pieces are participants in the group of peer readers, sometimes the critical overview is levelled entirely by other student writers with an interest both in writing and in publishing itself, that bridge from the world of the personal into the public world of print and authority.

When a new peer readers' group is formed with a selection task linked to a forthcoming book these are seven aims I would encourage this new group to have:

1. to work to their brief with a time limit for completion of the task;
2. to meet weekly (if sessions are too spread out, valuable time is spent recovering ground at each meeting and there is a risk that the group won't gather momentum and therefore won't offer gains either to the people who comprise it or to the writers whose work is discussed);
3. to work with pieces of writing which are anonymous but identified in some other way, for example by number (this focuses attention on the writing itself and enables those group members who may not be able to read a title comfortably to identify the piece of writing under discussion);
4. while being honest, to criticise as a sympathetic collaborator who acknowledges the effort involved in writing;
5. to produce reasons for their opinions and choices;
6. to draw writers into their discussion once their work is identified for publication; and
7. to evaluate the process after completion.

The Working Lives Group

In order to make this practice visible, I will describe the process gone through by the Working Lives Group which met at Gatehouse from February to June 1993. The task of this Group was not to select several texts for an anthology but to select one piece of writing from more than 50 sent in for consideration from groups in ABE both inside and outside Manchester. The pieces of writing were entries in a competition organised by Gatehouse and it was planned that the winning piece would be published as the second in a series known as Working Lives. The Group comprised five women and three men, recruited by a letter from me as the convenor, inviting them to join. Some were people I knew in Manchester ABE classes who were writing themselves and interested in talk about writing. Although they had not been through this editorial process before, they were willing to test out the spark of interest they felt in helping to choose material for publication. One (Alan) was a tutor. Others had been in earlier peer readers groups and had experience to share. Everyone committed themselves to meeting regularly for the nine meetings I estimated would be needed and, apart from unavoidable difficulties like illness, we kept to this.

We combined various skills and experiences related to our task. These included experience as a writer; experience of talking about writing; of examining it and encouraging it; experience of being a person with little technical reading or writing ability, which in this context is a positive asset in terms of responding appropriately to texts and pinpointing potential obstacles to understanding or deciphering; and experience of the publication process at first hand.

We met around a table on Friday afternoons, with a plentiful supply of tea and biscuits, and a mike in the middle to record our process. Individuals volunteered to undertake various tasks. Alan said he would organise keeping and distributing copies of writing round the group, Dorothy offered to time-watch our discussions, Pat was willing to take care of the cassette recorder so breaks and asides weren't recorded and tapes were labelled and stored. Peter brewed tea and coffee. I offered to note-take on behalf of the group, though people made their own notes too, and I was also convenor of the group. This sharing out of tasks was a sharing out of power, an insight I had learned from Peter, during the planning of other earlier workshops.

Each of us had a copy of the writing under discussion. We operated by reading each piece of writing aloud, then discussing, it, with a volunteer offering to read each time. Jim, Dorothy, Peter and Sheilagh said they would rather not read. Alan, Chris, Pat and I felt confident in this area, so this was fine. At the end of the first meeting we decided that we'd take home the writings for the following week's meeting to give us an opportunity to preview them. Some of us took audio cassettes, because listening worked for this task, while unsupported reading didn't.

Over the next three weeks we discovered that we dealt with between four and six pieces of writing each session. We evolved a system, suggested by Jim initially, that we'd begin each meeting by reviewing the writing discussed the week before. Any piece judged to deserve a second reading by any participant would be added to the 'short-list' we were keeping. When a piece of writing touched a personal chord, this was respected by the group and the discussion responded to this before coming back to the main task. We agreed that our cumulative comments would be relayed to individual writers at such time as we knew who the chosen winner of the writing competition was, and that she/he would be invited to meet with the group and tell more about what lay behind the writing for them.

After a few weeks I noticed a dynamism and sense of purpose in the group. The energy came from the writing being so absorbing and varied, the ideas sparked by it and from the strengths passing between participants. Peter and Alan, who hadn't known each other before our meetings began, exchanged tapes that were separate from the rest of us about Peter's own writing. Jim and Alan had an ongoing centre of interest too about playwriting and the use of video as an extension to writing, both of which Alan was using in his own writing development work with students. Pat regularly told us of the characters she was imagining and even dreaming about, which came to her after reading accounts of working lives at our sessions. And Dorothy was relaxing too. On one occasion she and Peter shared some Caribbean food, an event which was important to them both. The group itself was becoming the 'safe space' where individuals could feel stretched, listened to and encouraged, while ostensibly serving the needs of the group.

At our fifth meeting, Dorothy said she would read. This surprised me since it was a significant change in her attitude towards reading aloud. She read a long piece of writing hesitantly, often stopping to ask: 'Is that right?' At the end she looked immensely pleased. Spontaneously, we clapped her. Dorothy told us that she had practised in her home before coming to the workshop. I would judge that a number of factors were involved in Dorothy's decision to read at this and every session that followed. Most obviously, it was an opportunity to practise her reading; but also, reading aloud practised and demonstrated her emergent confidence publicly. As Dorothy said, 'When I look at what I've coped with and how I've come through it, I know I done well. I am a strong person.' Additionally, the act of reading enabled Dorothy to take a leading role in a communal activity. It expressed her sense of security within the group. She could count on our encouragement. I think also and importantly for Dorothy, by playing a more active role she gave something back to, in this instance, Gatehouse.

Peter too wanted the group to listen on one occasion as he tackled reading aloud part of a script. I think he wished to convey a series of messages through this activity: he wanted to use this bit of our time for his own literacy needs; he wanted to share in this solo aspect of our participatory activity; and finally, he wanted to demonstrate to people he trusted, who might assume he *could* read, how basic his skill as a reader is and, consequently, the loss he suffers (for he is passionate about books and language) in not being able to read with ease.

As well as the gains for themselves, peer readers were acting as a think-tank for the book which would emerge from their task, and were responding to the writers whose work they were reading. Writers were contacted by letter, at the end of our process. The group and Gatehouse needed to inform them that they had not won the competition they had entered, but that their writing had created a centre of interest and triggered new realisations for the group. We wanted to encourage and applaud them and pass on constructive comments about writing, noted at the time of discussion. These were added to a pro-forma letter about the competition results and sent to each competitor. Some responded by letter or phone apparently encouraged by the comments. The writer of the piece chosen as the winner of the Working Lives competition, Ken Sorbie, met the peer readers group to discuss his writing. At the time of writing, five peer readers have elected to meet at regular intervals, to steer the book *Never Ending Hours* through to publication.

These two activities (leading workshops for peers and acting as sympathetic editors/judges of writing by colleagues) are both extensions of the democratic publishing process we use at Gatehouse. They are about celebration; they are also about comparison, identification, dissent and discussion. This dynamic between critical thinking, self-reflection and the development of ideas is also part of the work I now want to describe between Peter G, the writer I introduced several pages ago, his text and me, working as his scribe.

Work with a Single Writer

In this section we follow Peter G's process of composition during an afternoon when he and I talked about his writing and I scribed his poem 'Morning'. Our joint work arose from two sources. First, Peter needed a scribe. Through the necessity of his lack of literacy, he has evolved a method of producing writing through people he feels a common interest with, who act as his scribes or 'right hands'. This limits his production of writing to certain people at certain times. For this joint work, Peter either uses 'legitimate' time to dictate, such as courses and workshops, or depends on the goodwill of others to attend to his needs as an extra activity. The opportunities for these collaborations are, in fact, occasional and fleeting. 'I'm aware of the time and involvement of the 'right hand' and that puts pressure on me.' But more positively, Peter feels that his writing mood is influenced though not controlled, by the person who mediates between him and the page, and he draws from this.

> If the 'right hand' is full of their own anxieties, I pick this up and I use it to my advantage. I will use my image from where they are coming from, so at all times they are offering me something, unknowing. I don't change my idea, but within what I'm feeling I'll make it golden yellow or really blue.

Peter uses images of 'hunger' or 'feeding' when he speaks about his need for writing and reading support. He can never get enough to satisfy him, because the balance between his dependence and a 'right hand's' interest in or time for the process of developing writing with him is often unequal. The downside of his ability to construct writing through a scribe is very deep anger at the unfairness of his dependency. But anger and unfairness can exist for a scribe too, if demands or expectations outstrip what it is reasonable to expect. Rights and freedoms are involved in transactions such as these. In this instance, Peter has a right to access and expression through literacy and another individual has a right to say no, when more is being asked than can reasonably be given. These are areas for negotiation and awareness of one's own needs as well as those of others.

The second source of our joint work is that I am interested in Peter's compositional process which is controlled and independent while his technical ability to read and write is basic and dependent. I shall demonstrate this apparent contradiction in what follows. These two factors created our mutual interest in meeting and recording our work.

Peter G is represented in the Gatehouse publications *Opening Time* (1986), *Yes, I Like It*, (1984) and *Telling Tales* (1992). His book of poems *The Moon On The Window* is published by Open Township (1989). He is a founder member of Pecket Well college, an independent residential centre for adult education courses in Yorkshire, set up by a group of volunteers, most of whom are basic education students.

Peter writing: First stages

During our afternoon of work Peter referred to 'two seeds planted four months earlier', which he hoped to develop during the course of the afternoon. These two were 'slender stalks with parasol leaves' and 'upon my flesh the words are spoken'. 'Seeds' for Peter are images or ideas he selects to write about and the initial choice of words for these ideas. The seeds are waiting for fruitful germination and for a successful time when a 'right hand' will be available to scribe. Peter had with him also a notebook in which he had written a poem using the first 'seed'. The image he held in this seed was of a small flower, a buttercup perhaps, which grew in ground where a tree seedling lay, waiting for germination. The flower as protector of the infant tree is the inspirational idea behind the poem Peter wished to write. Interpreting his first draft (reproduced on the next page) formed the first stage of composition. We read the piece through several times, finding continual difficulty understanding words in the central part of the piece, but having more success with lines at the beginning and end of the poem. This process, although incomplete because of these decoding problems, formed Peter's re-entrance to negotiation with the text and the original idea.

Words on the page, recording thought, are as necessary to Peter's success with writing as they are to any other writer. However, the process of solitary writing is incomplete for him because recovering the text from the page is difficult: he can only read back what he has written if he does so immediately after he has written it, and only then by relying on memory and initial letter sound (for there is no consistency of spelling for words that occur more than once in his texts). The piece is not recorded, since after a switch of activity, he cannot call it back from the page in its entirety. In this sense Peter's self-written writing is impermanent. What his 'hooks' or written drafts do serve to do, however, is to aid his memory in the recalling of 'seeds' together with certain key words he wishes to use in the final piece. They are first drafts, though limited for the

Liedk   Stoc

Lef Qeen Liedk Stoc Stading

toL pRade oping iti paRSoL

oV Levs op on The GReLod

Sading onR GRoth wi awt

SeL Levs is The paLRoR oV

pLoLan. to The dosing Bes.

theat weRing its kove pLoLan

Lesg it Fhe netR to RaRe tRen

a Gen to See a yoGR GRoth

Sos The GRawd VoLcknos with

moving SoL to ReveL a

Peter's first draft

reasons mentioned previously. In order to begin the technical business of decoding and transferring the original message, Peter needs a 'right hand' or scribe. Without this person, he could not review or add to it: 'It fetches it alive for me when people fetch it alive on a writing pad.'

Middle stage

At Peter's request then, I wrote the initial lines from the first draft and read them back to him. We then left behind this early attempt, and he began to dictate his poem afresh, pausing, thinking and then continuing as he worked to interpret the image contained in the seed. I wrote to his dictation, remaining silent, and judging the end of one line and beginning of the next according to Peter's pauses and gestures. When he asked to hear the piece, I read it aloud and he weighed the words carefully before deciding he had finished.

I offered to write the poem again neatly. At this stage Peter adjusted the shape of the poem on the page, instructing me how to position the lines, so that the finished piece had an internal and external symmetry which satisfied him. The transmission of the image to the page in this way completes the compositional process. This is Peter's poem 'Morning' which resulted:

Morning

Leaf green lean stalk, standing
Tall, proud, opening its parasol
Of leaves upon nature's own sky
Dome-like dance floor invites musical
Bees to dance upon
With honey pollened gaiters
Hokey-cokeying upon their own merry go round
Springboarding off a single leaf.
Shadows reflect upon warm earth
Becoming growth deafening silence
Of a volcanoed single thrust of life
Unfolding two specks of leaves
Born in music.

His speech for this page had come slowly and with pauses. I could sense a conscious manipulation of language and a detachment, a withdrawal. It was as if Peter was trying to achieve 'the optimisation of his performance,' which, as F. Niyi Akinnaso has argued, is usually only attained when a writer isolates her/himself physically and summons those features of written language which have been formally acquired and consciously learned (Akkinaso, 1982: 323–59, 112). The mode which Peter had chosen for this poem was quite different from his conversational speech. The latter is rapid, intended to vanish in thin air once its conversational purpose has been achieved, in contrast to the consciously ordered mode chosen here. As Sue Gardener and colleagues have pointed out (1992: 24), 'talking is relatively unselfconscious ... and as soon as you are writing, it's a very self-conscious process.'

The gap between Peter's agility with written language and his lack of technical literacy skills illuminates again the paradox of strength made apparent through weakness, a paradox which makes Peter's situation interesting but unenviable. Fortunately, his creative energy is taxed but not quenched by the circumscriptions surrounding his production of writing, as this example shows.

My Own Journey

As an editor and educator with people who are subsequently published by Gatehouse, I work with texts which are not mine and with writers who aren't me. My role is to draw out more from the writer, to plant seeds that might flourish, to discuss and negotiate. Working on my own writing, on the other hand, seems to mean a process of bewilderingly endless selection; discovering the unconscious suppressions as well as finding words to state what clearly has to be said. It is about marshalling my ideas and crystallising points of view and about narrative. Fortunately, like Gatehouse writers, I too have had editors to support me and narrow the distance between struggle and articulation. They have reduced the loneliness of writing and invited me into the safe space.

I am sure the books I read during childhood and the radio I listened to growing up in the 1950s, all of it scripted, formed my ideas about possibilities for constructing written language. My Dad, invalided from work with a weak heart for a few years, spent time reading to me when I was very young. I remember a haze of comfortable times, on his knee or the arm of his chair, looking at pictures and listening to the words — an early safe space. First from him and then from school, I learned that books can transport you, that you can change your mood and, for a short time, your identity, through words written on a page. Growing up in a house where there weren't many books and no television, I went fairly regularly to the library after primary school. I don't remember receiving advice about writers to look out for. My test, one shared by many other readers, was to read the first few pages and see if they invited me in.

My awareness of my skills as a writer was formed at school; and the teacher who listened to me through my writing and encouraged my primary school compositions is the influential figure behind my conviction that I can write. My primary classmates, who listened as my compositions were read aloud, the books I read, and radio, also formed my expectations of an audience. I moved from the *I* of myself as narrator in my 'compositions' to the *we* of secondary school and college, hiding as required, behind a passive construction as I juggled the ideas we had discussed in class about how other writers had achieved their effects. As I grew up, I built a picture of myself as someone who could use words and I actually enjoyed lessons where we went below the surface of a piece of writing to look at how writers had done it. I liked analysis and commentary. This combination of my power to use words, my liking for the *how* of writing and other writers' power to move and influence me through words sustained me first as a literacy tutor and then as an educator working as an editor for a small publishing house.

Accelerated spurts of learning and confidence have come for me through the provision of safe space, created through other people for me, and combining security and challenge. I continue to be absorbed in the work of making some voices louder and public, although there are untold struggles to survive and develop. I am enthused by the juxtaposition of community and 'small business' issues, and the strengths which are gained from the reciprocal nature of my work. I am passionate about production quality matching the writing and boosting the writers Gatehouse publishes. I want the expertise we have in print to match our openness and willingness to learn from our would-be writers and readers, and the development of new processes and practices to add to the range of opportunities for students to reflect on and re-interpret their past and present selves.

Conclusion

> Funny enough, even as a little girl the ideas and the ambitions, the dream, started from there. Think of a little girl between seven and nine, to have a dream from then. And grow up all the years from her life, turn fifty, and is at that stage to discover that a dream even from then could come true ... I looking back on those childhood years up to now, and achieving exactly what I always like. Because I always like pen and paper even though I couldn't hold it properly at all.

Dorothy B, whose warmth and enthusiasm for writing and, latterly, for reading aloud I described earlier, said this at the evaluation for the Gatehouse Course, which I describe on page 11. She chooses a dream metaphor to express the importance to her of reading and writing. But for her dreams to be possible depends on a set of ideas which we, as educators who are also learners, work to implement. We create the safe space through our attentive and critical listening and the listening we persuade others to do through our example, through the medium of our own writing and through the practices and processes we support and promote. This chapter has described activities and underlying principles connected with developing and making public writing from ABE sources. It is argued that ways of working such as these should remain within our practice as expressions of both the politics and practice of literacy work with adults. While continuing to develop a pedagogy and to define a framework of standardisation in ABE work, let us also continue to find routes towards literacy which recognise the whole person and provide opportunities to work in a dynamic way with technical weaknesses through individual and collective strengths.

References

Akinnaso, F. (1982) Spoken and written language. *Language and Speech* 25, part 2, 323–59

Barton, D. and Padmore, S. (1991) Roles, networks and values in everyday writing. In *Writing in the Community*. London: Sage.

Brice-Heath, S. (1983) *Ways with Words*. Cambridge: Cambridge University Press.

Curley, C. (1993) *The Cardigan*. Manchester: Gatehouse.

Fitzpatrick, S. and Grenko, V. (1994) Creating '*A Guide to the Monsters of the Mind*'. In D. Barton, M. Hamilton and R. Ivanic (eds) *Worlds of Literacy*. Clevedon: Multilingual Matters.

Frost, G. and Hoy, C. (eds) *Opening Time*. Manchester: Gatehouse.

Gardener, S. (1992) *The Long Word Club. The Development of Written Language within Adult Fresh Start and Return to Learning Programmes*. Lancaster: RaPAL.

Goode, P. (1984) As a castaway vessel. In *Yes, I Like It*. Manchester: Gatehouse.

— (1989) *The Moon on the Window*. Hebden Bridge: Open Township.

Grenko, V. (1991) *A Guide to the Monsters of the Mind*. Manchester: Gatehouse.

— (1992) The Snow Queen. In S. Fitzpatrick (ed.) *Telling Tales. A Collection of Short Stories, Poetry and Drama by Writers from Adult Basic Education*. Manchester: Gatehouse.

Horsman, J. (1994) The problem of illiteracy and the promise of literacy. In D. Barton, M. Hamilton and R. Ivanic (eds) *Worlds of Literacy*. Clevedon: Multilingual Matters.

— (1990) *Something in My Mind Besides the Everday: Women and Literacy*. Toronto: Womens Press.

Houghton, G. (1993) TEED, TECs and traumas. *RaPAL Bulletin* 22, 7.

Newsham, K. (1983) *Where Do We Go From Here? Adult Lives Without Literacy*. Manchester: Gatehouse.

O'Rourke, R. with Mace, J. (1992) *Versions and Variety: Student Publishing in Adult Literacy Education*. London: Goldsmiths College. (Available from Avanti Books, 8 Parsons Green, Bolton Road, Stevenage, Herts SGl 4QG.)

O'Rourke, R., Pearce, J., Ross, J. and Tinman, A. (1992) Wordpower and the publishing of student writing. *RaPAL Bulletin* 19, 60–70.

Rockhill, K. (1993) Gender, language and the politics of literacy. In B. Street (ed.) *Cross-cultural Approaches to Literacy* (pp. 156–75). Cambridge: Cambridge University Press.

Tyan, S. (1992) You never know the value till you see the vacant chair. In S. Fitzpatrick (ed.) *Telling Tales, A Collection of Short Stories, Poetry and Drama, by Writers from Adult Basic Education*. Manchester: Gatehouse.

2 Can't, Won't or Don't: Readers and Writers in Adult Education[1]

REBECCA O'ROURKE

> It is not difficult to make reading impossible. (Frank Smith, 1978: viii)

This chapter explores a complex issue shadowing writing development within adult education: reading. I define adult broadly across the continuum from the Workers' Educational Association and University Extra-mural Departments, through community education projects, to adult literacy and return to study provided in the adult basic education (ABE) sector.

Despite the differences between these sites of educational work — of an institutional, policy and practice nature — I argue that the uneven development of reading to writing is common to each. The Can't, Won't and Don't of the title is a shorthand reference to the disengagement from reading found in tutors and students concerned with writing, whether as part of basic skills acquisition, study skills or creative writing. They are all forms of refusal which, I believe, render the educational engagement with writing less complete than it could — maybe should — be.

My interest in reading arises from a number of sources. I had been aware of the greater emphasis on writing within ABE, but it was clarified by visits to Ireland during 1991–92. A second interest came through observing the way non-vocational adult education classes have developed two mutually exclusive stands: a literature based, reading focus and a creative writing one. Interest in either reading or writing might be expected to engender curiosity about the other half of the process, but this is rarely so. Students of each recognise that reading and writing are linked but, in general, readers are antagonistic to writing, writers to reading.

My third interest is the relationship between reading which is not educationally required and that which is. This developed from my argument that ABE has little expectation of, or guidance towards, a habit of reading. In exploring this I had to examine exactly what I, or anyone else, means by a habit of reading.

23

Two research experiences (looking at student publishing in adult literacy education and at creative writing in adult education) gave some scope to do this and they inform this chapter. I refer briefly to other research studies on reading, but the bulk of the chapter is split between trying to relate to adult reading some of the ideas proposed by one particular writer's arguments about children learning to read. I reflect on two episodes in my own experience of teaching, where students taught me new approaches to reading in ABE. Finally, I return to ideas about promoting the pleasures and uses of reading outside educational contexts which I have seen developed by librarians and would like to see extended into education.

Research Into Reading

The most extensive thinking about reading comes from those professionally involved in teaching reading to children and, to a much lesser extent, adults. Work is weighted to early readers: word recognition and acquisition of basic reading skills, including parental involvement and attitude, the 'real books' *versus* 'readers' debate, phonics, issues of multilingualism and the relation of verbal to literate skills.

There has been some attention paid to the effects on children of what they read. This aspect of children's reading has received disproportionate — often highly distorted — press attention. It is also, as I shall be discussing later, a preoccupation for librarians: the most articulate interest group concerned with adult readers.

It is commoner for the effects of reading ideologically biased texts to be inferred rather than demonstrated. Andrew Stibbs (1991) says there are no straightforward models of reading's effects — whether of an improving or degrading kind. A too simplistic model, he argues, 'does no justice to the idiosyncratic productive role of readers who can find the most innocent pleasures in the most corrupting texts and vice versa' (Stibbs, 1991: 135).

Recent years have seen a shift in the preoccupation with reading effects. The 1950s, 1960s and 1970s were concerned with the effects of comics and American crime novels on the newly emergent youth cultures. More recently, that concern has been displaced onto videos and computer games and the reading issue has now become whether enough reading of any kind takes place.

Feminism is concerned with two quite different types of reading and reader: the woman reader of romance and the male reader of pornography. The Arts Council (Van Riel, 1993) has recently signalled a concern to promote literature and some librarians are worried about the extent to which genre fiction provides the staple reading of most adults. This attention is rarely empirically based.

Unpopular Readers (O'Rourke, 1993), a study of genre fiction, was written as part of the Co-Media Libraries Projects. It contrasts the attraction textual analysis of popular genres has for cultural theorists with their lack of interest in exploring popular fiction's readership and the meanings they construct for themselves. It is based on a small scale survey of library users in Cleveland and argues for more research overall into readers of genre and non-genre fiction.

One of the few empirical studies of reading I found was West *et al.* (1993). Their starting point was that

> ... despite the general belief among educators that reading confers intellectual benefits, the effects of engaging in literacy activities remain under investigated ... [There are] actually very few empirical demonstrations relating print exposure to specific cognitive outcomes. (West *et al.*, 1993: 35)

They did their research in an airport departure lounge, classifying individuals waiting for flights as readers by the criterion of recreational reading for ten minutes. Thus identified, readers were approached and asked to complete checklists and a cultural literacy test, balanced for gender and ethnic bias. The researchers argue that ability demonstrated on these recognition checklists successfully predicts reading behaviour in real life.

They comment that reading research has tended to focus on the comparative information-processing skills of literate and non-literate societies and argue for a shift in focus towards the differences within literate societies.

This research links cultural and linguistic knowledge with reading, rather than reading of a particular type, and supports the view that it is less important what people read than that they associate reading with pleasure, choice and enjoyment .However, with children the assumption is that once the reading habit is established, reading choices will become more discriminating and selective. Quite where this leaves adult beginner-readers is less clear.

An argument frequently made against genre fiction is that it limits people's knowledge, moral outlook and language skills. The argument, and its obverse, that reading 'good' books is an enriching and improving experience is not proven.

Starting to talk, in very preliminary ways, to readers of genre fiction in Cleveland libraries I found reading genre fiction to be more complex than it seems. Before judging such readers — and predicting moral and educational outcomes for them — it is important to learn what exactly is involved in reading genres, which will also necessitate understanding reading as a social process. Academics cannot do this simply by reading popular fiction, because they have been socialised into a system of reading which values these texts and the act of reading differently. The most immediate difference is purpose, which cannot be inferred or imagined by them, but also significant is the range of other reading they have done which will, consciously or not, be in play with their readings of popular fiction.

Reading occupies a small space in most people's everyday lives, unless they are required to read for work or study. Very little is known about how and why people read, the uses they make of reading and the way their reading habits change during the course of a life. At different periods of life, different amounts of time and motivation to read are present for men and women, those in work and out of it, those with different educational experiences, those with and without children. Different kinds of life changes can encourage or discourage reading, as do certain types of work. The nature of reading needs to be established before claims can be made for the effects of particular types of reading, be they literary or popular genres.

The political momentum gathering on questions of reading, from educationalists concerned with young people's reading and the Arts Council and librarians with adult readers, suggests that people think they know what goes on when people read. The evidence from my research suggests they do not. The assumption is that it is easy to decide between good and bad books, good and bad readings. I think the issue is more complex than this. If changes in the way people read and what they read are possible — or desirable — then its first condition has to be a more detailed account from and about readers of their reading.

Reading with Frank Smith

Frank Smith (1978) argues that reading print utilises skills we have already developed as children learning to 'read' our environment — both its physical and its print rich features — and our carers. In my teaching experience I have noticed that when people have not been called upon to exercise either their reading or writing skills for a period of time, say leaving school at sixteen and returning to study in their twenties, their reading skills will have slowed down whereas their writing skills will have broken down. Is this because reading has become more naturalised within our society than writing? Because it is done to satisfy us personally, not an external, often judging figure? Because reading is more immediately useful and pleasurable to us than writing? I don't know. Reading skills appear to lie dormant, in ways that the technical skills of writing seem not to.

I can also see this difference in my brother and myself. On the basis of our writing it would be very easy to spot whose formal, secondary modern education ended at sixteen and whose continued to post-graduate university level. Our reading, however, is not so easily pigeon holed.

Although I read more than he does, our reading is not qualitatively so different. His reading habits and purposes are outside the intellectual and educational frameworks mine exist in, but he has his own framework, both intellectual and educational. He reads widely, adventurously and with some sophistication. Last time I was over I noticed the following books by his bed. Novels by Terry Pratchet and Ruth Rendell, Gramsci's *Prison Notebook*, Samuel Beckett's *Waiting for Godot* and two climbing books: the latest guide to his area and an autobiography. When I asked, I found that he was reading all of them, in dribs and drabs, because they interested him. He suggested I read Terry Pratchet and the climbing autobiography and had enough insight into my reading habits — and prejudices — to address my objections. He too had thought Terry Pratchet would be boringly formulaic but found the book witty and entertaining. The climbing book had the pace of a thriller and an unexpected spiritual dimension which, as he predicted, I enjoyed very much. Later that weekend he skimmed effortlessly through reference books to identify a mushroom I had seen on holiday. Although he exercises it only moderately, unlike my own almost compulsive appetite for reading, he is as skilled and as competent at the activity as I am.

I tell this story to underline something I want the people who read this chapter to be aware of: the rich reading life beyond education and educational purpose. I do not want to bring it under the yoke of educational purpose, but I do want to argue that highlighting its existence and value could usefully be extended to the practices of adult and ABE that are concerned with personal development and social empowerment.

Frank Smith explores the nature of reading rather than how reading should be taught, but the two are linked. His account builds into a subtle — and sometimes not so subtle— critique of the ways in which children are expected to learn to read. He distinguishes between informing and instructing, arguing that the teacher's responsibility is not to teach children to read, but to make it possible for them to learn how to read.

This injunction transfers well to adults too, except that when we contrast the resources available to schools and to the adult learner, it is hard to see how it could be achieved. Most adult learners come to classes for two, or maybe four, hours a week for 30 weeks of a year. They use shared classrooms over which they have little sense of ownership and their tutors may well be peripatetic and therefore unable to provide much in the way of books, charts and so on. The phrase is also charmingly imprecise: we can agree with it without really knowing what it means in practice.

Frank Smith is very critical of the emphasis put on comprehension as a form of memorisation, rather than understanding. This, I think, may be of particular relevance to adults learning to read. Smith argues that we do not learn to read by memorising words and the sequences in which they may occur. Rather, reading is a combination of memory, familiarity and predication. Readers learn to read by letting go of the words and catching the meaning.

> Poor readers read as if they do not expect what they read to make sense, as if getting every individual word right were the key to reading. But the more they try to get every word right, the less they will see, the less they will understand, and the worse their reading will be on every count. (Smith, 1978: 34)

I have seen this in adult learners who treat reading as something to be got through, in mechanistic, rote-learning fashion. These readers rarely go back to material they have read as something to be savoured or its meaning pondered. Unlike readers, these would-be, maybe never-to-be, readers are not motivated to learn by the pleasure of reading itself.

Blocks to Readings

Adult learners usually have three blocks to reading. First, they do not come to reading with the openness or urgency of children, but with the experience of prior failure. Such failure damages self-esteem and invokes enormous anxiety. Frank Smith successfully demonstrates how anxiety tangles the circuits of perception and concentration that are required for successful reading and this must be heightened for adult readers. Yet in my experience it is rare for tutors to discuss anxiety about reading, whereas it is now commonly understood that discussing maths anxiety or fear of writing is very helpful in setting that anxiety to rest.

The second block adult learners have to a receptivity to reading, which Frank Smith argues children have, concerns the naturalised skills of predication and perception. He argues these are the basis of children's ability to pick up reading. Were these skills absent in these adults as children or were they not stimulated in the correct way? Adults generally have lost much of the spontaneous and experimental learning that children engage in. Is something else happening instead? Is there a characteristic mode of adult learning? Can we re-stimulate adults to open up those childhood and childlike pathways?

Frank Smith argues that predictability is a key factor here and he demonstrates that when children start to use prediction to help them acquire reading skills, they are already proficient at predicting within a range of knowable alternatives. The key word here is knowable, which he is at pains to distinguish from known. If a thing is known a child has no incentive to discover it. I wonder how, if at all, this bears on adult learners? I am reminded of the discussions I had in 1991 with some ABE students who complained that publications written by other students all told the same story. The story, as they saw it, was: 'Schooldays, being unemployed, improving my reading and writing' and they commented: 'If you have a problem, you don't want it to be highlighted. You want to read something different to cheer you up' (ABE students, quoted in O'Rourke, 1992).

To sophisticated readers, with other agendas — like the common causes or subtle differences between the circumstances and methods of acquiring (or not) literacy skills, or how their own student publications compare with others — the reading has point and significance. But perhaps to a new reader, who does not yet have other contexts for reading or ways of making meaning from the text, the story is simpler and of less interest precisely because it is already known. And if it is already known then why struggle with a book to find it out?

We need to talk more with students about why they might want to read and what they could enjoy about it. Looking back I realise the groups I have worked with which have taken most readily to reading independently and widely have been the ones where I have done just that, as I hope to show in my account of work with a Fresh Start course in Hackney.

The final block to adults learning to read may be their tendency to equate learning with memorising. This is likely to be the case where, as so often happens, a person with reading and writing difficulties has developed their memory to compensate for those difficulties. I think sometimes as educators we compound this problem by feeling obliged to link books, or reading, to a purpose, rather than the simple pleasure of reading them. This is partly the degree to which we are hampered in the ways we can work. It is, for example, rare for a course to have resources like a book allowance and a borrowing library on site for its students. But it also reflects the anxiety about tutors being seen to teach and students being seen to learn which pervades the British education system at the moment.

Reading in Adult Basic Education

We've got a lot of student publications, but we don't expect any one to read them. (ABE tutor organiser, quoted in O'Rourke (1992))

An opportunity to explore reading a little more systematically came during a research project into student publishing in ABE that I carried out between 1991 and 1992. My brief was to chart the extent of student publishing, evaluate its contribution to student learning and examine the impact of changes in the organisation of ABE, specifically the introduction of schemes of accreditation. I visited literacy classes and projects throughout Britain and Ireland to talk with organisers, tutors and students about writing and publishing. This enabled me to construct a snapshot audit of current ABE practice, but it also helped me look critically at my own past practice as a tutor within ABE. Like any piece of research it generated, through unanticipated problems, areas for future study. The research was primarily about the rationale for students having their writing published or shared with others, but this issue was inevitably linked with reading. As the research developed I became aware of the uneven attention to developing reading skills, compared with writing, in the ABE sector.

This has two consequences for the practice of ABE. First, reading is usually taught only at the extremes of the range — either to people with virtually no reading skills or as study skills to those preparing for further study. The second consequence is to condemn student publishing, and I heard it condemned many times as I travelled Britain doing the research into student publishing later published as *Versions and Variety*.

It was deceptively simple: 'My students don't want to read that sort of thing.' And tangible proof was there too, pristine copy after pristine copy of students' writings displayed, or maybe stored is a better word, in resource room after resource room. It was depressing. Sometimes the uncracked spines were of books I knew, not just as words on the page, but as people who had written them.

Between 1982 and 1988 I worked for Centerprise community publisher and knew the tremendous amount of work and pride represented by what can seem to others simply 'limp grey curling things at the back of the shelf that you'd like to throw away, but can't' (ABE organiser, quoted in O'Rourke, 1992). It was uncomfortable to confront how unread much student publishing was. Had the bold rhetoric of the 1970s and 1980s been, in the end, only rhetoric? People had worked for years, struggling to make sense and meaning out of their ideas and experience because they believed others would read them. And they believed that because I, and people like me, told them their words were valuable and, if printed, would be read and valued by others.

I know too, that Centerprise, and other community publishers in the Federation of Worker Writers and Community Publishers, sold thousands of copies of the books. We had files full of letters saying how much the books had been enjoyed. We couldn't be deceiving ourselves, could we? So, what exactly was going on? It was quite simple really. It was not just student publishing that was unread; learners in ABE rarely read anything at all, beyond the worksheets put in front of them. Tutors did not always read student publishing so they couldn't introduce it and they rarely introduced any other type of reading.

The *Versions and Variety* project identified differences between groups of students attending literacy centres in Britain and Ireland in terms of student and tutor expectations regarding reading. During the research visits, we found that in Ireland tutors and students were as likely to offer examples of reading as writing when discussing how they worked together and where their sense of achievement lay. This was in contrast to the visits made in England, where it was rare for reading to be cited in this way and there appeared to be a big gap between the most basic reading skills and those such as skimming and scanning, summary and comprehension and critical reading. The habit and pleasure of reading, so often spontaneously named as the best thing about improving literacy by Irish students, was conspicuously absent in Britain.

A thread that emerged through this research, and seems to crop up elsewhere is the tension between reading being available and being *made* available. (I discuss this more fully in the final section.) Once I had identified reading as a problematic area in ABE I began to ask tutors and learners about it directly. I learnt from doing this that reading material was often introduced in the form of extracts and with the purpose of generating discussion. I also discovered a great deal of frustration on both sides. Tutors and organisers felt they did their bit by displaying books, and were disappointed at the lack of interest from learners, whereas learners often expressed frustration that they were not guided into reading by their tutors. Learning to read in terms of learning about books was rarely found.

This might loosely be called the promotion of reading and it has only recently begun to be taken seriously for adults, including adult learners in basic education. The work of Margaret Meek (1991), which encourages the development of reading as a meaningful and pleasurable activity and as a means of confirming and developing technical fluency, may well have been adapted to the needs of the new adult reader, but examples are not widespread. Putting literacy or creative writing classes in libraries, for example, is often a well meant but under exploited opportunity to explore the different relationships to books and reading that exist. Too often there is the assumption that learning about the books will happen by osmosis, simply from being surrounded by them. Likewise, the book resources that some ABE learners have access to need structured exercises to develop the freedom to explore that is vital if they are to become real to and valued by them. A learner in Dublin, discussing reading in a group where some read and some did not, made this important point: 'There are different books for different readers. Something must interest you. If you are a confident reader you can decide you don't like a book, if you're not confident, you think it's you.' (Quoted in O'Rourke (1992).)

The research found evidence supporting a number of explanations for why reading was given less attention than writing in ABE, including the difficulties of teaching reading, other than at the most basic level, and of monitoring progress. Learners come to adult literacy projects wanting to learn to write more often than they want to read; but it is also sometimes the case that tutors are more confident in their ability both to teach and monitor a student's progress with writing. Whether or not I, as a tutor, actually manage to behave in a way that empowers and does not patronise the learner I am working with, there are strategies for working on writing that give me the confidence to believe this is the case. Scribing a person's spoken words, discussing strategies for organising a piece of writing, deciding what the purpose of a piece of writing is all allow for negotiation, giving the learner space to question and discuss. Writing is also visible and tangible; it is there on the page between us, and I and the learner can see when it is longer, neater, fuller than the last piece.

Reading is more difficult, both to develop and to monitor, and teaching a mature adult to develop as a reader is never simple. Of course, there are those who argue that it is possible to measure 'progress' in reading via the monitoring of increased technical skills. However, if we, learners and teachers together, are engaged in the development of a richer experience of reading in terms of meaning and content, the problem of how this development can occur, and in what way it can be monitored, cannot be solved merely by tests of technical competence. As a tutor, I can never observe someone reading silently, as I can watch them write. I therefore cannot know when to intervene or when to simply encourage and prompt. Nor can I help them re-cap or review what they have read. There are two strategies to which tutors often resort. Either we ask the student to read aloud or we ask them to reflect on something they have read, orally or in writing. The problem with both of these (which can, in context, be useful and necessary classroom practices) is that both, for older adults particularly, may recall school experiences they associate with disempowerment and humiliation.

To explore this further I offer two examples from my own ABE teaching and use the work of Frank Smith (1978) to reflect on them. One example, where work on reading had a high profile, is prison teaching. I taught part-time in HMP Pentonville for eighteen months between 1987 and 1989. The second example comes from Hackney and a Fresh Start course, where I learnt the need to distinguish skills from purpose in the teaching of reading.

Frank Smith asserts that children learn to read in spite of the efforts of teachers to teach them. A seductive idea, but what would its implications be for adult learners, those children who did not learn to read despite, or because of, what their teachers did? Two men I worked with in Pentonville illustrate the effect of motivation on learning to read. Both men had varying degrees of anxiety, but what differed was the power of their desire to read to override that anxiety. As far as learning and using reading is concerned, prison is unlike other adult education contexts. First, students attend classes every day. Second, reading is valued because it can offset boredom and draw imaginary boundaries, creating privacy and distance in overcrowded and claustrophobic conditions.

A man I will call Joe arrived in prison with no reading or writing skills at all. I worked with him at least once a week, and sometimes three or four times a week, for a period of about 10 months. He also worked with other tutors during the week. Joe was dogged in his pursuit of language skills and he made enormous progress. By the time he left, he was a slow but enthusiastic reader and a careful and considered writer. The methods used to help Joe learn included a wide range of materials — flash cards, tapes, language experience, small beginner books, copying, cloze exercises and worksheets — and were used by tutors of differing experience — no previous literacy experience through to fifteen years in the job — who held different views on the best method of teaching and learning.

In a way Joe illustrates Frank Smith's thesis perfectly. No one but Joe himself can lay claim to his achievement. Such a variety of learning and teaching methods and personalities were involved that the only common factor is Joe's ability to take something from each and use it. What struck me then about Joe was how singleminded he was in learning to read and write. He was serving his first prison sentence and determined that it would be his last. He wanted to make prison as positive as he could, which for him meant coming out with the ability to read and write. He didn't want to feel ashamed when his kids started to read and write and he wanted something to occupy his mind in prison.

The man I will call Don was completely different. Like Joe he was in his early twenties with no reading or writing skills to speak of, but he never expressed the same motivation as Joe. Don wanted to read and write without any real idea of what that might entail, either to learn or possess those skills. He was angry with his tutors, disrupting lessons with tense exchanges about the babyish work we set. He held the books or worksheets upside down and attempt to read the words backwards. Sometimes, with pieces he liked and had worked on before, perhaps language experience, he read with his eyes shut. He would read gibberish, nonsense strings of words tracing his finger along the page, then off the page and across the desk and along the table.

Don pushed tutors to the point of despair with him and then rounded on them for not helping enough. With hindsight, I think he knew more than he pretended to know, certainly enough to mock the process of teaching and learning, but one source of his anger was not knowing enough to become independent of his tutors. What I don't think he had, and I doubt any of his tutors could have supplied him with, was his own desire to learn. And I think he knew this and it bothered him because he antagonised other members of the class in direct proportion to their willingness to work.

Don was happiest when the man I will call Bill joined the class. Bill, a much older fairground worker, was amazed anyone wanted to read and write. It held an outsider's attraction for him: he had no need of reading and writing and it had no place in his world. Bill was happy to opt out of lessons with Don who, I think, felt validated that there were worlds, even if they were not his, where reading and writing were abnormal.

My experience on Hackney AEI's Fresh Start course alerted me to the need to support and develop reading habits and purposes. Fresh Start is a three day a week return to learning course for women, designed to meet both social and educational needs through counselling, help with basic language and study skills and introductions to a range of subjects: health, history, maths, books and writing, computers. One student, who I shall call Lin, was incredibly anxious about reading although it was clear that she had no technical problems with it. She lacked confidence, but more significantly, she did not understand why people read books other than reference books. The course's compulsory Books and Writing module, with its requirement to read and report on various books, was a torture to her.

As her tutor I encouraged and chided and did the kinds of things reading tutors do: I suggested small books, with big print, about things I thought might interest her. I told her not to worry, to relax. But I could not help her with the main problem because it was only as Lin overcame it that she was able to identify it. And, confident in a sense of purpose both for my own reading and for Lin's, it had not occurred to me that she — or any other reader with technical skills — would have such a problem.

'I never knew what a book was for', she said, bounding into class the day after she completed *Jackie's Story*. What she meant was that she hadn't realised readers could bring themselves to a book, and enter into its world, feel *with* its characters as well as thinking and feeling *about* them. She hadn't realised that it was okay for a book to move you to tears, anger or laughter. That you would remember fragments of its story and characters long after the book was closed, that they could change the way you viewed the world or yourself. Lin also hadn't known that once a character or story involved you to the point of compulsion it was absorbing and enjoyable to read on. She really hadn't understood the pleasure and power of reading.

This experience alerted all the tutors to the dangers of assuming students knew why reading was a good thing for them to do. We began to promote reading more. Some of us were avid and wide-ranging readers so we consciously brought more of our reading into the classes. The maths tutor, Hashida Dave, used a collection of poetry about infinity as part of a maths lesson. Denise Brown, the health tutor, used fiction, poetry and historical writing to illustrate topics such as childbirth and ageing. Jo Temple, the study skills tutor, who had always talked enthusiastically to the group about books she was currently reading, now took them on visits to libraries and bookshops.

That year, too, we took the reckless step of handing the book allowance over to the students, as a result of which I learnt one of my most important lessons about working with students and their reading. The lesson was: trust them, especially their enthusiasm. A student I will call Vivienne had been entranced by the TV serialisation of *Oranges Are Not The Only Fruit*. She bought the paperback tie-in, which pleased me no end. She had also bought, in hardback, a copy of Jeanette Winterson's latest novel, *Sexing The Cherry*. I was less thrilled about that. Jo, however, was characteristically unperturbed: yes, of course we could have bought three paperbacks for the money but we couldn't renege on our decision. The money, though, was less of an issue than the degree of difficulty I knew Vivienne would have with the novel.

Uncomfortable though it is to admit, I realise I would never have introduced that group to such a complex literary text. And by protecting them from that challenge I would have denied them the confidence that only comes from attempting something initially daunting.

Vivienne, and the other members of that group who read *Sexing The Cherry*, did have enormous difficulty with it. They also had fun trying to work out just what was going on and gained knowledge and pleasure from the book, precisely because it was so puzzling, so rich and so new to them. It was also important to recognise how much of their pleasure in reading *Sexing The Cherry* came from the book itself being so beautifully produced. Their pleasure counter-pointed that frequent complaint in ABE, from tutors and learners, that so many of the books they are offered do not look like proper books.

HMP Pentonville provides another neat example of what a tutor can teach when she doesn't try to. It is, although entirely unintentionally, a good example of making reading possible, rather than attempting to teach. A man I will call Simon was in the prison hospital where I ran a weekly drop-in class providing whatever students wanted. Simon's interest was creative writing, our discussions about reading almost incidental. I certainly never thought of myself as teaching reading to him, and I never prepared work around reading. He sometimes talked about various books he'd read and sometimes asked for things: a copy of Keri Hulme's *The Bone People*, as he and his girlfriend used its Maori glossary for their love letters; endless copies, for other prisoners, of popular poems such as T.S. Eliot's cat poem, 'McCavity'.

One week I had with me the book I took the copies from — Ted Hughes' and Seamus Heaney's anthology, *The Rattlebag*. Simon started to flick through it and asked to borrow the anthology. I said yes, as long as I got it back. Each week he mentioned what he was reading, particular poems he liked, whether I could get him collections by various poets. Then he wasn't there: moved back to the wing and then to another prison. So much for *The Rattlebag*, I thought but some months later it came back with an appreciative note inside from Simon and two other links in the returning chain. All had thoroughly read and enjoyed it.

Had I used the anthology as the basis of a lesson I doubt it would have been so attentively read. It would have become work, or lessons, and not reading. It illustrates well Frank Smith's warning that we should not conflate *learning to read* with reading, especially with older students 'who may be restricted to activities that do not make sense to them so that they can acquire "basic skills" '. The truly basic skills of reading, he goes on to argue, 'can never be taught directly and are only accessible to learners through the experience of reading. And not only does meaningful reading provide the essential clues and feedback for learning to read, it provides its own re-inforcement' (Smith, 1978: 128).

This does cause problems for students when there is a period of transition, that may feel like stagnation, while the work necessary for this independent reading takes place. Students in ABE do not seem to make the transition to independent reading as often or as easily as they do to independent writing. In his conclusion to *Reading* Frank Smith argues that there are certain pre-conditions for reading in children. These can be summarised as follows:

1. the ability to distinguish words;
2. the insight that words are meaningful, for example CAT does not just say cat, it means cat — in other words, print has a symbolic function;
3. an understanding that there is a relation between spoken and written language.

To what extent are these the same for adult learners? Have they been scrambled or modified in some way? Do things have to be unlearnt, such as, for example, that there is a one-to-one correspondence between written and spoken language?

One point that does strike me after reading Frank Smith's lucid and persuasive account of the nature of reading is that many of the strategies children and their teachers employ are not readily available to adults. Those children who are nurtured into reading and the world of books through colourful, pictorial representations are guided into and along the print. They experience blissful and sociable occasions of being read to: at night, on journeys, as special treats from teachers and storytellers. They are surrounded by books which give full rein to the imagination, books which are about them and their worlds and interests. The adult beginner-reader, who may not have enjoyed such nourishment as a child, does not fare nearly as well. I believe that if reading is to be promoted to non-readers and infrequent, maybe anxious readers, then a more imaginative range of methods will have to be devised. Children ask for or assume help when they are stuck: they ask what words mean and are read to and with as they move towards control of the medium.

We need to find corresponding means to support adult readers. The recent increase in both availability and range of spoken word cassettes (Wright, 1991) could be important here. They can demonstrate reading's value — its ability to distract, entertain, inform — without the remedial associations of simplified or beginners' texts and they can be used alongside print to support the learning of technical skills.

Repetition is a key point of divergence between learning to read as an adult and as a child. Young children learning to read have a huge stake in repetition. They ask for passages to be read over and over again until they have them word perfect. Adult beginner-readers, in contrast, do not like repetitions. They are often critical of stories which are effectively a repeat and get annoyed or bored by unsubtle repetitions within pieces of writing.

There are two possible explanations for this. Adults may genuinely be bored, having passed whatever cognitive stage of development children are at when repetition excites and entertains them. However, it might also be the case that learning to read requires repetition, not just to internalise print's conventions, but its way of constructing meaning. Perhaps adult beginner-readers actually need the repetition they eschew so strongly, rejecting it because they recognise its association with childhood and their need to demarcate themselves as adults?

Reading Outside Education

Pat Coleman has spent much of the last decade at Sheffield and Birmingham libraries, giving time, energy and resources to promoting reading. She is also a major contributor to debates about the changing role of libraries. However, towards the close of her career in libraries (in 1993 she moved into social service management) she became a powerful exponent of anti-populism in reading promotion.

> The librarian's job is to promote the best and we don't do that. We used to promote only the best ... A very elitist view: it's now changed — maybe there's been an over-reaction. It's gone to great lengths now. Mills and Boon — anything available. (Hughes, 1991: 16)

She does, however, identify a real tension for all of us concerned with promoting reading: that of balancing what people want with what people could — or might — discover they want. This applies to reading itself and to choices within reading.

The spirit of the Sheffield work has been carried forward by Rachel Van Riel and Chris Meade, who both worked with Pat Coleman on 'Opening The Book', the 1989 festival of reading in Sheffield which marked the shift in emphasis librarians gave reading promotion. Rachel Van Riel now runs a successful consultancy agency which promotes the status of reading, largely through libraries. Her work challenges certain assumptions: that reading is passive, a retreat from the world, a poor second to writing yourself. She has contributed to reading promotions — in general, rather than privileging certain types — for Sheffield and Birmingham libraries, where Chris Meade worked as an arts development worker before taking over at the Poetry Society. Some of the promotion has been simple, others have a baroque ambition to them, such as a huge installation where people literally walked through a book making choices and encountering various activities to do with reading.

Less ambitious in scope, although as original in its concept, has been a series of reading guides, including books to read when you are ill, a travel list which includes book titles and information under such headings as: books to impress other people you are travelling with, books for long journeys, books for short journeys. These, and other innovative reading lists, were complied by Mary Cutler, appointed in 1991 as Britain's first reader in residence. Birmingham also has a permanent, changing display of books recommended by all the library staff, from the librarians to the caretaker.

Birmingham's Centre for the Book, established in 1991, has regular changing displays around themes rather than particular authors. These use a lot of colour and large text and are designed to draw the reader on into the book. In autumn 1993 its theme was books chosen by local Black people, some with high-profile jobs such as singers and weather readers on TV, others not, which had made an impression on them. Extracts from the book and its cover were displayed alongside their statement.

The housebound service, after consultation, set up a surprise system whereby the reader would get five requested books and one surprise. Follow up surveys found that people enjoyed this very much and even if they had not liked particular choices, still supported the idea. In 1989 Southern Arts initiated the Well Worth Reading fiction promotion, linking libraries, book shops, arts associations and the media in themed promotions of modern fiction. And from the late 1980s onwards, various themed reading promotions, such as the nationwide Borrow A Penguin or Leicester's Fiction Addiction, were organised. Birmingham, however, by asking the question 'Why Read?' brought a fundamentally different approach to bear.

Some of these promotions work directly with the ABE providers, others could be persuaded to do so. They would all give ABE learners a taste of the pleasure and variety that reading generates.

However, as Rachel Van Riel's work demonstrates, it is not just new or beginner-readers who benefit from or need reading promotion. Readers at large are often set in their rather narrow ways. Technically competent readers, especially on return to study or indeed formal courses, would benefit, especially as writers, from being encouraged and guided into wider reading. Writers and would-be writers are one of the most puzzling groups of reluctant readers. In a piece of recent research for Leeds University into creative writing (O'Rourke, 1994) I was struck not just by how many writers didn't read, but how they rationalised this. For some it was a decision to spend what little free time they had writing not reading. For others, reading was simply market research — sampling possible publishing outlets for their own writing. Others felt reading would influence their style or lead them into unconscious imitation. Far fewer than I would have predicted read to learn about their craft or to expand their sense of what was possible. Where such writing was happening as part of an adult education class, tutors were reluctant to bring reading into the class, although in some cases this was simply bowing to student pressure.

Reading is an issue across the educational spectrum, and beyond it, in arts and leisure. It may lack the immediacy with which writing, as a means of empowerment, claims our attention, and generates its own problems for political literacy campaigns — individualistic, harder to incorporate into collective and shared ways of working — but I believe these are surface problems. Reading is equal to writing in its capacity to engage consciousness and generate knowledge. Work which sets out to develop writing, from whatever point in the educational continuum, can only claim to be fully developmental when it also addresses the issue of why and how such work might be read, and the relationship of that reading to other readings.

Note

1. For my brother, Danny, who died 6 January 1995.

References and Further Reading

Batsleer, J. *et al.* (1985) *Re-Writing English*. London: Methuen.
Fowler, B. (1991) *The Alienated Reader: Women and Popular Romantic Literature in the Twentieth Century*. London: Harvester Wheatsheaf.
Hughes, T. and Heaney, S. (1982) *The Rattlebag*. London: Faber.
Hughes, V. (1991) *Literature Belongs to Everyone*. London: Arts Council of Great Britain.
Meade, C. and Van Riel, R. (1990) *Opening The Book*. Sheffield: Sheffield Library Services.
Meek, M. (1991) *On Being Literate*. London: Bodley Head.
O'Rourke, R. (1992) *Versions and Varieties*. London: Goldsmiths' College. (Available from Avanti Books, 8 Parsons Green, Bolton Road, Stevenage, Herts SG1 4QG.)

— (1993) *Unpopular Readers*. London: Co-Media.
— (1994) *Getting Critical: The Relationship of Creative Writing to Adult Education*. Leeds: Department of Adult Continuing Education, Leeds University.
Phelan, K. (1993) *Libraries and Reading Promotion Schemes*. London: Co-Media.
Smith, F. (1978) *Reading*. Cambridge: Cambridge University Press.
Stibbs, A. (1991) *Reading Narratives as Literature: Signs of Life*. London: Open University Press.
Van Riel, R. (1993) *Reading The Future*. London: Arts Council of Great Britain.
West, R. *et al.* (1993) Reading in the real world and its correlates. *Reading Research Quarterly* 28 (1).
Winterson, J. (1985) *Oranges Are Not The Only Fruit*. London: Pandora.
— (1989) *Sexing The Cherry*. London: Bloomsbury.
Worpole, K. (1984) *Reading by Numbers*. London: Co-Media.

3 Working With Words: Active Learning in a Community Writing and Publishing Group

MICHAEL HAYLER AND ALISTAIR THOMSON

QueenSpark Books, a Brighton-based community publishing project, is one of about 50 member groups of the British Federation of Worker Writers and Community Publishers (FWWCP). We use it here as an example of the much wider range of activities that take place within the Federation. There has been much debate about and analysis of the FWWCP since it was formed in 1976. This has concentrated largely on debates about Writing and Literature, Politics and Nostalgia, and whether the movement is Socialist or Working Class (see Gregory, 1991; Morley and Worpole, 1982; Samuel, 1981; Worker Writers and Community Publishers, 1978). After years of disparagement and neglect by the guardians of national literary culture, the FWWCP is now generally regarded as both a serious producer of writing and a significant oppositional movement. It is widely recognised as a valuable contributor to, and reflector of, the 'culture' of this country and, in recent years, has taken a leading role in the development of international networks, with associate members in Australia, New Zealand, South Africa, Ireland and Spain.

There are dangers in success. Support from the arts establishment — the FWWCP now receives core funding from the Arts Council and several member groups have been created by literature development officers funded by the Regional Arts Associations — has provided money and cultural status. Yet there is a fine line between support and a dependency which *could* undermine an oppositional political commitment and the voluntary nature of local groups. Other changes within the FWWCP over the last decade and a half reflect changing views on class and self-representation. After some furious debate, there has been general acceptance of a broad definition of cultural oppression which recognises that many people's writings and histories have been excluded or denied in dominant culture, because of class inequalities but also because of inequalities of gender, age, disability, ethnicity and sexuality. In recent years members of the Federation have recognised the need for separate spaces for other voices to be heard, and have benefited from the cross-fertilisation of writing by disenfranchised groups (see Thomson, 1990).

The arguments about the nature and politics of community publishing are still relevant in the context of the 1990s, but we want to focus here on issues about the learning and education which occurs in Federation groups. In 1982 the authors of *The Republic of Letters* introduced issues about education through chapters on the 'Struggle for Self Representation' and 'Literary Institutions and Education'. More than ten years on from that seminal book, we use an account of one member group to focus on the experience of informal learning in community publishing, and to consider the challenge it offers to the present government's push towards formal and functionalist education for learners of all ages.

Twenty-two years ago QueenSpark (QS) began as a campaign to save a Brighton building and create a nursery school. Its street newspaper ran a column of old photos and reminiscences from elderly residents. In 1974 Albert Paul came along with his hand-written life story, and this became the first QueenSpark book. Now, 40 books later, QS is one of the leading community publishers in the country.

Over the years, QS has gradually shed its locally based campaigning role — in that sense reflecting the decline of 1970s style community politics — but it has developed a structure and approach to community writing and publishing which has contributed to its survival and provided a basis for change and growth. The core of active QS members — a constantly changing group of between 50 to 80 people — come to QS with different backgrounds, motivations and needs. Several writing groups offer a cooperative forum for the development of writing confidence and skills. A manuscripts group reads and responds to writing from within and outside QS, and sets up book-making groups to organise publication. Volunteers give their time and develop their skills in sales and administration. A paid worker employed for 12 hours per week supports volunteer members and coordinates QS activities, and a writing development worker is employed for 4 hours per week to support the writing groups and to develop new groups and events. Representatives from all the groups make up the QS management committee, upon which we, the authors, are both current members. In the early years of QS there was no formal management structure and articulate academics or professionals had an influence disproportionate to their numbers — described as 'a sort of Fabian set-up' by one member. The current structure has created a steadier balance of influence, and makes it easier for all members to have an input into decision-making (Deakin and Hayler, 1991).

What follows in this chapter are, first, personal reflections on what our experience with QS has meant to our own learning about democratic practice and writing.

Using accounts written for us by other QS members, we then describe the varieties of their participation and learning in QS. We explore how and why people get involved in such projects, how the groups create a particular forum for learning, and how they enable people to recognise and develop themselves as writers and as active participants in making literature. We recognise certain issues and tensions within community writing and publishing, but argue that 'becoming a writer' happens most effectively in contexts which provide collective and collaborative support, which value writing from people's own language and experience, and which encourage people to build upon that experience and expand their writing into new territory and new languages.

We begin with our own experiences of education and development. We come from different sides of the world and have very different experiences of formal education. In common we have the key role that QueenSpark Books has played in our learning and our lives.

Mike Hayler

I had some happy times at primary school but must have failed the eleven plus and I went to a secondary modern school in Brighton. By the third year it was all over and I'd given up on my education. So had the school, except for one teacher who encouraged me to get down to learning while I had the chance. I'm not sure that I had the chance and I certainly didn't want to take it. I was expelled in 1975 and spent six months listening to David Bowie in my bedroom.

Ten years later I got some 'O' levels and 'A' levels at evening classes and went off to Brighton Poly to begin a degree course in Humanities. As the first year came to an end, I began wondering what this was all about and why I was subjecting my family to penury while all my old mates were 'out there earning good money'. Not much of it made any sense as far as my life was concerned.

I first contacted QS as part of an 'Independent Learning Assignment'. At that stage Al was the paid worker at QS, and he suggested that I sift through the boxes of records, minutes and correspondence for my research. I decided to join one of the writing groups and work on my own writing. I never made it. I got side-tracked into the manuscripts group and the management committee, with several book-making groups along the way.

QS made sense of the education I had decided I needed, and provided an education that I never knew existed. It gave me a reason to acquire the skills of higher education which had previously seemed useless in themselves — just like algebra when I was 13. At QS I began to understand communication and the use of language and writing. I could do things: I could learn; I could share that learning; I could support and lead other people's learning. Most of all, I could participate. It made me believe that it was possible and necessary to learn without becoming a different person, and without forgetting that lonely, angry boy who sang along to Hunky Dory and considered failure at close quarters. QS showed me that learning happens in all sorts of ways and in all sorts of places. Being part of QS has taught me more than I can say.

I have been teaching in a primary school for two years and I have run some workshops and courses for the Centre for Continuing Education at Sussex University. Continuing education makes sense to me now.

Al Thomson

By comparison with Mike, I had a privileged and successful experience of initial education. Growing up in Australia, my parents were able to afford to send me to fee-paying junior schools, and when I was 11. I won a scholarship which meant that they could send me to one of the country's private secondary schools. I went straight from school to university, and after getting a degree I won a second scholarship which brought me to England for postgraduate studies. I now work as a lecturer in Continuing Education at the University of Sussex.

People often construct life histories which characterise their lives as a steady journey of progress and success. When I look more closely at my own educational life history, and at the position of writing in my life, the neat account by which I introduced myself becomes more fractured and fragmented, and less smooth and steady. Before the school scholarship exam, my parents organised writing tuition from a teacher friend because I seemed to have particular problems with writing. The only moment of the exam which I can recall was turning the page of the 'English expression' section, to discover with horror that I had to write creatively about a murky image that looked like a cave. I could not see the point, and I did not know what to do. Throughout my schooling I always felt that I was an awkward, clumsy writer, and at university the completion of essays was a traumatic experience; at one stage I dropped out for a year when I couldn't finish (or even start) a piece of writing. As a graduate student, writing continued to be an incredibly arduous and painful experience.

While I was a student in Melbourne I got involved in community history, and when I came to England I became a volunteer with QueenSpark Books. Over time I served as a paid worker for both QS and the national Federation of Worker Writers and Community Publishers (FWWCP), of which QS is a member. I began to learn a new range of skills in organisation and administration, in book-making and marketing. I also found new ways of writing: for reports, funding applications, press releases, news articles, polemic and, on rare occasions, a poem for performance. I found that this writing was supported and acknowledged. I enjoyed writing for a purpose and for an audience, and I relished collaborative writing. Through observing with admiration the courage and extraordinary efforts of other members who overcame great obstacles in order to write, to be heard and to be published, I began to understand more about the process and difficulties of writing, and about ways to make writing easier and more accessible. Influenced by these experiences, my own writing became less precious and less difficult. Writing articles like this is still not easy, but the learning and understanding I have gained from my involvement in community writing and publishing has made writing a valuable and affirming experience, and an essential tool in my life and work.

The spelling, grammar and punctuation rules that were drilled into me as a school boy taught me to 'write properly', but that emphasis on rules and mechanics may have been one of the obstacles that blocked me from writing with pleasure, confidence and ease. The functionalist training in writing certainly did not make writing a positive or valued experience. That came from recognising that writing was something to be shared and discussed rather than guarded with pride or embarrassment; it came from recognising the creative potential of collaborative writing; it came from writing on subjects about which I felt passionately, for readers who cared about what I was saying. These have been learning outcomes of my involvement in community writing, history and publishing.

Like many members of QS we too have become writers. However, in researching and writing about QS we have realised that most of our writing energy is not engaged in the poetry, prose and non-fictional creative writing which is the focus of QS writing groups. Through QS and other activities we have developed confidence and skills in other forms of administrative and analytical writing. Though we sometimes feel that we would like to develop our 'creative' writing, we believe that a strength of groups like QS is that they enable a diversity of writing forms and approaches.

We also recognise that our role in QS has often been to facilitate other people's writing, and that while there are mutual benefits in this enabling role, it poses further issues about the relationship between editor or facilitator and writer. How does power work in such relationships? Whose story is written and published? What drives us to adopt such a role? Are we hiding from or concealing our own stories? These issues in community writing and publishing have been explored by Maggie Hewitt (1990) and Stella Fitzpatrick (1988), and deserve further consideration.

Researching QueenSpark

We began our research by asking members of each of the QS groups to respond to a simple, open-ended questionnaire which outlined our project and invited people to write in narrative form about their experiences with QS, guided by four general questions. How and why did you get involved? How are you involved now? What do you get out of your participation in QS? What have you gained or learnt from your involvement? As well as writing individual responses for us, some members discussed the issues as a group. We received 24 written responses, about a third of current QS members and including most of the active members. We refer to these members who responded to our questionnaire as 'participants' to indicate the significant role which they have played in shaping the findings of our research. We used our participants' responses as the basis for a first draft of this chapter, which we circulated to members for additional comments and suggestions which, in turn, informed the final version of the chapter.

The backgrounds of the research participants — in terms of age, gender, class, ethnicity and educational experience — are significant because a different combination of people in another community publishing group, such as the Gatehouse Project for beginner-writers in Manchester or the Ethnic Communities Oral History Project in West London, might well have different comments to make about their involvement and learning. Further research might consider the contrasts between different FWWCP member groups as well as their common aims and approaches.

The participants in our research project were a fair cross-section of current QS members, including representatives from several writing and book-making groups, the management and manuscript groups, and administrative volunteers and paid workers. Many were active in two or more QS groups. In the past people often became involved with 'a project' rather than with 'the organisation' and frequently moved on when the project was completed. With improved organisation, communication and resources — including an office and meeting room and a set of second-hand computers — members are now able to develop their involvement and move from one area of interest to another, for example, from writing group to manuscripts group to book-making group.

The gender balance of the participants — 7 men and 17 women — reflects the gender make-up of the organisation as a whole. We were surprised that no one highlighted gender as an issue in their QS experience (for example, the silencing of women's voices in mainstream writing and publishing; or the supportive role of other women in the writing groups), though these ideas were implicit in more general comments about, for example, the supportive nature of the groups, and take effect through participation in a women-only writing group.

Also difficult to assess is the employment status of participants, as ten of the responses did not include such information; in most cases they are women and are either retired, in part-time employment or with family responsibilities. Of the others, four are in full-time employment; one is part-time employed; seven are retired and two are in full-time school education. Again, this mix seems to approximate to our impression of QS comprising a low proportion of members in regular or full-time employment, and a high proportion of members who are retired (though the full-time students in higher education, who in term time often make significant contributions to QS, are not represented, perhaps because the questionnaire was circulated during the summer). Age and retirement are significant categories for many of our participants, and important factors in their involvement with QS. Arthur Thickett explains that his voluntary work with QS helped him to 'save face' with family and friends after his enforced retirement. QS has helped Margaret Howells to maintain self-confidence in her retirement, and for Nick Osmond it has provided a focus for new activities after taking early retirement. At the other end of the age spectrum, the two teenage members of the Hove Writers write very positively about learning from the insights of older members.

Judgements about class status and identity are almost impossible to make, partly because of the nature and aims of the questionnaire, but perhaps also because it is not a significant category for many of the participants. Nick Osmond is self-conscious about the mixed blessings of his middle-class background, and Arthur Thickett explains the value of collaborating with 'like minded working people', but most participants do not mention class and none are explicit about the relationships between class and the politics of writing and publishing or their own participation in QS. Nor is ethnicity highlighted as a significant factor by participants, perhaps because the small proportion of QS members from non-Anglo-Celtic backgrounds mirrors the racial mix of Brighton as a whole.

Participants rarely refer explicitly to prior experiences of formal education. Doris Hall writes movingly about her dyslexia being recognised and supported by QS people who came to talk about publishing her childhood autobiography: 'What a joy it was to talk over my problem with them, and then to put my memories into book form.' Others talk about having previously lacked the knowledge or confidence to create stories or put thoughts into writing. We were surprised by the relative silence about negative prior experiences of education, which we have found to be a common theme in the educational life histories of students in literacy classes and other Federation writing groups. What is clear is that QS does not serve as, and is not perceived as, a basic skills literacy organisation. None of our participants are members of adult basic education (ABE) classes or describe themselves as beginner-writers, though new links are being forged with

ABE groups. Most participants, and indeed most QS members, are people who have previously attained at least the basic skills of writing, but who feel the need for support and encouragement to develop their writing and identify themselves as writers (for writing and publishing in ABE, see Judy Wallis' chapter, and O'Rourke and Mace, 1992).

Apart from the backgrounds and identities of our participants, we were fascinated by the different ways in which they replied to the questionnaire. The forms of the responses and the use of various ways of writing are suggestive about different writing identities and different experiences of QS. The majority of responses (15) are hand-written and use the bottom and reverse side of the questionnaire. Some of these writers answer our four guiding questions in point form; others respond to those questions by producing a short chronological account of their involvement with QS. All of these short hand-written responses are from women, apart from two by 16-year-old males.

Of the eight type-written responses, two are in the form of letters or memos addressed directly to us, and six are longer narratives with an analytical or self-consciously literary approach. Several of these longer narratives used headings, such as 'Queenspark Books — An Experience' or 'Putting My Feet in the Water', or introduced their response with a quote. Arthur Thicket commences: 'QueenSpark is a very small pond almost lost in a corner of the Southern Jungle, where little fishes jump quite prettily: a couple of pike lurk … in the depths …'. All of the adult men produced a type-written narrative response, as did two women, each of whom had had a central administrative role within QS.

Our hunch is that members of this latter group of participants not only have ready access to type-writing or word-processing technology, and a technical confidence and competence with written expression, but they also have relatively self-assured identities as writers. In some cases this identity as a writer has been forged through years of work with words; in other cases QS itself has helped individuals who were attracted to writing to identify themselves as writers. Another, related hunch is that some people are more self-assured with the public writing form of the questionnaire or directive response. Gender is probably one explanatory factor. It seems that men are often more able or willing to adopt a self-confident writing identity and to write in public forms such as surveys. By contrast, women may often be more comfortable and familiar with the comparatively private autobiographical forms of diaries, poems and letters.

Motivations for Joining QueenSpark

Many members were introduced to QS by family members or friends, and word of mouth is certainly an effective form of publicity because it often involves a recommendation or encouragement. Others had first heard about QS from a source of public information, such as the local library, a town hall notice-boad or an events column of a local newspaper. A few people had known about QS for many years (from early community politics or from the books) and then got involved when changes in their lives, such as retirement, made it possible. In many cases, the participation which followed an initial, impersonal contact (such as a bulletin board) was dependent upon the friendliness and encouragement of the first personal contact.

Our study revealed some of the reasons which caused these participants to join (and others not to join, or to leave) the organisation and, for those who stayed, the sense of the 'warm sea' of community they enjoyed. The initial motivations for joining QS are relevant to this research because they can help us to gauge what people have gained or learnt from participation. Three participants wrote that one reason they joined QS was to attain skills which might help them find employment, though each of these three stressed that QS had been a learning experience with many other unexpected benefits. Several other participants joined QS after retirement, either because they now had the time to follow up previously frustrated interests, or because they were seeking active, sociable fulfilment or a focus for a new stage of life. Members of the two stroke writing groups joined because the group offered an opportunity to share and explore the personal experiences of stroke.

Most members of the writing groups had had a previous, often long-term interest in creative writing, but felt that they wanted to develop their writing confidence and skills through participation in a group. A few members had a more specific aim — to write about local history or to produce an autobiography — though these participants noted that in the group they had learnt from other writers and their different forms of writing. A very few members of the writing groups were, at least initially, less interested in developing their writing (Arthur Thickett explains his belief that you cannot be taught to write, and notes that he had other writing support systems) but rather wanted ideas about getting published or receiving public feedback about their writing. In many cases initial, narrowly defined aspirations have developed into a more diverse involvement in QS, and unexpected learning and achievements.

This is particularly true for members of the manuscripts group, who are often active in several different QS activities, and who identify themselves most strongly with the organisation as a whole. Membership of the manuscripts group usually involves administrative and decision-making responsibility, and interchange with the diversity of QS people. Manuscripts group members look beyond their own writing to consider not only other people's writing (the writing groups also serve that function) but also issues about editing, publishing, marketing and reading. It connects people more directly with what might be described as the core ideals of QS, and with active participation in enacting those ideals. By contrast, some members of the writing groups tend to identify themselves primarily with that group and their own writing. This is partly due to different interests and motivations, and partly the result of meeting at times and places which set the writing groups apart from other QS activities. Within an organisation like QS there is an underlying tension between aspirations for personal writing development through the writing group, and a commitment to the collective politics of community writing and publishing. This is a theme to which we return later.

We did not survey people who had left QS, but it is important to reflect upon the reasons why people have left or even rejected the organisation. Some people use QS as an introduction to the publishing industry, learning and offering skills before moving on to professional work in publishing or the print media. Some see QS as a stage in their writing and learning journey, and move on to write their own books or plays in the commercial culture world. Others use QS as an informal progression route into further or higher education. Though many of these people end their active membership of QS, they have often made valuable contributions to an organisation which provided an accessible path to educational and career development.

Some active members, particularly those who take on paid or unpaid administrative roles, have left QS because the organisation has not had the capacity to coordinate their input in fulfilling ways, or because of burnout or personal alienation. In this regard QS is typical of over-stretched and under-resourced voluntary organisations. Other members become disillusioned by the QS attitude to writing. The notion that anyone who wants to can be a writer challenges not only the literary establishment, but also those who regard their own values and opinions about writing as universal. Several members have left claiming that QS encourages and produces mediocre uses of language, that the writing groups do not understand or respect form or structure, and that fellow members do not want or try to push their writing forward (to 'write like Henry James'). QS does make its ideals prominent in its publicity, and writers with such attitudes usually stay well away! But people relate to writing and publishing groups in different ways and few of us recognise the strength of our own individualism until we are confronted with it. At that point QS writers have to decide whether they accept or reject the shared approach to writing, and whether their own learning journey is linked with the journey of others. Even those who leave at this point have learnt something at QS.

Writing groups can also be difficult to join and can create their own conservatism. For example, the longstanding QS women writers group has tried to encourage new and younger members but comprises mainly older women.

Younger women wishing to join a QS writing group have found that the group did not provide an appropriate forum where their common interests and issues could form a basis for writing, and have usually left the group after one or two meetings. The recent expansion in membership and meeting space has allowed for a wider range of writing and publishing groups and, in turn, a broadening of the background, age and interests of QS members.

That Sparkling Warm Sea of Community

Many QS members refer to friendship or community when asked what they have gained from their involvement with the organisation. 'QueenSpark gives its members a sense of belonging', says Wilma De Souza,

> of being part of a family. QueenSpark has members from all walks of life, but what we all have in common is that our personal identities are some-how an issue, and therefore we are looking to belong. For the majority, QueenSpark is a place that provides this sense.

Nick Osmond explains, 'I get a lot out of my involvement at QueenSpark. Comradeship and making one or two good friends has been important.' For Arthur Thickett community is a central theme:

> I quickly and willingly jumped into that sparkling warm sea of community again ... This spontaneous 'magic of community' at its best, its peaks, its flights when the spirit soars — is the greatest feeling in the world (OK there's sex) and all I want to do at these times is share it with those I feel I can tune in to ... and that's just about everyone around.

Other participants refer specifically to the friendliness and trust available in the writing groups. Violet Pumphrey identifies a 'meeting of like minds' with-in the women writers' group, despite the fact that 'we all write so differently', and she cherishes the 'friendliness and greetings on arrival ... the feeling that I am a welcome member'. This sense of belonging is never linked to a partic-ular style or subject of writing, but refers always to the way in which the groups operate. Sixteen-year-old Robin English finds the Hove writing group 'very helpful yet fun, in the friendly atmosphere in which I look forward to working each week'.

Friendship, and the enjoyment of working in a 'community' of writers and publishers at QS, creates, and is created by, the essential element needed for gaining confidence and for progressive collaborative learning — trust. For some writing group members this sense of trust enables the group to serve a therapeu-tic purpose. Margaret Howell finds the writing group 'therapeutic': 'It relaxed my mind, and at the same time stimulated my brain.'

For many members the atmosphere of trust provides a basis for overcoming under-confidence. Several participants in our QS survey write about their lack or loss of confidence in the past, and the feeling that they were unskilled and uneducated. 'I knew I sadly lacked the the knowledge of how to put a story together', writes Sylvia Calvert, while Doris Hall recalls the debilitating experience of dyslexia. Violet Pumphrey writes of the impact of QS in her life: 'Confidence — lost over the years is returning (gained). That everyone has a story to tell (learnt).' Marjorie Batchelor summarises the common conclusion that QS 'has opened up a whole new world for me'. The key to this new world is Violet's word, 'confidence'. All our participants reported that this was what involvement in QS activities had given them. Indeed, any new learning in supportive contexts is capable of generating this feeling; just as, in turn, a sense of confidence in one area enables any of us to embark on further learning in another. We will now focus on learning in three areas which this study highlighted: writing development, social and personal development, and democratic practice.

Working with Words

Members of the writing groups highlighted, above all, the specific confidence they had gained in using words. Andrew Grinstead speaks of a new confidence in his 'writing skills'; Sylvia Calvert says that she is 'beginning to understand how to structure a story'; Sam Royce, that 'by listening to others I have found an improvement in the content and quality of my work'. Within the group process of writing activities there is clearly a lot of learning going on. Group members are recognising the effect of a particular writing style, or the use and meaning (and perhaps the spelling) of unfamiliar vocabulary, or how punctuation can affect the pace and delivery of writing.

Tim Shelton-Jones describes what he has observed in the groups about other people's writing talents:

> After a while it hits you — the wealth of near-genius you've immersed yourself in. It's not the kind of talent that takes the Literary World by storm, because it's far too individual for that (it's the less original ones who get published). But a talent, nevertheless, to send shivers down your spine; like finding a Picasso at Portobello Road market. Sometimes it's poetry, sometimes fantasy, sometimes autobiography. Nor are these top scorers rarities ... We've had them at QueenSpark Books, too — plenty of them.

Many of the writing group members explain that they learn from one another and that this goes beyond gestures of mutual support. What they write about and the styles in which they write are influenced not just by the workshop convenor or the QS organisation, but above all by the other members of the writing group.

Thus June Drake comments that the members of her group 'are giving me the push I needed to get started in writing my autobiography', and Violet Pumphrey emphasises the importance of 'like minds'. Within the workshop atmosphere, participants ask the questions that their teachers should have answered long ago, except that now there are no teachers and the writers themselves set the agenda and learn from one another. This usually happens in the process of reading and hearing each other's work, and sometimes by writing as a team, when the results can be wonderfully strange but the process is vital and rewarding, as Tim Shelton-Jones recalls: 'We wrote a collective play, a joyous journey it was into the realms of the practically impossible. The play was a ragbag but the learning was a treat.' Members of the writing group will often disagree and they will always take different routes to writing, but in such an atmosphere ideas are formulated, experiments are attempted and new skills and confidences are forged.

Involvement with QS does not always lead to experimentation with different writing approaches and styles. Ironically, while QS has aimed to publish alternative histories and new forms of autobiography, the writing itself has sometimes adopted very conventional forms. Indeed, the successful publication of over 40 books with a wide local readership has perhaps established a narrow genre of local history and autobiography. Writers who submit manuscripts to QS, including members of our own writing groups, use the books as a guide to appropriate form, tone and content. When Sid Manville (1989) wrote *Everything Seems Smaller: A Brighton Boyhood Between the Wars* he deliberately excluded his trade union activity because he thought that QS readers would not be interested, and that it could reduce his chances of publication. QS published the book with very few changes — and without probing or enquiring about Sid's union activity — because it was an interesting, local working-class autobiography which was also 'a good read'. Both writer and publisher were constrained and guided by an establised and successful genre of life-history community publication. We are now learning that both community publishers and writers need to be more critically reflective about our motivations and decisions, and about the types of writing and histories we produce.

The process of constructive criticism within the writing and book-making groups at QS plays an essential role in this reflection. Hearing other people whom they trust and often regard as friends criticise their writing gives writing group members a feeling that they are respected and that their writing, and therefore they themselves, are worthy of the time and attention of others. To an even greater extent, people feel that commenting upon the work of others, either in the writing groups or the manuscripts group, is evidence that their opinions and impressions are valued by others, and that they have an equal share in making decisions about what QS will publish.

Members of the manuscripts group, like Margaret Howell, get 'a great buzz' from being part of the process which leads to book production. This is an entirely new experience for most people. It puts members firmly into the driving seat of publication and empowers them in public life, often for the first time. Manuscript group members often feel hesitant at first about commenting upon the writing of others, but they quickly learn to begin with positive comments before suggesting ways of developing and presenting texts. These suggestions frequently affect decisions about publication. Members of the group often become involved in book-making groups which work closely with writers. People learn, at an individual pace, the skills of collective and collaborative editing along with the practical tasks of book production. As Helen Ridgeway concludes, 'I shall never take a book for granted again! I didn't realise how much work went into it. I certainly learnt a lot about the book publishing side.'

Though members of all QS groups highlight the value of mutual support and learning, within the QS writing groups there is, however, a tension or ambivalence about the role of the group convenor. In the past, QS has employed writing group convenors, but at present the groups are convened by volunteer members with the assent of other group members. Some participants in our survey are critical of formal writing classes which employ tutors. Leila Abrahams joined QS because she was disillusioned by previous experiences of adult education writing courses, in which she was at the mercy of a teacher's whims or prepared programme, and confined by the bureaucracy of formal education. Tim Shelton-Jones explains that when the Nightwriters had a paid convenor it was a creative writing class and not a writers' circle, and his account of 'tutelage' and 'a regime of exercises' suggests his dislike of the taught approach. A rather different perspective is provided by the teenage members of the Hove group, who argue that it provides a positive contrast with school work: there is no pressure to write; they receive help to finish unfinished writings; and they relish the diversity of experience.

Yet members of the writing groups are also positive about the role of the convenor. Leila Abrahams recalls that the experiment of rotating the convening role among the Brighton Women Writers after the departure of its last paid convenor was 'unhappy', and another group member, Margaret Howells, expresses a preference for an 'enthusiastic convenor'. Between the lines of Tim Shelton-Jones' account, too, we detected a nostalgia for the collective energy and inspiration generated in the Nightwriters when their paid convenor's work helped to motivate and sustain the membership. Members of the Hove group value the supportive role of other members, yet they also stress the importance of the volunteer convenor's leadership and support. Ambivalence about the role of the convenor is clearly an unresolved tension within QS and other community-based writing groups, and requires further consideration.

We have already noted that few of our QS research participants referred to negative prior experiences of education. Nor did they explicitly discuss the difference between QS and formal education. It is clear that members have mixed feelings about the term 'education'. Many would not regard QS as having much to do with education — although they all recognise that they have been or are learners in different ways. They do not wish to be seen as students and some feel very uneasy about being identified as 'slow', 'backward' or 'needing help'. These are damaging terms which people remember from their school days and identify with 'education', and which can carry a self-perpetuating, stifling of confidence. In a sense, QS is valued precisely because it is not seen as an educational organisation. There are dangers as well as advantages in this disassociation; not being readily perceived by potential funders as an educational organisation, QS has sometimes been cut off from educational resources and status. Renewed links with the local adult education networks are only gradually shifting these perceptions, both within and outside the organisation.

Learning from Diversity

Active QS members learn from exposure to a diversity of personal experiences, and from their own experience of putting ideas into practice within the organisation. Violet Pumphrey summarises the common theme of recognising that 'everyone has a story to tell'. Learning that 'everyone has a history and that anyone can be a writer' is a liberating experience when you have always been taught that history is about those with power and influence, and that the title of 'writer' belongs to those who make their living from the published word. Jackie Lewis, who until recently was the paid worker at QS, agrees that the organisation encourages members to 'look beyond the conventional and see people for what they can be rather than what they are', and in so doing changes their view of particular situations and stimulates a broader outlook on life. This exchange and insight is expanded many-fold within the context of the FWWCP. QS members who have made links to the 'Fed' are rewarded and educated by meeting many different people with diverse experiences of life, and by direct personal access to those experiences through Federation writing and performance.

Within QS we have often wondered about the extent to which members are committed to the politics expressed in *The Republic of Letters*. This matters for our research because what people learn is shaped by their aims; perhaps also because learning the politics through experience within a group like QS is part of its value and achievement. Some of us came to QS with a commitment to the politics of community publishing, though we have often learnt more about the politics through trying to live it in practice. Wilma De Souza joined QS as a student committed to a politics of representation ('giving a voice') but learnt about democratic process, about looking 'beyond a person's face value', and about the 'liberating effect' of creative writing workshops. Jackie Lewis explains that when she came to work with QS she had little knowledge of community publishing, but in the course of her job she learnt about cooperative and democratic ways of working; about new ways of understanding the world of writing and publishing; that 'anyone can do anything and anyone can write', and was herself empowered by this recognition.

Other members joined QS with a primary intention of improving their own writing, but developed a more reflective and critical sense of issues about writing through collective work and by witnessing other people's writing experience and progress. Several participants use the QS slogans 'finding a voice' and 'everyone has a story to tell' not as empty rhetoric but because they have learnt the meaning and value of the slogans through participation, as Hazel Marchant explains: 'I have learnt that there are a lot of untapped skills within the community of the unemployed and retired. And that everyone has a story to tell and has the right to be heard.'

As we have already indicated, not everyone in QS shares what we called earlier the 'collective politics of community writing and publishing'; people relate to writing and community publishing in different ways. We were familiar with this from our own experience of QS. What this research did for us, however, was to put into sharper focus the diversity of perspectives that participants have, and the tension there can sometimes be between balancing personal interests in writing with a collective politics of community practice. Tim Shelton-Jones' advocacy of the ideal 'writing circle' — an equal group of writers which excludes politics or criticism of the contents of writing from its discussion — is arguably at odds with the ideals of *The Republic of Letters*, which pose an explicit challenge to the social, educational and cultural inequalities that have silenced so many people's voices. Another member, who wrote of sharing a national concern about the causes of illiteracy among the young, allied herself with arguments which have often led to the denigration of the very practice of creative writing and collective publishing in education and community contexts which QS represents.

We found that in responses from members of the writing groups, the value of the collective politics of writing and publishing was less explicit than in those from other members. Nevertheless, replies from members of the Hove Writers and the stroke writing groups, for instance, all affirmed the importance of collective support, if not of collective politics, for their development as writers. An explicit purpose of the stroke writing groups is to explore and publicise the experiences of stroke, even though they do not necessarily articulate the underlying political significance of this desire.

Learning about Democracy

As we have indicated, QS offers a choice of ways to participate; as Mike's experience shows, some who join with the intention of writing then choose to participate in the organisation in other ways. We wanted to find out more about what learning to work with others in a community organisation might mean. In terms of writing, as the responses told us, participants learned above all as Stevie English put it, to 'have a go' at different kinds of writing. We knew from our own experience that members also learned about selling and distributing books, about finance, and about office administration. So we were interested to read the response, for instance of Hazel Marchant, who came to QS in 1989 from a Re-start secretarial course, with little knowledge of writing and publishing and with limited confidence in her own abilities and potential:

> Since that day I have helped in the office, have convened the Hove Writing Group and held the position of Chair for one year. I've written short poems for anthologies, recorded oral history interviews and illustrated several Market Books [QueenSpark's short run book series].

While Hazel herself chose not to say this, others in our study told us that she had also learned something else: to be a confident and inspiring communicator. Hazel now writes regular columns for a local and a national magazine, and has given many public talks about QS to gatherings of various sizes. Her education and self-development over these four years has clearly been about more than confidence in herself as a poet. She has also learnt other forms of self-expression, partly from watching other QS volunteers, partly from actually doing those things, and partly from showing other people how to do them. She was able to develop her skills as a convenor in a non-threatening, although challenging, atmosphere of support, and then to take those skills to the sometimes less friendly world outside of QS.

QS members also learn about management. The management process at QS is time consuming and can be frustrating. Despite the increasing cross-fertilisation within the organisation, there are tensions within groups, and more often between groups, caused by clashes of interest and ideas. The paid worker is sometimes a target for less than gentle criticism when such clashes come to a head. But the QS management process is also, eventually, democratic. Each group is represented by its own elected member on the management committee and this leads to a feeling that everyone is able to have their say and to be involved in the running of the organisation. QS members recognise that they make the difference throughout the organisation and that, collectively, they really are in charge at last. Although members are not always willing or able to accept the responsibility of power, 'Who's in charge? You're in charge' could become a motto at QS. This practical realisation of the nature and potential of

empowerment is, perhaps, one of the most significant learning experiences provided by QS, especially when it enables members to take more control over
other aspects of their lives.

Our Own Learning

For those with experience of higher education, including the two of us,
Queenspark offers what Wilma De Souza describes as 'a very definite extension
of my education'. She mentions 'practical skills in production and negotiation
skills' as examples, and goes on to list 'unexpected skills; how to adhere to a
democratic process, and how to look beyond a person's face value'. Nick
Osmond has found new skills through participation and through leading the
learning of others: 'I love combining the writing/editing and the practical phases
of book production. Working with QS has been a process of learning and self
teaching and I now feel quite multi-skilled.'

Several other men within QS, including, again, the two of us, recognise that
they have gained many skills from their involvement. Responses from women
are often more modest and self-effacing. When asked what they have gained at
QS, women often refer to the ability to understand and support others. Yet
examination of women's roles in QS shows that they make a major impact: all
but one of the paid workers have been women; most of the writing groups
have been convened by women; a majority of the members are women; and
women members seem to have been more ready to diversify their work within
QS. By contrast, local women send less manuscripts to QS than do local men,
and it has been relatively difficult to find books by women for the Market
Books series. This may be because women are less confident about going public with their writing because the forms in which they are writing are more personal, or because the forms of QS books do not always suit women's writing.
Both gender and genre are critical issues for future reflection upon the processes and products of community writing and publishing.

By exploring our own and others' experiences as QS members we have in
this chapter begun to articulate a number of key themes. We have learnt that
many adults are wary of the language and formal processes of 'education', and
define their own learning not as 'education' or even 'learning', but rather as
'personal development'. We have learnt that shared possession and responsibility (as opposed to formal teaching) for writing usually encourages involvement
and creative and personal development — but that some people have inter-
nalised traditional models of 'education' and resist more collective or mutual
approaches.

We have recognised that writing takes many different forms — fictional,
autobiographical, oral history and reminiscence, administrative and analytical —

and that some people prefer to work with one form of writing while others benefit from cross-fertilisation. We have also realised that developing writing is just one part of the wider range of learning in QS — that embraces learning about democratic processes, about making and selling books, about running a voluntary organisation — and that these learnings, in turn, shape the development and production of writing.

It has become clear to us that people have very different commitments — some more to their own writing and others more to a collective enterprise — but that active involvement often changes the nature of commitment and leads from one to the other. Above all, the exploration for this chapter has reinvigorated our belief that people develop 'literacy' skills best when that development is part of a broad approach to learning and personal development. 'Becoming a writer' happens most effectively in contexts which provide collective and collaborative support, which value writing from people's own language and experience, and which encourage people to build upon that experience and expand their writing into new territory and new languages.

Note

For a QS publications' catalogue write to QueenSpark Books, 11 Jew St, Brighton, BN1 1UT, or phone 0273-748348.

References

Deakin, A. and Hayler, M. (1991) QueenSpark Books. *Mailout*, April/May.

Fitzpatrick, S. (1988) *Working Around Words: An Account of Editorial Work for Two Gatehouse Books*. Manchester: Gatehouse.

Gregory, G. (1991) Community publishing as self education. In D. Barton and R. Ivanic (eds) *Writing in the Community*. Newbury Park: Sage Publications.

Hewitt, M. (1990) The invisible hand. In A. Thomson (ed.) *Community Publishing Information Pack — Making Books*. Brighton: FWWCP.

Manville, S. (1989) *Everything Seems Smaller: A Brighton Boyhood Between the Wars*. Brighton: QueenSpark Books.

Morley, D. and Worpole, K (eds) (1982) *The Republic of Letters: Working Class Writing and Local Publishing*. London: Co-Media.

O'Rourke, R. and Mace, J. (1992) *Versions and Variety: A Report on Student Writing and Publishing in Adult Literacy Education*. Goldsmith's College, London. (Available from Avanti Books, 8 Parsons Green, Bolton Road, Stevenage, Herts SG1 4QG.)

Samuel, R. (ed.) (1981) *People's History and Socialist Theory*. London: Routledge and Kegan Paul.

Thomson, A. (1990) Community publishing: *The Republic of Letters* revisited. *Adults Learning* 2 (1), 15–16.

Worker Writers and Community Publishers (1978) *Writing*. London: Federation of Worker Writers and Community Publishers.

4 'You Can't Write Until You Can Spell!': Attitudes to Writing Amongst Adult Basic Education Students

JUDY WALLIS

In this chapter I explore the attitudes towards writing that many adult students bring to their classes when they return to education and use their experiences to inform the debate about English teaching which is currently raging in our schools. Calls for a return to traditional English teaching have inevitably rubbed off onto assumptions about adult literacy practice. As perceptions of Adult Basic Education (ABE) are increasingly replaced by Basic Skills Training, so functional literacy competencies which can easily be accredited have been promoted at the expense of wider, more open-ended and democratic approaches to working with adults. I argue for a greater emphasis on personal writing and publishing in the ABE curriculum as a way of developing more confident creative *and* functional writers.

'A Golden Age of Literacy Teaching'?

In recent years it has become a popular pastime among the tabloid press, politicians and right-wing educational theorists to paint a romantic vision of the English teaching that went on in schools before it became 'tainted' by progressive and liberal teaching. Dr Sheila Lawlor, Director of the Centre for Policy Studies, for instance asserted categorically that 'no longer can pupils write the clear, correct English that was second nature to their grandparents' (quoted in Dickinson, 1992: 20).

Newspaper letter pages and radio phone-ins have become havens to those self-appointed guardians of the English language for whom any misspellings or mispunctuation is regarded as a symbol of moral decline and the decay of modern civilisation. The split infinitive and double negatives (like single mothers and foreign social security scroungers) have become causes for national concern.

Terms like 'progressive', 'liberal' and 'student centred' have become terms of ridicule and abuse; synonymous with self-indulgence, lack of rigour and a general decline in the standards of behaviour in society as a whole.

This view of language is based essentially on a deficiency model — that students lack the 'right' language and that such deficiencies have to be made good. It marks a return to the old style 'remedial' English teaching in which the emphasis is always on identifying weaknesses within a framework of 'good' and 'bad' English. The emphasis is on technical skills and correctness rather than on creativity and the powers of self-expression. Its methodology is to give unconfident writers more of the same in the hope that the message will finally 'sink in'; a theory of educational practice which Freire saw as the 'digestive' concept of knowledge. The illiterate is:

> under-nourished ... starving for letters, thirsty for words .... The word must be deposited, not born of the creative effort of the learners. As understood in this concept, man is a passive being, the object of the process of learning to read and write, and not its subject. (Freire, 1972: 23–4)

Yet if you walk into any ABE class you will find people oppressed by feelings of powerlessness, dependency and low self-esteem. These adult students are the products of this so called 'golden age' of English teaching. They have been thoroughly imbued with the notion of the immorality of 'bad' English; that if you can't spell it you can't write it. They sit before the blank page frozen with self-doubt and fear of making a mistake. One student with whom I was researching early writing experiences at school described the physical symptoms of 'fear, sweat and shivering as if with a chill' when he was asked to write. The idea of writing as enjoyable or in any way empowering was absolutely alien to him. If there was a literary equivalent for 'tongue-tied' this would be it.

We emerge from the educational system with the clear message that good writing is synonymous with correct writing. Accordingly, the process of written communication is reduced to a purely mechanical activity. One student recalled for me during an interview I had with her in preparing this chapter:

> I had a vivid imagination and loved making up stories for my brother but when I wrote them in class the teacher made so many corrections particularly with the spellings that I did everything I could to avoid doing any writing.

Many students describe the sense of being the victims of some mysterious set of codes and rules from which they have been excluded. A facility with language is reduced to a series of booby traps designed to expose the unwary writer to ridicule and contempt. Another student's experience of writing was dominated by 'all those funny little whirly things, those dots and squiggles'. The written word becomes a source of humiliation and marginalisation.

'Finding a Voice … and Finding a Spelling Mistake'

I have been involved in ABE ever since the campaign was first launched nearly 20 years ago. In 1989 I found myself employed on a Flexible Learning Project in Dorset. One of my initiatives was to set up a Drop In Workshop. The idea was that students should work through a nice tidy set of competencies carefully enshrined in their personal learning plan. The trouble was that they kept on straining at the leash to get together as a group and, worse still, no matter what 'useful' tasks I set them to take home they would persist in coming back with the most wonderful pieces of writing about themselves and their own experiences which had nothing to do with alphabetic order or form filling! Perhaps I'm not a very efficient workshop 'manager' but personal writing soon became a subversive activity and when I needed to demonstrate the outcomes of the workshop at the end of the project those were the 'products' of which I felt proudest.

Between 1991 and 1994 I was employed to coordinate a project funded by the Regional Arts Board to extend opportunities for creative writing with students in ABE schemes. While I was in the process of collecting my thoughts for this chapter in June 1993, an incident occurred within the project which crystallised the sort of educational attitudes which have so damaged adult students. I was organising a residential writing weekend for ABE students. The students spent the first day in workshops talking, sharing ideas and struggling to express them on paper. In the evening we all gathered together to read our work to one another. Anyone who has participated in an event like this cannot fail to recognise their power to move and inspire. This was no exception. Over 50 people were crammed into a smoky lounge just off the bar. A student introduced the writers. The Autobiography Workshop started off and the first writer stood up to read her piece. The hand holding the paper shook, the voice stumbled and trembled slightly. Fifty faces watched expectantly, sympathising with the reader's nervousness, nodding in agreement, grinning encouragement. The concentration was so intense you could almost touch it. The reader finished. The room erupted in cheers, feet stamped, people stood up, arms raised, clapping. This atmosphere carried on for over two hours. The elation and excitement never faltered. It was the most simple and basic form of publication. For many of those present it was the first time they had experienced the power of the written word, of finding their own voice, a voice which was listened to and respected.

The following week I was back at work dealing with the aftermath of the weekend — paying bills, writings reports for funders. Amongst the piles of paper was a message from a tutor whose student had been at the weekend. Yes, the student seemed to have enjoyed the weekend but the tutor had been very concerned to find some spelling mistakes on the handouts that the student had brought back from the weekend. They were considering a formal complaint. My

anger almost immediately subsided into despair. We had spent the whole weekend saying you don't need to be able to spell in order to write and yet the first
thing the tutor had noticed about the handout was the spelling mistakes. The
handout had, in fact, been produced by a student who was leading the Workshop
and I decided to find out what the response of the participants had been. This is
what one student wrote:

> I have not had very good experiences with teachers, they have never
> seemed to understand my problem. Teachers have always shouted at me
> and bullied me, telling me that I am stupid. I believed this and always
> thought that the teacher was right. I always looked up to them, putting them
> on a pedestal. As I grew older I became quite nervous of teachers, even my
> children's teachers. Teachers to me were never wrong.
>
> With Steve (the student/workshop leader) at first I felt very nervous. I felt
> tense because I know I cannot spell. I didn't think I was going to be able to
> do the morning workshop but when Steve explained that he had problems
> too, I began to think of him as a person, not as a teacher standing in front of
> the classroom. It meant so much to me to be amongst people who have sim-
> ilar problems with spelling. Suddenly the workshop and writing became
> enjoyable!

This is one of many examples I have observed in this work of a difference
between the attitudes of tutors and their students towards the authority of 'the
teacher' in literacy education. This student found Steve an empowering teacher
not *in spite of* Steve's evident weakness in spelling, but *because of* them and
because of Steve's confidence in revealing his own vulnerability. It was this that
helped her see Steve more fully as 'a person, not as a teacher standing in front of
the classroom'; and it was this recognition that enabled this student to feel
released into the pleasure to be found in the struggle to write.

For most students, accustomed to seeing teachers as free from their own difficulties in literacy, and for many of their tutors too, used to assuming that this is a
model to which they must also conform, the notion that writing can be something enjoyable, something to experiment with, is incomprehensible.

For them the writing content and the means of expressing it are inextricably
bound together. If your spelling and grammar are faulty then your writing and
the thoughts expressed in that writing are faulty. If your thoughts and ideas are
not worthy of respect then what is the point of trying to communicate them anyway? By putting the emphasis on *how* students write, teachers risk undermining
their confidence and invalidate *what* they write.

Seen from this perspective the whole issue of writing and language assumes a
deeply political significance. A whole section of society is disenfranchised from

the written word. This is the section of society most likely to be suffering from educational underprivilege. Because they do not feel they have the necessary skills to articulate their experience in writing, the expression of that experience is effectively stifled.

Self-expression and Spelling

I am not arguing that the teaching of formal writing skills should be abandoned. ABE students know better than anyone that it is important to spell correctly and to write in standard English because people will discriminate against those who can't. Students need to be given access to as wide a range of writing forms as possible, particularly those forms which will give them access to power in society, such as formal letter writing, essays, reports. The issue is not *whether* students need to acquire formal writing skills but *how* they can acquire them most successfully.

Grammar, punctuation and spelling are all needed in order to communicate clearly to an audience. However, they are only part of the writing process. The crucial first step for anyone working on their writing is to gain an awareness of their reader and a conviction that they have something worth saying to that reader. This ability to 'find their voice', to experience the creative power of writing, to validate their own experiences and lives through the written word is absolutely central to their progress as writers. Until students experience that sense of power and ownership of the written word, until they trust the authority of their own words, they will always identify themselves as the victim, or as inadequate and illiterate, and never feel in control of these sets of rules and codes of language. Personal writing fuses the content with the means of expression in a way that no other form of writing can.

Yet the whole issue of the place of personal and expressive writing in the ABE curriculum is coming under increasing attack as literacy skills become dominated by the need to demonstrate competency in a set of narrow occupationally related activities. For some, the crusade against personal writing has come to embody a whole set of values, approaches to teaching and implications for the teacher/student relationship that they find distinctly threatening.

'It's Too Wishy Washy'

Those that dismiss expressive writing as 'wishy washy' claim that such writing lacks discipline and rigour. It is self-indulgent and is only of interest to the writer. How do you measure progress?

The trouble is that expressive writing does not fit neatly into the framework of narrowly defined objectives which can be used to demonstrate measurable outcomes. Programmes of work which concentrate on the technical acquisition of skills are able to quantify very precisely whether the learning has been successful or not. There are no grey areas. The teacher is put firmly in control of what is correct or incorrect.

It is tempting for tutors to become obsessed with spelling and to concentrate in great detail on every mistake their student has made. I have worked with tutors who regard the ideas that have been expressed in their students' writing as almost inconsequential. Such responses, which reduce writing to a purely technical expertise, have a totally demoralising and demotivating effect on students: 'My ideas are worthless because my spelling is worthless. So what's the point in working on my writing if I haven't got anything worth writing about.'

Cynthia Klein in her article 'Learning to Spell — or Spelling to Learn' supports this view that good spelling comes before creativity and expressiveness in writing and she argues that 'it is only automatic spelling and handwriting which enable free and fluent expression' (Klein, 1992 : 23).

These views ignore the fact that there are two processes at work in any written task — the creative process and the critical editorial process. Placing good spelling and handwriting as the lynchpin of any writing activity ignores the need to generate ideas and to provide the circumstances in which those mechanical techniques can be meaningfully applied. When the instruction takes place in the context of the student's desire to communicate something which is important to them the opportunity to learn the conventions follows quite naturally. Cynthia Klein's argument ignores the crucial importance of motivation; that it is the purpose and interest of the subject which generates a wider commitment to all the other aspects of writing.

A learner may come to an ABE group with a request for help with punctuation. The literacy tutor knows that judgements about whether to use full stops and commas are best developed when the learner is producing written text which actually *needs* punctuation in order to clarify the meaning. Punctuation marks can then be understood as useful symbols in the context of written communication. (Clarke, 1993: 16)

Writers write for readers. Establishing a sense of audience is crucial in developing the critical skills of the editor. This is most readily achieved by publication of students' writings. If we define 'publication' as anything which enables writing to be shared then it can range from a wall display or a reading to a glossy desk-top-published production. The main, although not sole, purpose of writing is to have an effect on someone else. Writers need to know that they have communicated something they care about to an audience who they respect.

Functional *Versus* Expressive Writing

> My students have come to a Brush Up Your English class. They need to write
> business letters and reports. It's got nothing to do with Creative Writing.

This view is typical of a backlash against expressive writing and its place in
the ABE curriculum. It was most starkly expressed by Sue Slipman speaking at
the 1991 ALBSU Annual Conference when she accused tutors of using student
writing 'as a way of confining students to an educational ghetto', and dismissed
student publishing in adult literacy education as the ' "Valium" of basic education — an excuse for lack of planning and rigour and a poverty of expectation'.

This backlash against texts published from personal writing appears to stem
from an assumption that functional writing tasks are necessarily the best and
only way of gaining functional competency. It does not acknowledge that once
you have achieved a sense of control and the power of the written word in one
context it is readily transferred to other situations.

All writing is part of a continuum which encompasses many different forms
of writing — reports, letters of complaint, short stories and poems. Students
need to experience a repertoire of different kinds of writing and to investigate
the different uses of language which are contained in them. They need to be
given time to explore, to experiment, to expand, to try out different roles and
hear different voices.

Report writing does not exist in a form of quarantine from any other form of
writing. As Harold Rosen argues: 'one important feature of genres ... is *their
capacity to absorb one another*. Genres cannibalise other genres. They have
strong digestive systems' (Rosen, 1993: 182). Even the most practical uses of
language cannot be conceived without the use of creative thought — the ability
to express complex ideas simply, to choose the most appropriate words, to
develop ideas, to shape narrative and create meaning — all require imaginative
intelligence on the part of the writer.

By encouraging rigid distinctions between formal and informal writing we are
in danger of reinforcing the notion that transactional writing is dull, remote and
stuffy while personal writing is fun. One ABE organiser whose students had
been doing some reminiscence work in a creative writing workshop as part of
the project commented: 'They have produced some wonderful writing and have
really enjoyed the workshops but now they need to get back to some *real* work.'
I often wonder why celebration, enjoyment and active involvement should be so
incompatible with 'real' work!

We should encourage our students to use their personal experience and to
employ it whenever it helps to clarify and elucidate. Adults who want to

improve their formal communication skills often commence with the belief that such writing has to be impersonal and to obey a rigid set of rules which govern that particular form. As Sean Taylor argues elsewhere in this book the pressure to write in order to 'impress' and not to appear dumb is overwhelming. As a result newcomers to literacy classes sometimes produce writing which is unnecessarily verbose, unclear and smattered with a liberal dose of inflated gobbledygook. Worse still it can be stultifyingly boring and totally unilluminated by the light of human passion and personal experience. When students' feelings become isolated from their thoughts they become woolly, inaccurate and dishonest.

One example among many in my experience is of the woman who asked me to help her with an essay about the experiences of mature students returning to education. She herself is a mature student who after a series of low-paid jobs, an early marriage, children and divorce had enrolled on an Access course at the local FE College. Although nervous and unconfident, she did not conform to the 'passive victim' stereotype of the woman returner. She was a strong assertive woman who had reflected upon and valued the challenges she had faced in her life. Over a number of months since she started the course she had struggled with objectivity, of trying to write in an impersonal mode without acknowledging her own experience. The frustration and tension of powerful feelings being deliberately suppressed were painfully evident in the end product. It was as if she was wearing someone else's shoes — they didn't fit! The feet belonged to her but not the shoes she was forcing them into — similarly the experience that belonged to her did not fit into the language in which she felt obliged to express it.

We started again from scratch and started to adopt an autobiographical/ reminiscence approach to her subject. In making connections between her life experiences and learning she actually began to gain a sense of control and power over her writing. She started to use her own feelings and personal history to make sense of the 'objective' points she needed to make. Suddenly the piece of writing came to life as she used her own passions and deep concerns as evidence to support the impartial truths with which she was wrestling. The writings flowed with an assurance and ease which had been totally lacking in the original efforts. The essay marked a turning point in her confidence in coping with academic writing.

What I have set out here is a context within British ABE practice in which the use of personal writing and publishing has come to feel like a subversive activity and is increasingly regarded as marginal to 'mainstream' literacy teaching. It does not sit easily with notions like 'measurable outcomes' or 'setting *realistic* learning aims'. It seems like a luxury in terms of the demands it places on our time and resources. In the short term it may be difficult to justify as 'cost efficient'.

Yet if our aim is to produce powerful, self-assured writers who are in control of their own words, there is no quick fix solution. We need to halt students' life-long withdrawal from the writing process, challenge their (and our) assumptions about what makes 'good' writing and show that writing can form a meaningful and vital expression of all aspects of their lives.

References

Clarke, Julia (1993) Unpacking student centred learning. Unpublished thesis, University of Southampton.

Dickinson, Trevor (1992) Passionate intensity, myths and realities: a backcloth. In *Made Tongue Tied by Authority New Orders for English?* Longman York Publishing Services.

Freire, Paulo (1972) *Cultural Action for Freedom.* Harmondsworth, Middx: Penguin.

Klein, Cynthia (1992) Learning to spell or spelling to learn. *ViewPoints* 13.

Rosen, Harold (1993) How many genres in narrative? *Changing English* 1 (1).

5 Working on Writing with Refugees

HELEN SUNDERLAND

It is 9.15 on a quiet, bright August morning in Clapham, South London. I walk into the Adult Education Centre, unlock the office, take the registers out of the drawer, begin to get the day ready for the 10.00 o'clock start of our six week Summer School for Refugees. I am not the first in the building. In the activities hall, sitting round groups of tables, students are already working — there is a young couple from Iran, the husband is writing in Farsi while his wife works on a drawing symbolising oppression in her country and their child does laps of the hall, waiting for the creche to open. An older African man, his hair beginning to grey, is fleshing out his account in English of the education system in Ethiopia. Farah, tall, slim and very young, only just out of high school, is working on a poem about leaving her parents in Somalia. What has made these men and women, who have a full day of studying ahead of them, so eager to work?

They are people keen to share their pride and knowledge of their countries with others, to demonstrate their skills. They are eager to explain what has led them to take the drastic step of leaving everything they know behind them, and to turn the negative image of themselves projected back to them by British immigration systems, press and (some) people, as seekers of asylum who need help with English, accommodation, money, jobs and health-care into a positive one of people with skills, talents and experiences that they can contribute to this country.

It is one of the shibboleths of adult education that as teachers we all recognise the previous learning and experience our students bring. In fact, how much do we use or allow the students opportunity to demonstrate this learning and experience? The following from Mike Baynham, written in 1988, still rings true today, in spite of all the weasel words about accreditation of prior learning:

> Too often as teachers we behave as if we were teaching people how to communicate (tell stories, request politely, insist), instead of recognizing that they already know how to communicate, they come to the task of

69

learning another language with a lifetime's experience of communicating in one or more languages. We need to enter into a dialogue with our students which can include their experience as language users, their understanding of the process of learning a new language, their crises of adaptation to the ways of another society, which may greet them with racism and the denial of opportunity. (Baynham, 1988: 122)

Working with students through personal and creative writing is one way to initiate this dialogue. In the case studies that follow I will show how teachers were able to learn as well as teach — learning about the history and culture of students' countries and about human experiences that hopefully the teachers will never have to go through.

In the 1990s, however, adult basic education (ABE) funding is increasingly being driven by ideas of *performance outcomes*, measured in discrete language or literacy tasks which, too often, limit or deny students' previous experiences. At the same time, the teaching practice of ESOL[1] has, since the 1970s (when I first began teaching ESOL classes myself), all too often been concentrated on students' abilities to communicate orally. Writing, when practised at all, has tended to be of the functional variety — initially in the 1970s and early 1980s concentrating on the 'letters to school' type of survival writing and, more lately, on the writing needed to study or obtain work effectively, such as note-taking or job applications. In this chapter, I want to re-assert the importance of an educational approach to ESOL which, in my experience, by giving value to students' capacities to reflect on and share their life experience in writing provides an effective means to student progress and confidence, and is an essential complement to these other approaches. First, I will describe, from two different examples, an approach which, through working on writing, enabled teachers and students to enter a dialogue that gave the students opportunities to express what they knew, felt and had done, and gave teachers opportunities to learn about other countries, cultures and human experience. Secondly, I go on to pick out the key arguments for persisting with and developing this approach.

From Pain to Pride

In 1988 and 1989, as ESOL organiser for Clapham Battersea Adult Education Institute, I was responsible for organising and working on summer schools, each catering for approximately 90 newly arrived refugees. These were run in response to demand from organisations working with refugees. Refugees arriving in London in May and after found it was too late to be admitted to ESOL classes which generally finished at the end of June. When they came back in September, as they had been told, it was often too late to get a place on a college course. The idea of the summer school was to give an intensive ESOL course, plus advice about suitable courses for the next academic year, plus orientation into life in London (visits and visiting speakers on essentials such as income support, housing etc.).

An essential part of the schools were the Open Days which were run each year. Students created displays about their countries which were made up of student writings, plus pictures, books, maps, artefacts, clothes etc. that they had brought with them. During the Open Days students then talked to visitors about the displays and about their countries. The first one had been put on with the aim of publicising the school and raising money for the following year. However, it was such a successful event in itself in that it provided a focus for the language work we did in classes, and the students and tutors enjoyed it so much, that we decided to repeat it in following years.

The writing for the first school was done in separate classes (levels varying from elementary to advanced). Teachers talked about the Open Day and discussed with the students in their classes what they wanted to write about. Nearly all chose to explain why they had left their countries. Most were fluent writers in their own languages. They were keen to write and needed little encouragement, just some help with transferring their skills into writing English. This was done through discussion of differences in students' languages and English of discourse organisation, register and style, as well as the more obvious help with grammar, punctuation and vocabulary. The writings were proof-read, re-drafted, typed on a computer and mounted for display on Open Day. They were also collated into a book which all students took away with them at the end of the school.

It is often said among teachers working with refugees in English classes that students do not want to talk about their experiences — they are too painful, and students should be given more neutral topics. If this is true, it may be that writing gives people an opportunity to broach areas of their experience they cannot bring themselves to speak about. Looking back at the books of writing produced by the students in the first summer school, I see that about a third of students wrote of atrocities that most of them had not previously talked about in the school. The following are typical extracts from these writings. The first is from a young Colombian woman who fled to this country with her sister, husband and baby:

> My eldest brother was murdered, my second brother was tortured when he was in prison. By who? The Police ... The government is very bad.[2]

The next piece is by a young Ugandan, in his middle teens:

> What I have seen and experienced such as arbitrary roadblocks or the sexual abuse by three men of one of the girls from school will always be part of my personal history. No-one has any right to stop me from saying all these things.[2]

I could quote several similar passages written by different students, possibly less blunt, but with the same kind of content. No ESOL teacher who has worked with refugees will be surprised by these writings. They encompass the almost universal experience of the students we teach. It can be very difficult for teachers to know how to react to writings such as these, it is a very human reaction to feel guilty about not having suffered or to feel collusion (through being British) in the situation that caused the students' suffering, and it is possibly fear of their own pain as much as the pain of students that leads teachers to avoid such work. I have been told by case-workers working closely with refugees that it is important not to appear shocked by such stories, but to listen (or read) almost dispassionately. However, I have also been told that it is important to give students the opportunity to give voice to these experiences *if they so choose.*

This proved to be the case in our summer schools where reading the writings of others helped to bring cohesion to the group and to lessen the feelings of isolation that many of the newly arrived refugees felt. Students were interested in reading each other's writings, and in discussing the similarities in their experiences. Discussions were an essential component of the writing process — they preceded the writing, went on as drafts were examined, and followed after final drafts were read out. As well as comparing experiences, students had linguistic discussions about vocabulary and meaning and helped each other to phrase their ideas into written English. Politics was an integral part of these discussions, and I have a very vivid memory of one communist refugee from Turkey connecting his experience with that of a refugee fleeing a communist regime for many of the same reasons that he had fled Turkey: 'He's left because he's not a communist, I've left because I am a communist, and now we're both the same — refugees!' He was typical of the students who gained a lot more than learning English from the schools. Through writing and through discussing and reading each other's work they formed friendships which outlasted the school, and recognised bonds of common experience which strengthened them, and they left at the end of the school visibly more confident than when they had arrived.

In the second summer school we organised the writing for the Open Day differently. As well as writing, teachers and students decided to produce a collage for all the classes, consisting of drawings and writings by the students about their countries. For one hour of every day (five days a week for four weeks) all four classes met together in the activities hall to plan, write and draw. There were approximately 90 students. The main group were young people from Somalia, but we also had students of all ages from Eritrea, Ethiopia, Kurdistan, Vietnam, Colombia, Iran, Angola, Cote D'Ivoire and Peru. Their educational and professional background was as varied as is usual in an ESOL class, with doctors, engineers, farmers, journalists, sociologists and freedom-fighters sitting alongside school-leavers. Students with the same language, but at different levels of English, sat and worked together. This time, they mainly chose to write factual accounts of their countries — sharing out the topics: 'I'll write about politics, you write about education.' Some wrote in English, others in their own languages as well as in English. Students illustrated the writing or drew for the collage. They produced flags, political cartoons, sketches of their villages, traditional designs. As happened the year before, they seemed to need very little encouragement to start writing, and the finished product in terms of visual and written display materials was impressive. Again, most were accomplished writers in their own languages. They already had skills of composing, proof-reading, re-drafting. Where they needed help with English phrasing, grammar or vocabulary it was given by other students who shared a language, or by teachers all working together in the hall. The writing and the drawing process appeared to prove cathartic — students were obviously enjoying themselves, and arguments and discussions were generated among the students about what they had written. Students were impressed by each other's skills and spent time moving round the hall looking at each other's writing and drawing. Their motivation was infectious. They came into the hall to work before classes started, at lunch-time and in the afternoons if there were no other activities planned.

All the teachers were impressed by the range and content of the writing and art work produced. One student, an educationalist in his own country, wrote what amounted to a book about Ethiopia, giving details of history, culture, government, education and the economy. Another, who was a writer in his country, produced a play. A third wrote out, illustrated and translated old Persian proverbs. Others concentrated on the political backgrounds which led to them becoming refugees. Even those who spoke very little English wrote something — for instance an acrostic poem describing their country:

Eritrea liberation
Rights for people
Independence
Tigrinya is the national language
Revolution
Eritrea never kneels down
Arrive — the time will arrive. Paulos (ILEA, 1990: 11)

As an English teacher it is interesting to look at the vocabulary already available to this student, a beginner in English. Liberation, independence, revolution, kneel down — these are not usually the meat of an ESOL beginner lesson.

Making the collage and mounting the writings and pictures for display was the culmination of several weeks of hard but collaborative work. I feel sure that the motivation to write was fuelled by the desire to inform, and students told me, individually, and in the school newsletter that they produced each week, how much they had enjoyed seeing information about their country on display at the Open Day. They were also keen to expand on and discuss the display with visitors. For those of us working with the students it was an exhilarating experience, and for everyone who visited the Open Day an informative and sometimes eye-opening insight into the different countries.

A Day in the Life — Then and Now

This example gives an account of working on writing with a very different group of students. They were refugees too, mainly from Vietnam, and had been in the country for several years. Most were ethnic Chinese, and could write only a little or not at all in either Chinese or Vietnamese.

We worked on the Archive Project, the idea of a member of the Art Department who wanted to do something different for the end of the summer term. It was based on the theme of a time-capsule and all classes in the Adult Institute were invited to make a record of Clapham in the 1980s which would be deposited in the local library for posterity. Art classes drew views of Clapham, poetry classes wrote poems. In the Clapham ESOL classes, we decided to base all our work, eight hours a week for a six week period, on contributions to the Archive Project, culminating in a display. We were working mainly with classes at an elementary level of English, 95% of whom were refugees. We worked on several different themes — taking, developing and printing photographs of the Clapham used by the students (as opposed to that used and viewed by the Art Department) and writing captions; facilities in the area that students used; a map of the Clapham area and local journeys; interviewing each other; recording music that students liked and saying why they liked it. In the main, we worked all together — over twenty students, usually three teachers, squashed into one room. Though cramped for space, it gave the atmosphere of a workshop rather than an ESOL class, and was more productive in terms of students working collaboratively.

Unlike the groups in the summer school detailed earlier, most of the students did not write fluently in their own languages and had not previously been given much opportunity to focus on personal writing in their ESOL classes. The educational thinking in ESOL has borrowed much more from the EFL than from the Literacy tradition, and the emphasis was then on communicative competence, writing skills being practised through worksheets to back up the oral work. As I have already said, where literacy was tackled (and we had set aside two out of the eight hours a week to focus on literacy) the concentration was on the functional such as filling in a form, and on skills such as using a dictionary. Although my experience has changed my thinking, and this chapter is about how and why I feel working on writing from experience is essential in ESOL, as I visit classes and institutions as a teacher-trainer, it seems to me that practice has not changed. Wordpower may have replaced the RSA Profile Certificate, but the thinking that underpins both are still task rather than process orientated, and the products required are still pieces of functional writing.

The main writing focused round comparing 'a day in the life' in Clapham contrasted with 'a day in the life' in students' own countries. The first pieces they came up with were thin in the extreme — 'I get up at 7.00 o'clock. I go to school. I come home at 12.00 o'clock.' But when they started on accounts of their own countries, the interest level rose and the writing began to flow. Prompted by discussion and questions to write fuller accounts, they started to get more involved. Where they had difficulty with vocabulary or expressions, they asked each other, us, their families at home. Students wrote and re-wrote, they expanded their texts, they corrected grammar and spelling, they read each other's work. This was before the days of ready access to computers — we had two ancient typewriters in the room, and some students used these. Most seemed to take great pleasure in re-drafting again and again and the final versions were neatly written out, with interesting content, and informative for people from different countries.

> In my country I used to wake up everyday at 4.30 am and have my breakfast of soup and rice. At 6.00 am I would go to work in the fields — it was very hot, about 30° in May and June ... (T. P. Vuong)

> My family had a coffee shop. I used to get up at 5.00 and go to open my coffee shop at 5.30. All the people came for breakfast before they went to work. We served noodles, rice and soup. In Vietnam many people eat breakfast in the coffee shops ... (Nguyen)

The final display was of a much higher standard in terms of content, vocabulary and grammatical accuracy than we had anticipated (to our shame) and taught us what it was possible for this level of students to achieve. Visitors to the display from the art and other departments were surprised and informed by the students' writings. With mostly English or European students, members of other departments had not had much contact with people from other cultures and appeared interested in reading about their lives and realising that the people they bumped into in the canteen had interesting stories to tell. The students were pleased with the product (their writings and the display), but also appeared to grow in confidence through the process — sharing their knowledge of their countries, producing an extended piece of writing in English where before they had attempted nothing longer than a sentence on a worksheet. The result was an improvement in English language skills altogether, students who generally communicated in a purely responsive way in English, through one or two broken sentences, had for the first time initiated a piece of extended discourse in English.

Issues and Reflections

What issues need to be considered in order to encourage good student writing?

Today's educational/political climate

As teachers we must recognise the importance of the processes in education when the current climate concentrates almost exclusively on products. Funding in adult and further education is directed at accredited schemes that recognise measurable outcomes, often highly inappropriate for refugee students of English. It is insulting, not to say faintly ridiculous, to tick boxes accrediting the ability to read a map (one of the competences in a widely used scheme) for someone who has travelled through several countries and two continents to get to here. Meanwhile there are no boxes to tick for improved confidence, lessening of isolation, increased motivation to learn. No boxes either for a dialogue between student and teacher or for teacher learning from students as we learnt about student experiences, cultures and countries in the examples given earlier. It is vital that the lessons from the more liberal days of adult education are not lost in the current appetite for performance targets and measurable outcomes.

Recognition of prior skills

As I said at the beginning of this chapter, this is currently a fashionable concept. But before prior skills can be acknowledged, we need to find out what they are. We should be asking what writing students have done before; in which language(s); and in which script(s). We need to know if they have written in a professional capacity (for instance journalist, academic). We should consider asking students to write in their own language(s) as part of the initial assessment. Through discussion, we can find out how much story-telling was part of students' experience, how used the student is to narrating a story, developing it and holding audience interest. The skills of writing and of story-telling need to be separated from the English language skill, and it needs to be recognised that just because someone cannot write English it does not necessarily follow that s/he cannot write. The following is a small extract from a piece about Kurdestan written by a Kurdish journalist, an extremely accomplished story-teller, at the time of writing, a student in my ESOL reading and writing class. That he already has a powerful style of writing is evident even in his second language, all we needed to do in the English class was to look at the nuts and bolts of grammar, spelling and punctuation.

> No world radio, TV, newspapers or magazines write about this country that is oppresssed and needs help. They are only interested in business and profit. Something very little is made big news — if a race horse belonging to a millionaire breaks a leg, all TV and newspapers write about it. But here is a

country that is divided and looted, its people kept in poverty, repressed and put in prison if they protest. Who writes about it? There has been no power to this day, truthfully to help and look after this people, to allow them to breathe freely in their country and their lives. (Hossein)[3]

Acceptance of the political dimension

ESOL has a history of focusing on the functional — visits to the hospital, shopping in the market, using the telephone. Initially when English as a Second Language began in the 1970s, this was to differentiate ESOL from the then very grammar-based English as a Foreign Language practice and to concentrate on the kind of English that students were expected to need. There are still good reasons for including this kind of English in a syllabus for newly arrived refugees who will have to go shopping, use the telephone and visit the doctor. However, to concentrate on this to the exclusion of everything else puts students in the position of only practising the English that reinforces the view of them as people in need of coping strategies. It also gives very little opportunity for extended writing practice — letters to the milkman are the most that will be expected. To acknowledge and include a political dimension in the content of ESOL teaching gives refugees a real opportunity to talk about what they know and why they came, as well as widening the scope of discussions, reading material and reasons for writing. It opens up the dialogue I have already talked about and gives teachers as well as students an opportunity to learn and change. This is so even with students who have an elementary knowledge of English — one group I worked with were very keen to talk and write about their flags — from discussion about when countries got their own flags came issues of history and colonialism, from discussion about which flag they supported came issues of civil war and partition.

Many teachers are worried about possible disagreements between students — between Iraqis and Iranians during the war or between Eritreans and Ethiopians. I have seen arguments turned into opportunities for writing by asking people from different sides in a conflict to write down their point of view. The argument becomes diffused and the students are motivated to write.

Expectations

Are our expectations high enough? I fear they are frequently pitched too low. Often ESOL teachers refer to students as 'illiterate', yet how many people have no literacy skills at all? Maybe some of us teachers do not feel comfortable with writing. Do we then project these feelings onto our students? With suitable facilities, time and encouragement the students may well surprise us. In the Summer School for Refugees one student wrote a play about despotism and choice, another almost a whole book about his country.

Time and facilities

No-one is likely to produce a piece of good writing in fifteen minutes at the end of a language lesson. Students need to be given time to think up and discuss their ideas, draft and re-draft, show and discuss their writings with others and re-draft yet again as a result of this discussion. And yet the structure and methodology we have inherited from English as a Foreign Language rarely allows students this time. Teachers are expected to present and practice language items, to encourage students to communicate — the emphasis being on production rather than reflection. As teachers, we need to be aware of the length of time it can take to produce a finished piece of writing and be confident enough to allow students that time. Students should have facilities to produce their work — adequate paper (this is a serious comment in this time of cuts, I have visited classes where there is no paper), typewriters, wordprocessors, software utilising their languages. They need to be taught the skills of using computers and keyboards. If possible there should be room available with facilities for them to continue writing outside lesson time.

Recognition

Though in my experience students are very keen to write whether or not there is an end product, it is good to have a focus for the writing. This may be to record their lives in an archive, or for an exhibition, as described earlier. It may also be for a reading event (an idea borrowed from Adult Literacy and not much used in ESOL) or for publication — and again ESOL schemes are still much slower than literacy schemes to publish their students' writing. Research on materials for teaching ESOL resulting in the publication of a bibliography (Sunderland, 1992) found very few collections of students' writing and identified this as a gap in provision of published materials. Alternatively, the end product may be something for students to keep for themselves, a book about their lives to give to their children, a diary to look back on.

Other chapters in this book discuss blocks students may have to writing. In my experience and the experience of others working with refugees, this has rarely been an issue. Refugees have almost always been eager to share experiences. In an article about working with refugees, Meena Wood describes the following experience:

> One of the students, when asked the question why she came to this country — without prompting — produced a written sheet with a detailed account of her journey here ... which included witnessing numerous deaths and violence. (Wood, 1991: 37)

This may be because the refugees are experienced writers in another language or languages already, but it may also be because it is the only time since their arrival in this country that they have been asked to share their knowledge, culture and experiences instead of having to learn about Britain and the British and, as I said at the beginning of this chapter, thus have the opportunity to present a positive image of themselves as proficient, educated and knowledgeable people.

But if the students are fluent and experienced writers in another language already, why work on writing more? There are many reasons for doing so. The first, and most obvious, is that the people I have been describing have deliberately made a decision to learn English, which, as I am suggesting, means developing their fluency in English literacy as well as English language. Writing, as well as reading, is therefore of central importance to them: fluent writers in their own language as some (but not all) of them may be, they have now a declared interest in learning the conventions and possibilities of English. This means exploring, both in their reading and writing, the differences in style, register or discourse with their own language(s). There are also practical reasons — refugees may need to improve their writing in English for jobs, further study or personal satisfaction. There are psychological reasons — producing good writing that people want to read validates students' experiences and improves their confidence; many appear to want to write and write eagerly when given the opportunity; writing can be a cathartic experience and a way of expressing what refugees do not feel able to talk about. There are pedagogic reasons — writing is a way of demonstrating students' skills, knowledge and experience. And there are social reasons — writing gives refugees a voice, a basis for sharing their experience with others and, as was shown in the account of the Refugee Summer School, a lessening of isolation. And finally it is worth working on writing with refugees because readers (including teachers and other students) can learn from and enjoy their work.

Notes

1. Reference to ESOL (English for Speakers of Other Languages) in this chapter refers to English that is taught to refugees and long-term immigrants intending to settle and/or work in this country. It has distinct aims, content and methodology from EFL (English as a Foreign Language) which is for visitors who have come to this country with the intention of learning English and expect to return once they have done so. Until the late 1980s ESOL was known as ESL (English as a Second Language), and in fact this term is still used by some people. Those in adult and further education who made a decision to change did so because of equal opportunities implications. It was considered more positive to define people in terms of what they could do (i.e. speak other languages) rather than what they could not. The association of second language with *second rate* and *second best* was also considered unfortunate.
2. Student writing taken from *I Can't Tell Everything*, Clapham Battersea AEI, 1988.
3. Extract from *I am Kurdish*, taken from student magazine *Hello 3*, Clapham Battersea AEI, 1987.

References

Baynham, M. (1988) Talking from experience — writing and talk in the ESL classroom. In S. Nicholls and E. Hoadley-Maidmont (eds) *Current Issues in Teaching English as a Second Language to Adults*. London: Edward Arnold.

ILEA (1990) *Refugee Writings*. London: ESL Publishing Group, Language and Literacy Unit, ILEA.

Sunderland, H. (1992) *A Tutor's Guide to ESOL Materials for Adult Learners*. London: Language and Literacy Unit.

Wood, M. (1991) English for refugees: an enabling process. *Language Issues* 4 (2, Spring/Summer).

6 Writers in Search of an Audience: Taking Writing from Personal to Public

PATRICIA DUFFIN

My Writing Journey

I find that when I look back to my childhood that the landmarks I remember are connected to reading rather than writing. I have very vivid memories of being read to by my two great-aunts, watching as they pointed to the words on the page. Eventually, they would stop reading just before the end of the story, and insist that I could read the rest myself. I can remember the frustration of knowing that the rest of the story was there, if I could only find a way of unlocking it. I only remember the one book, *Snow White and Rose Red*, and eventually knew it by heart. The highlights of my schooldays were getting access to the glass-fronted cupboard in P7 where the school library lived, and then, joy of joys, when the town's public library started a children's section. Riches indeed. I also have good memories of being read to: fairy tales by my mother, and tales of Ireland by the teacher, in the last half-hour of the school day. What a treat!

Writing I remember as a task that school demanded I undertake. I first wrote poetry out of homesickness when I went to college and found in it a real sense of satisfaction at being able to build pictures from words. However, I never showed it to any one, anymore than I could share how miserable I felt. I know now that I wasn't alone in those feelings but we all pretended different. Again, writing became a task — lecture notes, essay deadlines, counting the words to see if I'd got there yet. It was only through working at Gatehouse that I rediscovered how writing could be a pleasure.

In the early days between 1977 and 1981 when we ran lots of writing workshops it was common practice to join in and write whenever possible. Snatches of this soon gave me a taste for more, and eventually I joined the first women's writing group set up by Commonword (Manchester's other community publisher). I found that to be both a scary and exhilarating experience, especially when we published and launched our first book (*Home Truths. Writing by North West*

Women, 1981). It created all sorts of parallels for me with my work and with the students I was encouraging to go through the same process. Certainly it confirmed my feelings about how exciting and valuable it was to put some of yourself onto paper and to try and pass that onto others. Probably that is where I first began to develop some sense of audience. This was partly through the analysis that happened in the women's writing group but, quite dramatically, through that first public reading, in September 1981.

There was the audience, and I could see and feel their interest as it leapt out and died down throughout the performance. Then, when I got up to read, I found myself in a stark empty space that had to be filled in a way that reached them and held them until I stopped. I was lucky to get it right that first time because it meant that I wanted to try again.

The Gatehouse Project (now Gatehouse Publishing Charity Ltd and Gatehouse Books Ltd) was set up in 1977 as a response to the needs of adults with reading and writing difficulties for appropriate reading material. In those early days, of what was then known as the adult literacy campaign, adults who had the courage to come forward and seek help would often end up working on children's reading books. It took the insight and energy of various individuals and organisations such as *Write First Time*[1] to begin to present a very exciting alternative to this way of working. The alternative was to use those adults' own experiences and their own words to create new and relevant reading material. Gatehouse set itself up in Manchester with two primary aims: to publish and distribute nationally some of the writing already generated in local groups; and to continue stimulating and supporting this specific group of new writers.

The experience of community publishing projects, such as Gatehouse, and others described in this book, is that anyone who sits down to write is in search of an audience of some kind. Rebecca O'Rourke, in preliminary discussions about this chapter, reminded me that even when writing only for oneself, such as a diary or to work through any kind of crisis, the act of writing it down, of doing something different with the experience, turns oneself into an audience. It is important for writers to be aware of this range of complexity of audience as soon as words are formed on the page. The audience may be a teacher or tutor, the rest of the group they belong to, their family or a faceless public: in any case, it is more than just themselves. This means that all writers need to search out and engage with critical comment on their work. The dictionary definition of 'criticism' is 'judging of merit especially of literary or artistic work'. As I skimmed the page to find it, I realised that I had inadvertently read the definition of 'critical' — 'censorious, fault-finding'. I think that this is what many of us anticipate when criticism is talked about. Therefore, little wonder that we find it so hard to receive others' views without feeling under attack. The purpose of this chapter is to outline a number of models which will hopefully provide a shift for both the writer and the critic in terms of finding other ways of giving and receiving criticism. In order to explore this I want to consider some of the ways in which the search for an audience takes place, and some of the moves from personal to public writing that this search entails. The process itself can be mapped as an intricate circular diagram with numerous points of entry and exit. There is no neat straight line, rather, given the opportunity, there is a whole range of exciting possibilities.

First, I will describe the struggle of one writer, Chris Curley, working over a period of six months with me, as editor, to take account of the response of four groups of other student readers, to his writing and prepare it for publication. Secondly, I will relate some of the work of a specific readers' group, meeting over a period of three years, whose declared purpose is to provide an 'audience' to other writers, like Chris. In discussing this work, I want to set out some of the power issues raised by the situation of a group taking on the role of critics and reviewers for peers. In preparing this chapter, I interviewed Chris and four members of the readers' group about their reflections on these different 'searches for an audience'. These were in no way interviews by an outsider: I was talking with all these people from a position where I too had been a participant in the search.

Writer *Versus* Reader: Problems and Solutions

> I thought it was just going to be what I put on a piece of paper. I didn't think about editing or worrying about how other people read it. (Chris Curley)

These are the words of the author of *The Cardigan*, one of a series of books that Gatehouse publishes for beginner-readers. This specialist set of books is designed to combat the frustration that readers often face when moving from reading their own language experience to reading books. Often, it can be the struggle to read a short section of a longer book that can produce a new sense of despair: as if the goal posts have been moved. It has always been very difficult for us at Gatehouse to find a piece of writing that is both the right length and works well as a story which we could publish in order to provide a transition for a reader in this position.

The Adult Basic Education (ABE) class which Chris attended in Manchester had been asked to write about 'something funny' as homework. He came up with a memory of the old cardigan he had grown increasingly attached to in his working life as a joiner. It was a very short piece of writing, less than a page, but it had in it all the elements of a good story. There were glimpses of the relationship he had with his wife, and with his dog, an intriguing insight into life as a joiner, and a fourth character: the cardigan itself. Passion, conflict and loss have their parts to play before the story draws to a close. So, when his tutor brought it to Gatehouse it looked to be ideal as a text for a beginner-reader. However, in order to be certain of that, we need to test it out with the readership we wanted it to reach. As new or beginner-readers form part of mixed ABE groups, we circulated this and another piece of writing to four such groups across the city. The reading and discussion were done in class time prompted by a set of questions that I had prepared, which could be used either as direct questioning or as prompts for discussion (see Appendix). I also asked groups if they would tape their sessions so as to catch the debate itself as well as the conclusions. This is a routine practice we use with all Gatehouse work. It means that the tapes are always there in order to check the progress of debates leading up to decisions. (As a worker it can be a salutory experience to play these back and have to recognise how one may have unduly influenced the outcome of a discussion, often quite unconsciously.)

The returned questionnaires without the tapes would be less than the full story; and it was by listening to the tapes made by the four groups that I, as editor, met the first audience for Chris's writing. I had designed the questions to guide the readers to focus on particular aspects of the text. I was fortunate that all the tutors I approached were interested in working in this way and I left it to them to decide how best to make use of the questionnaire. The first three questions were deliberately wide and open-ended and elicited fairly brief responses. The next question, however, asks: 'Is there anything else that you want the writer to tell you in the story? Imagine that they are in the room and you could ask them questions.' Perhaps it was the second sentence that acted as a trigger, but it is clear from the answers that there was a whole range of things that readers were eager to know more about behind the story line (in particular, more detail about the lives of the characters.) There were also plenty of responses to the question: 'Are there any parts of the story that you think would work better if some parts were left out altogether? If so can you explain this for the writer.' It was at this point that quite specific critical comment began. In Chris's case this focused around the swear words he had used in the story — 'leave strong words out' was the consensus among the groups.

As I said, the questionnaires on their own reveal only part of the picture: it was the tapes that gave me the shrieks of enjoyment produced by one group, and the depth of discussion behind the brief written replies to the first three questions come into their own. I could hear how they recognised Chris's move from dislike to a strong attachment to the cardigan that became his favourite garment as it grew more disreputable. One reader matched it with the story of her own 'lucky jumper' that she associated with the first time her driving lesson went well and so she kept on wearing it. Others saw it as 'like a comforter' and also 'like the cornerstone in the Bible — he rejected the cardigan but now he want it!' None of this richness of oral exchange could find its way into the questionnaire. The tapes also gave me a much fuller picture of people's reaction to the swear words, e.g. bloody, piss off. For some, 'bad language is everyday life' while for another: 'It knocked me off it, ruined the whole story. Makes you think of a stereotype working-class person, only vocabulary four letter words.'

Most telling of all, however, was the way in which the tapes gave a voice to the reaction of beginner-readers in the groups, such as these two:

> You could follow the story because you read it (out loud) but if some-one was reading it all alone they wouldn't be able to understand it. Maybe if it had pictures in it, maybe you could make the words out. [The groups had been sent the writing in book form with blanks where the illustrations would go.]

> Would work if read to or put on cassette; would easily remember it after two or three times as so funny.[2]

When it came to reading one of the swear words, a new reader said in a surprised voice: 'I don't think I've seen this word before.' On being told what it was, he added: 'Mind you, you say it but you don't come across it, do you? You don't read it.' It was comments like these, indicating surprise at seeing 'swear words' in writing, together with the evidence of others who, in trying to read these sentences, either omitted the words or just couldn't read past them, that were, more than any wish to censor this language, the motive for leaving them out in the final publication.

As soon as the writing had been selected by the pilot groups it was necessary for the writer to begin to get to know his audience.

Chris had been diagnosed as dyslexic and was working on various techniques for dealing with this, including teaching himself to use the wordprocessor. Originally his concern with the piece of homework he had written was to use it to work on his spelling. When he discovered that Gatehouse wanted to consider it for publication he was interested and excited and he and I met initially to take his page of writing and begin to convert it into the format we use for our beginner-reader books. This means first selecting a small number of sentences to go on a page then subdividing these in such a way that the reader can pause at the end of a line and still keep hold of the sense of the text. Once his writing was chosen to be published Chris presumed that this would happen very quickly. However, my task as editor was to take him through the publishing process as Gatehouse does it: by helping him to gain a picture of who the book was for, and then to consider what adjustments this might require. I began by showing Chris copies of other beginner-reader books and discussing the ideas for learning that lay behind them. We also looked at the feedback questionnaires and listened to snatches of tapes.

Part of our job at Gatehouse is to encourage and support students to develop their sense of themselves as writers. Gradually, I began to realise that, in this case, a contradiction was being created. As a result of my encouraging Chris's sense of himself as a writer, he began to extend his story and go into more detail about the characters. Unfortunately, this began to take the story out of the reach of new readers as it grew longer and more complex. I had to keep redirecting his attention back to their needs and away from his own. When I asked him later how he felt about this stage of our work, he said, 'I felt a bit inferior' and, in effect, that his audience was taking his story away from him.

Previously, Gatehouse beginner-reader books have been written, taped or dictated by students who were themselves beginning to read. Frances Holden, author of three books, talks about this in her introduction to would-be readers in *Keep Your Hair On*:

> At first I thought I wouldn't be able to do anything, but I can read quite a few words and I'm quite satisfied to read so many words. I can do my name and address. And when I look at my story, how do I do it? I go back in my memory for stories to write down. Sometimes I tape them and then I get so many words down myself, and I have somebody to help me with the rest. (Holden, 1983: back cover)

These are short books with approximately 10–15 pages, each page having illustrations and just a few lines of writing. So, through the use of language experience Frances had worked to produce her words on paper and then use this as reading material; a process which Wendy Moss discusses in her chapter in this book. When asked whether this work had helped her to learn, Frances said:

> Oh, yes, it's helping me a lot. I can go over the words again. I can look at my exercise books and read it all again. I can write the words in other stories and I know them when I see them in other places. (Holden, 1983: 1)

Frances had been free of Chris's conflict; for, unlike him, her reading ability closely mirrored that of her audience.

The tension created for Chris and, inevitably, for me, as editor, sprang from that difficulty described earlier of finding and writing appropriate material for a person who is, like Frances, a beginner-reader. As the gap between writer and reader widens so the dilemma of their conflicting needs becomes more apparent. Chris, as a reader, far outstripped his skills as a writer, and it was as reader, as audience, that he wanted to extend what he had written. However, my job as editor was to represent a different audience, that of readers just starting on the journey. Their needs were quite specific in terms of content and presentation: the book we were to produce together had above all to be appropriate and accessible to them in a context where few such books exist. Even with Gatehouse, where all our writers are ABE students writing for their peers, beginner-reader books like this one make up less than a quarter of our published list. As this had been clearly identified as an area of need in our development plan, we were now committed to publishing at least one of our titles every year for beginner-readers. In practice, it was proving difficult to find appropriate material to do this. Earlier books had been developed from the language experience work that tutor-scribes had been making with students who were beginner-readers. However, changes in the structure of adult education in Manchester and the national move towards accreditation was, we found, causing a reduction in this work. We had, therefore, moved to publicising among the Manchester ABE groups our search for short clear texts, using existing beginner-reader books as models for this. From our experience we knew that for the new reader a book needed to have a sense of natural progression, of hand and toe holds that enabled them to negotiate their way across the rock face of the text. The model that seemed to work best for this, we found, was the story: characters who were introduced and then sustained throughout and a narrative that worked its way through to an ending. Our invitation to groups to submit this kind of work obviously meant that the writer might not be themselves a beginner-reader.

The compromise that Chris and I reached was that he would continue to work on a longer story at the same time as we prepared his writing for beginner-readers. Despite the contradictory effort this meant, when I asked whether he would encourage other students to go through the same process, Chris's answer was a very emphatic 'Definitely'. What then did he get out of it all himself? This is what he told me:

> Before, I didn't like letting anybody read anything I wrote. I didn't like reading it myself, never mind somebody else reading it. But the finished product gave me a bit of confidence and it made me a little bit more assertive. Now I can talk a bit better about my feelings and stuff like that, that I've kept hidden for years. I got anxious while we were editing and working on the book itself but at the end of the day, I got rid of a lot of the anxiety I had all my life.

As well as shifting his perception of himself the process also changed his awareness of others:

> Instead of thinking of myself, I've got to think about other people. If I write letters I've got to think of them, the people who've got to read it.

At the end of our work together Chris did agree with what was changed, including the replacement of swear words by more acceptable ones. For him, the hardest aspect of the editorial work had been having to leave out from the short piece about the cardigan a much more substantial account of his life. He told me that he planned to go on to use the skills that he had acquired through making this book to turn his longer piece of writing into a book also. (Those skills had involved planning how the book would look: typeface, spacing, illustrations, cover design; writing an introduction and copy for the back cover; and doing a mock-up for others to comment on.) He also said to me that before getting to the stage of publication with this longer piece he would show the writing to others to give him some idea if he was on the right lines.

What Chris evidently gained, then, from this process was a keener sense of readers as other people than himself. For the students who worked as his readers, the benefit was one of learning how to be the kind of critical readers I referred to earlier: in the sense, not of 'censorious fault-finding', but of 'judging the merits' of Chris's work.

Because ABE students are extremely conscious of the struggle behind even the shortest piece of writing, often their prime concern is to praise the writer for putting pen to paper in the first place. (I can remember in a *Write First Time*[1] editorial meeting in the late 1970s, when we were selecting from writing sent in from all over the country, one student arguing fiercely that in rejecting writing from another ABE student we were also rejecting that individual's struggle to write.)

These groups, however, had learned to move on from bland comments like 'very nice' or 'I'm not keen on that' to pinning down more clearly the *reasons* for their judgements. This is a move I have seen taking place in every Gatehouse editorial group. At early meetings, the preoccupation is to recognise the value of another student's writing and the risky step this writer has taken in asking them to consider it for publication. At this stage, it has felt tempting to deal with the selection procedure for publication as some kind of division sum (so much space available divided by the texts submitted), making the choice dependent solely on matters outside the editors' views of the 'merits' of the pieces submitted. However, from our experience, it is precisely the debate about the criteria for choosing some pieces rather than others, in a situation focused on reading with the purpose of making editorial choices, which offers a vital opportunity for students to make sense of what writing development means.

For this to be valuable to student editors, an important condition is having enough pieces of writing to enable them to compare and contrast them. Usually this only happens on the second reading of submitted writings; for, as I have said, the first response which student editors want to ensure is a recognition of the writer's work in its own right. This stage, too, provides an important check on an educator-editor like me, who has read innumerable scripts and can begin to falter at the task of greeting each new one as unique, and means that the process is educative on more than one level: a learning experience for both students and tutors. The Readers' Group which I look at later illustrates this work in more detail.

So, is it worth it? Should students be put through this process of dealing with other people's reactions to their writing? As I have suggested, it makes a difference whether that other person is a tutor, their fellow learners or people beyond them. I think that the answer to this depends very much on being clear about what the writer's purposes may be. Some writing may be intended for sharing in a limited way, perhaps only with a tutor or group. It is when the writing is intended for a wider readership that the issues discussed in this section need to be taken on board. The audience may be the group, the centre or much wider; but the best possible route out to the general public is to begin with the familiar group.

Giving Feedback to the Writer

So far, I have looked at the issues that arise when giving feedback to a writer preparing for publication. Obviously, this represents only a small proportion of all those interested and involved in writing. So, what about those others? Are they interested in some kind of critique of their work, and if so, how might this be done? In 1991 Gatehouse began exploring these questions through a specially convened group known as the Readers' Group. Writers regularly send their work in to Gatehouse asking for comments, whether we might publish it or where else they could send it in the hope of being published. Inevitably, this includes a whole range of writers, not exclusively from ABE, who see us as sympathetic to new writers. After responding to this in a fairly haphazard system (very much worker based) we decided to try and find a more satisfactory and democratic way of handling these requests. We looked at a number of models operating among other member groups of the Federation of Worker Writers and Community Publishers (FWWCP)[3] most of which are not ABE groups. We invited Mike Hayler, a member of Queenspark Books, Brighton (and co-author of another chapter in this book) to come and tell a group of interested students and tutors about their Manuscript Group. What was attractive to us about his account was how clear and independent they were about their task. The group were, he told us, all volunteers, sharing the work among themselves. The outcome of our meeting with him was the establishment of the Gatehouse Readers' Group. It consists of four ABE students, two tutors, Ann McDowell, our administrator and myself.

It is important here to distinguish between the role of the Readers' Group and that of any other Gatehouse editorial group. The latter have a clear brief: to select for publication. They are provided with specific guidelines on subject matter, length, target audience, timescale and budget. The Readers' Group, on the other hand, was set up to deal with any writing that a writer chooses to send to Gatehouse on their own initiative, often in isolation from any knowledge of either Gatehouse's publishing plans or indeed, even, of the aims of the organisation. Inevitably, the majority of this writing is returned. It is the Readers' Group that has the responsibility of doing this in a fair and constructive way.

In October 1993, I invited the Group to meet and discuss their experience for me. Airinne, a recent member, described its task as 'to read people's work and encourage them to keep writing. Also, to give constructive suggestions about their work and about possibilities for publication.' Gatehouse's aim is also for the group to develop their own skills in reading and criticising writing, both for their own development as individuals and also for our benefit, as it creates a rich pool of expertise to be called on by editorial groups. Pat, a second member, reflected in these terms on her experience with the Group:

> I can look at a piece of work now and perhaps think, 'Well, it could be improved if …' where before I used to think, 'Somebody's work, this is sacred. I can't be cruel to this person.' But now I'm thinking to myself, 'Well, we've got to be. If they've got to improve we need to say what needs to be done. So, I've got a bit harder really.

Initially the Group decided that its aim was to read and give feedback on writing by ABE students in Manchester for possible publication by Gatehouse. It soon realised that quite a bit of the writing sent in did not come from our target group. Before long, it was revising its original stringent guidelines — in particular, when some writing came from an ABE student in Wales. Who did we suggest he could send it to instead? We recognised that for many students Gatehouse was now virtually the only publisher of student writing nationally. Did we just return it? The Group identified strongly with the writer and decided to make an exception here. They read, discussed and sent comments back, including suggestions for getting the work published locally. Some months later we received copies of three booklets that the writer had produced as a result of our advice. From this the Group decided to revise its original policy and be much more flexible. In practical terms, we set up a system for receiving the writing and dealing with it. This consisted of a number of short standard letters with space left for readers' comments to be added on. Gradually, the Group has seen itself as increasingly more about encouraging and supporting new writers. Copies of writing are sent out and read by members before the meeting. Everyone comes with their own opinions on the pieces that they have read. The discussion in the Group centres on what people like in the work and what they feel the writer still needs to do for their audience. Jimmy, a third member of the Group, describes the importance of this group discussion:

> To be in the Reading Group is to be part of a team. We can obtain a better insight from the other members of the team, thereby enabling us to give a clearer and more detailed feedback to the writer for her or him to put into practice on their next piece and, hopefully, publish.

They will also try to suggest ways of getting work published, from using local resources to sending it to magazines, for competitions etc. The premise is that each writer is already launched on the road to seeking an audience and wants to continue working on that. The Group is very strong on encouraging writers to do more sharing of their writing in order to get constructive criticism: using their own ABE group; finding writing groups; starting a writing group.

No writer produces a single perfect piece of copy that needs no discussion and adjustment. Yet this is the kind of pressure that many put themselves under when writing is required. (In an attempt to change this way of seeing writing we regularly include in our publications copies of the original handwritten draft, next to the polished typeset piece and in our workshops we encourage writers to put worries about handwriting and spelling aside and to concentrate on what they have to say.) At the moment, I am wrestling with this particular paragraph in order to include valuable comments from two colleagues in such a way that the final version appears seamless to the reader. For adults returning as students with models of what is expected when they write, we need to be more explicit about our own struggles to find routes into writing and help them to recognise that while there isn't a point where it stops being difficult, the drafting process does eventually yield results.

For the purposes of this chapter I am concentrating on the stage after the first draft when writers are learning to move into engaging with an audience. This is what Pat is referring to in speaking of how she has moved from feeling, 'I can't be cruel to this person' to a position where she 'can look at work and can think, 'I know how that can be improved.' The crucial issue then, for the Readers' Group, was working out how to pass on that awareness to the writer in a positive and clear way.

The Group works on two key principles: first, that no writer should be given the impression that either they or their writing is being rejected; and second, that every writer who submits writing to them should receive back constructive editorial feedback. The struggle is then to find positive words to express what may otherwise have a negative impact. This is an extract from the Group's discussion about how they approach this issue:

Pat: We read a piece the meeting before last that I was totally disgust-
ed with. I didn't like the material, I thought it was smutty rubbish
but I thought to myself, 'Well, I'm not here really to judge the
morality of it.' But I'm thinking as a consumer what I would buy,
I would not buy anything by this person.

Airinne: So, I suppose, it's separating in your head whether you're doing
it as a consumer or a commentator or whatever, separating your
own personal feelings about the subject from the way they've
done it.

Pat: Yes, there's me reviewing, this is the sensible me because I've
got to be sensible because this person obviously would like good
advice. And there's me, the consumer, who some stuff I wouldn't
touch with a barge-pole.

Airinne: I suppose, we have to be careful we don't leave people with the
feeling that they shouldn't be writing about anything they really
want to, or feel the need to.

Patricia: Also, we are doing two things all the time. We're saying that anybody who wants to write should be encouraged but, at the same
time, that if they are sending writing to other people and they
want to know what their opinion of it is, then you have to know
certain things about changes.

Airinne: I think just encouraging people to write is important, a good thing
to do.

Every writer then receives back some kind of critical comment; sometimes
they have asked for this; at other times the writing has been submitted in the
hope of publication. The brief of the Group, as I have said, is to respond to writing that has been sent to Gatehouse as a publisher. Writers may not be clear
about who it is that we publish and sell to; but as Gatehouse is seen to be sympathetic to the new writer so we receive a whole variety of material. The role of the
Group then is to consider carefully how best to help these writers. Invariably,
this begins with a constructive response to the material before advising on presentation, other more suitable publishers, possible contacts, routes for investiga-
tion and so on. Airinne qualified Pat's claim to be 'hard' on these writers with

> It's constructive, though, isn't it? It's to help them. So the aim is to give
> them something to think about if they want to change it. It depends on how
> it's done, doesn't it? But you always send back something positive. I think
> that's an important part of the philosophy.

How does the group go about responding in this 'constructive' yet critical way?
It meets every six weeks and at each of these meetings it considers three or four
pieces of writing that have already been read beforehand. Usually, the discussion

begins slowly with general comments about the whole piece. Then, gradually, we focus on particular lines or passages. Invariably, there are different perspectives from the six or seven round the table, and a fair amount of debate. For instance, as one of the pilot groups 'test-reading' the first draft of Chris Curley's *The Cardigan*, we engaged very quickly with the issue of profane language in this piece. We had already discussed the use of bad language in other pieces and had decided that sometimes this was essential to the writer's purpose. Some group members were not convinced, however, that this was the case in this instance. At the same time, they expressed an appreciation of the pace or tempo of Chris's story as it built up, concluded that it was very professional and recommended illustrations and a description of the writer to encourage others. This is one of the few occasions that the Group had been able both to engage with a text which we subsequently published and to discover a writer's reaction to their comments.

The issue of writers not feeling rejected as people has been the other central concern of the Group and we have developed a number of ways of dealing with this. Our initial concern centred on ensuring that feedback was sent in a positive and helpful form by framing letters in a friendly way with positive comments being listed before more critical advice. We then searched for ways to find out how writers felt when they received such a letter, either by asking the writer to respond to the group or by inviting those who were members of Manchester ABE writers to come and have a fuller discussion with the Group. One writer sent us this entirely spontaneous response:

I've written a few short stories and poems
in fact it's a hobby of mine
I've sent one or two off to Gatehouse
and they've always acknowledged my rhyme

Gatehouse is a group that helps budding writers
they try to help you understand
you can't just write a best seller
because you hold a pen in your hand

This group deserves more publicity
it's hard working, it's honest, and fair
information is there if you need it
so to Gatehouse 'Thanks for being there.' (May Allen)

Dorothy, a fourth member of the Group, sums up what they hope they are getting across to writers:

Nobody should see themselves as a loser if not accepted for publication because you gain two things (by asking for constructive criticism): you gain the courage and the idea of writing.

These accounts of ABE writers engaging with their readers have parallels in any writing situation in which a writer is developing an awareness of what needs to happen when putting pen to paper. The realisation has to be made that drafting in one's head in order to get it exactly right for the page is much less useful than scribbled messy drafts. This means recognising that writing is only the start of a process working towards getting it right for the audience. It involves being rigorous with oneself without becoming despairing. It means asking others to read and comment. It requires being reasonably comfortable with what has been written while maintaining an openness to change. This is hard. However, it can also be an extremely fruitful stage providing the right commentators are involved. Not just clarity but new insights can be the eventual outcome.

For the tutor, it is about making drafting and redrafting a visible process and one to be encouraged. It is also about enabling individual writers to recognise and share their variety of ways of working. In terms of engaging writers with their audience a whole range of possibilities can be explored. Peers working together in small groups can provide fruitful feedback. As in the example of *The Cardigan*, peer groups can correspond through taped or written commentaries. The description of the Readers' Group provides a more distanced model of a critical response to writing that still maintains a positive and supportive connection with the writer.

As for me, what surprises me when I write about the work that I do, as I have here, is how it always provides a tool for my own learning, and an opportunity to track beginnings, middles and ends. It creates a space where I can pin down uncertainties and begin to unravel and deal with them. In offering me another audience, it means that I am forced to look again at how best to hold the reader's attention and pull together elements of all my previous writing experiences. With this book, there has been the opportunity to sound out my writing ideas with an interested group of peers and get their constructive feedback. At the same time there has also been the pressure of deadlines to meet, words to count and moments of despair which it is good to have confirmed by other contributors that they share.

These models have been presented in the hope of sparking a recognition of what can happen with good working practice, and to validate the importance of supportive and constructive criticism. The ultimate aim is to provide some flexible approaches to enable writers to recognise their search for an audience and, on finding it, to ensure that the audience goes away satisfied. Finally, I can only re-iterate that all of us who write do so out of struggle and fear of failure. It can help to remember this and to share our learning with each other.

Notes

1. *Write First Time* was the national literacy paper distributed regularly for ten years (1975–85) to literacy centres across the UK. It published writing by adult literacy students and pioneered the involvement of students as equal members of the editorial team. A comprehensive archive is lodged at the library of Ruskin College, Oxford.
2. Gatehouse has now produced a cassette tape to accompany a subsequent publication, *Never Ending Hours* (Sorbie, 1994).
3. The Federation of Worker Writers and Community Publishers is a federation of groups which are committed to writing and publishing based on working-class experience and creativity.

References

Curley, C. (1993) *The Cardigan*. Manchester: Gatehouse Books.
Holden, F. (1983) *Keep Your Hair On*. Manchester: Gatehouse Books.
Home Truths. Writing by North West Women (1981) Manchester: Commonword (out of print).
Sorbie, K. (1994) *Never Ending Hours*. Manchester: Gatehouse Books.

Appendix

Questions for pilot groups.

Questions to think about:

1. What did you think of the story?
2. Did it make you want to keep on reading?
3. Was there a clear beginning, middle and end?
4. Is there anything else that you want the writer to tell you in the story? Imagine that they are in the room with you and you could ask them questions.
5. Are there any parts of the story that you think would work better if some parts were left out altogether? If so, can you explain this for the writer.
6. This story has not yet had any drawings done for it. Have you any ideas about that?
7. Were any of the words particularly hard to read? Can you suggest other words?
8. This story has a *title*. Think about whether it works for you. Did it make you want to read the book? Does it help you guess what the story might be about?

Have you any other suggestions?

These two stories are being considered by Gatehouse for a new Beginner Reader book. So, the readers will all be quite new to reading and this may even be one of the first books that they read. We want to find out what adult basic education students think of these. Your comments will help us to choose which writing to publish. They will also help the writer and the Gatehouse worker to think about any changes that will make the book more useful for new readers.

Thank you for taking time to read, talk and answer these questions.

Patricia Duffin
Gatehouse

7   Reminiscence as Literacy: Intersections and Creative Moments

JANE MACE

A reminiscence group is a group, usually of older, or elderly people who have come together in order to share recollections of their past experience. An adult literacy class is a group of people, of any age over 18 or so, who meet in order to improve or develop their reading and writing. A creative writing group or a writers' workshop consists of people who have a common interest in exploring ways to write creatively, ultimately for publication. My own work, since 1974, has included all these activities. The question I want to explore in this chapter concerns the first: the reminiscence group. In my experience of setting up and convening six of these since 1980, the people who agree to join them do so because they see an opportunity to reflect aloud, with others, on their life experience. They do not, in the first instance, see their role as writers, nor, for that matter, as listeners: but as tellers; and when I and others invite them to take part, we are inviting them to see themselves primarily as oral historians. The work of facilitating such groups means, certainly, encouraging participants to be attentive listeners, as well as narrators; but, in addition, we also invite them to see themselves as potential or actual writers. The question I want to explore in this chapter is this: why do we, who as adult educators work with reminiscence groups with older people, have this preoccupation with writing? Isn't it enough to ensure a democratic and affirmative oral exchange of experience? What is the reason that I, and other reminiscence workers, seek to persuade older people that they could also choose to write, and even publish, some of the narrative they share orally?

Part of the answer which I will discuss is offered in a contrast which Frank Smith proposed over ten years ago between the expressive value of speech, and the equal, but different value of writing. First, he argues for that of speech:

> There is one advantage that every speaker has over writers, the possibility of using intonation for subtlety and for emphasis. Punctuation, italicizing, capitalizing and underlining offer only a shadow of the modulating powers

of the human voice. And in face-to-face situations the speaker's repertoire is enlarged enormously, not only because a wide range of conventional facial and other physical gestures exists, but also because the speaker can respond from moment to moment to the listener's understanding and uncertainty. (Smith, 1983: 127–9)

Having acknowledged these undoubted advantages of speaking, he then goes on to assert one still greater advantage which writing possesses, namely that 'it is superbly more potent in creating worlds'. Writing, he says, 'enables us to explore and change the worlds of ideas and experience that the brain creates' (Smith, 1983: 127–9).

Reminiscence work, approached as a process which is about literate as well as oral narrative, entails a series of moves between talking, listening, writing and reading. Ever since, as a literacy educator, I first began doing reminiscence work, I have become increasingly fascinated with the meaning of these moves. What I find attractive about Frank Smith's view is the general argument on which he bases it that neither writing nor speech are as much about *communication* as they are about *creation*: that we use language, whether spoken or written, not merely to transmit something ready-made from our experience or thinking, but in order to *create* new meanings and new worlds.

The work of reminiscence, taking this view, is primarily a creative activity, and it is because I share Frank Smith's view about the creative powers of writing that I am interested in how oral accounts may become written texts, through a process in which participants have time to reflect on and develop the first version of a story — and, if they choose to do so, to be able to edit, amend and elaborate on it as a piece of writing. The published version of this process is, by definition, selective (just as any of the earlier interviews, group discussion or written drafts were). For those who make the choice to have their texts appear in print, the process entails, first, reading back a transcribed version of their talk on the page and then deciding how far that written version accords with the version of themselves that they feel willing for others (unknown) to read — rather than for a group or individual (known) to hear. Such a process raises many of the same issues of power and selection discussed by Wendy Moss in her analysis of language experience work.

In this chapter, I want to analyse some of these issues as they occur during the course of a specific approach to reminiscence work with elderly people which I call 'lines and intersections', in order to explore in what ways a move to *writing* changes what was originally an *oral* reflection on experience.

I will begin with some general points about reminiscence itself, setting out the idea of lines and intersections as a means to describe the relationship between talk and writing (or the literacy events) that it entails. I will then briefly describe three of the reminiscence projects on which I have worked, from which I will go on to delineate something of the power relationships in which participants and reminiscence workers/adult educators are engaged, and how these relate to the issue of historical significance which this work raises. Finally, I will pick out one example of how the intersections between reading, writing, talk and listening combined to produce a written text with specific choices being made by me (as editorial partner) and author as to style, order and shape, in order to return to the original question: what are the relative values of written, rather than spoken narrative, and what dilemmas are raised, in terms of making a transition from one to the other? For me, as I will indicate, these dilemmas include a difference — and even a conflict — between ideas about writing which the participant/speaker may have in her head, and those that I have myself.

Reminiscence

Reminiscence is a complex process. The telling of a tale is a present activity, situated in one particular place and time, with a different relationship both to the listener(s) and to the historical time of the tale being told. As Phillida Salmon has put it:

> For elderly storytellers and their listeners, one obvious fact glares out: their predicament … For human stories go on and, from the vantage point of their telling, earlier events are seen as leading up to later ones; and the current end of the story in some sense governs what is to be made of its earlier phases. (Salmon, 1992: 219)

To put it another way: our perception of our present circumstances colour and shape that of our past experience.

Since the mid-1970s, the use of reminiscence as an activity capable either of providing the teller with healing to present pain (reminiscence therapy) or the listener with information about an aspect of social reality (oral history) has taken the form of a social movement in its own right (Bornat, 1989). My own interest in it, as a community educator and literacy researcher, is in its two other functions: as an activity of educational value to the participants and as a research approach of interest to literacy and community education.

The basis of this approach to reminiscence is an effort to redress inequalities in power relationships between people seen, conventionally, as 'experts' and others seen as not; and between those few people set apart as 'writers' and the majority who are not. Like others, I have certainly gained theoretical strength in pursuing this effort from the work of researchers like Shirley Brice Heath (1983), David Barton (1991) and Brian Street (1993) who have pulled apart old (but still dominant) ideas about the relative status of oral and literate cultures. Challenging the orthodoxy of the 'great divide' between the two, these and other writers in the last 15 years have analysed the realities of social context in which speech, reading and writing constantly interrelate.

Over the period of a reminiscence project's life, I see a series of intersections between what seem to be lines of speech and text, creating and re-creating. At the point where these lines intersect there is a new kind of creative moment. One line, for instance, is that of an individual speaking while others are listening. Another is a group following a text while one person reads it aloud. When such reading causes one of the group to look up and offer their own comment or begin a narrative of their own, I see an intersection, exactly the kind of moment that this kind of reminiscence work is intended to encourage, with the aim of enabling a mutual enrichment between the oral and the written work.

Other examples of what I mean by such intersections are:

- when one person's account of an event (re-read as transcript) is echoed and re-told by another;
- when one member's text is brought in for others to read, following it on a copy as they listen to it being read aloud; and this reading causes another to look up and add her own anecdote or reflection to that of the author.

Two other intersections which interest me are the delayed effects of oral work in a group or an interview, as when

- recollections expressed in speech (in interview or group) stimulate either speaker or listener later to seek out documentary sources (diaries, old reports, letters) to bring back for sharing in a later discussion; and
- when the recollection of the voices and thoughts prompted by talking with others leads an individual, later and alone, to contemplate writing as they have not done before.

To some extent, the process of writing this chapter has entailed these intersections for me, as well. Each time lines of speaking, reading, listening or writing have intersected, I have had some sense of another shift of my thinking — a creative (if sometimes confusing) moment. The text began as a paper I wrote for a conference held in August 1993. This was not publicly printed, but circulated at the conference to the 50 participants, along with the other conference papers. Comments from the 15 people who attended the workshop where I 'presented' this paper gave me new perspectives, as did discussion in two subsequent seminar groups I led in the autumn, and in a workshop at a second conference (which, in this case, did publish the proceedings, as well as providing a space for discussing the ideas at the event itself).[1] At other times since, I also talked these over informally with friends and colleagues, including contributors to this book.

In addition, during that period, I gained new insights from reading other people's writing about issues to do with autobiographical writing, oral history and literacy. All this process of listening and re-articulating, of searching and re-wording, worked to change the paper I first wrote in June 1993 to become this chapter, completed in March 1994.

Another experience, just as I was nearing final draft, gave me pause for new reflection. I learned of the death of the woman from whom I had first gained my fascination with these things: Dolly Davey. I met Dolly in June 1979, when she came to a meeting of the first reminiscence group I convened. We worked, together and with the group, on what became her published autobiography. Early in the morning before I was to attend Dolly's funeral with her family, I replayed at home some of the tapes of our conversations 15 years earlier. As I listened, I recalled how much I had enjoyed listening to her talk to me and to others about her life. For me this pleasure reminded me sharply of my position as 'story-taker', working with Dolly, the 'story-maker' (Steedman, 1992). I remembered that those of us who choose to do reminiscence work do so not only in order to rescue lost history, or in order to provide educational space for others; but because we ourselves long to be told stories.

All the intersections I have described depend, as they had done in my work with Dolly, on a central inter-connection: that between the individual interview and the group meeting. Individuals agree to be interviewed; some, but not all of them, subsequently agree to join a group which meets several times; during the group meetings, individuals are given the attention of the whole group. At each stage, the job of the adult educator coordinating the project is to set up these lines and encourage these intersections. I now want to illustrate these rather abstract notions by a brief description of the practical work of reminiscence projects.

Approaches and Settings

From our observations of our own practice and that of others, Jane Lawrence and I suggested (Lawrence & Mace, 1987: 22–3) that reminiscence work in an adult education setting tends to follow a series of phases over a period of 18 months to two years, from outreach and interviewing to an open meeting, after which a group forms and meets regularly, to exchange recollections and prepare some of these recollections to share with others in the form of a display, publication, or performance. This pattern was true for my own work with three such projects: the 'S.E.1 People's History Group' (1979–80), the 'Now and Then Group' (1981–84) and the 'Cottage Homes Making History Project' (1992–93).

When I was invited to initiate a project in 'people's history' in North Lambeth, I was working as a teacher and organiser at Cambridge House

Literacy Scheme and founder member of the *Write First Time* collective, which published three times a year writing by individuals and groups in literacy education up and down the country.[2] My work with the S.E.1 People's History Group began in January 1979 and ended when I got a new job (as Head of Goldsmiths' College's Lee Community Education Centre) in March 1980. I began by attempting to convene a group, in a room in the Waterloo Action Centre. Despite various forms of publicity, via the community newsletter distributed on the estates and contacts of the advice workers in the Centre, no-one appeared at its first meeting. The idea of then visiting individuals in their homes, with their consent, evolved, therefore, from trial and error. Only after visits and interviews to some 12 individuals, did I try again and publicise an open meeting, for which, by this time, we were able to prepare a display and copies of a duplicated text from one of our interviewees. That evening 40 people came (many of them relatives and neighbours of the more elderly residents), some 15 of whom agreed to meet again, and begin working as a group.

For 18 months, we met once a fortnight in the branch library in the adjacent street to the Action Centre. Several people worked with me as volunteer assistants to the project (including three Lambeth librarians) and we often divided into small groups, with one of these volunteers 'chairing' the discussion and recording it, either with tape-recorder or notes. During that period, we published duplicated texts from interviews with four local residents; and, as a printed book, the autobiography of one of the group members: *A Sense of Adventure* by Dolly Davey (1980).

In contrast, the Now and Then group which Dave Rogers and I convened at the Lee Community Education Centre from 1981 to 1984 originated, not as a literacy and community publishing idea, but as that of providing a response to the request from some members of an existing 'retired group' which met regularly at the Centre for 'interesting discussion'. The group's name was chosen to express this interest: for while the group was certainly about sharing and reflecting on the past life experiences of the older people who took part, it was also to be a forum for discussion of current issues in everyday life, and an opportunity to test out ideas about 'how things had changed'. So, unlike either of the other groups I describe here, or other later reminiscence groups at the Centre, this one, like an adult education course, regularly planned a termly programme of topics, invited speakers and outings. During the course of three years, however, we also published three duplicated booklets of the group's writing (a mixture of edited transcripts from talk and of their own compositions).

The third project I want to refer to is one which I coordinated with a group of pensioners resident on an estate in North London, at the invitation of Ruth Lesirge, the Chief Executive of the charity ('Cottage Homes') which managed the estate where they lived. By this time, I was employed (as I still am) as an academic researcher and trainer in literacy and community education at Goldsmiths' College. The 'Cottage Homes Making History Project' began in September 1992 and ended a year later with the publication of recollections from participants (Mace, 1993). The project took place on one of Cottage Homes's three estates of housing (the other two are in Derby and Glasgow), built at the end of the 19th century to provide care and accommodation for the retired employees of the retail and manufacturing trades in drapery and clothing. On the Mill Hill estate live some 250 residents, varying in age from 60 to over 90, a majority of whom are women, most of whom live independently in one of the cottages, and the more frail of whom live in the nursing accommodation. Flower beds and grassy spaces spread out between the one-storey cottages, each with its plaque commemorating the store or individual who endowed it; and in the middle of the estate, stands Marshall Hall (endowed by Marshall of Marshall and Snelgrove Department store).

This environment, and the source of its funding (philanthropy and fund-raising by the trade) were a constant reminder to me, as I walked through the gates each Monday, of Phillida Salmon's comment about the effect of the 'current end' of life stories. I often wondered whether other pensioners, from these or other department stores or shops, living in less attractive conditions or with less sense of gratitude to an erstwhile employer, might well have other perceptions of the working lives behind them. Meanwhile, we were meeting at a time of increasing pressure both on pensioners' incomes and on the retail trade they had worked for.

In the first two months of the project (September–November 1992), as in Lambeth, my assistant Kirsty Robson and I visited, interviewed and revisited people individually in their homes. Subsequently, 25 people came to an open meeting, held in Marshall Hall; and over the eight months that followed, an average of 10 or 12 people attended the weekly group meeting.

From these projects I now want to offer examples of three intersections and the creative moments they represented.

Telling individually and re-telling to a group

Publications from reminiscence work, as I have already said, can only provide a very selective account of the authors' recollections. But their function is not only to provide a slice of social history: in an important sense, the publication from reminiscence activity is the creation of and a souvenir from the reminiscence work itself. In the same way that *Write First Time*, the adult literacy paper, and Gatehouse have included in their published work something of the handwritten drafts which preceded it (as Stella Fitzpatrick illustrates in her chapter), so reminiscence work, if it is to convey something of its making, needs to include something in its published work from the interchange which preceded the individual narratives. This both makes the creative moments more visible to other readers, and brings them back to mind to those who were originally part of the group itself. It was for this reason, in Dolly Davey's published autobiography, *A Sense of Adventure*, that I proposed interleaving Dolly's first-person narrative with extracts from group discussion between Dolly and other group members.

There was a sequence of events (and creative moments) by which Dolly's text evolved between June and December 1979:

1. First, Dolly came to a meeting of the group as companion to an older neighbour, and talked (on tape) to three people.
2. I sent Dolly the transcript, went to see her at her home, and we talked again, on tape.
3. I transcribed this, too, and sent it to Dolly.
4. She read the transcript and wrote some additional pieces.
5. I copied parts of the transcripts and Dolly's writing, and other members of the S.E.1 group read these.
6. At further meetings of the group, Dolly talked some more and her husband, Fred, joined the discussions. Again, I transcribed the tape and returned the transcripts for participants to read.
7. Finally, Dolly and I separately read the whole, I wrote an introduction, and she and I agreed the completed text.

The book which resulted consists largely of Dolly's narrative. In brief, this relates how she left her home in Yorkshire in 1930 to come to London. After four years working as a domestic and lady's maid, she met and married Fred. This is an extract from the text as it appeared in the finished book, when she relates a historic day soon after that:

> It was 18 months after we got married that he was invited to come up to my home, and he did. He rode from London to Yorkshire, on a pushbike. I left on Sunday morning at 10 o'clock on the twelve-and-sixpenny excursion, and he left on the Friday and arrived at my home the same time as I did — just in time for dinner! It was really an achievement, because he had never been up there before, and he didn't know the route. It was one great north road then. There wasn't an Ml or anything like that. (Davey, 1980: 22)

On the same page, immediately after this, we included the following extract from the discussion in which Fred, with Dolly recalled this event for three others of us (Jenny, Gladys and me) in one of the S.E.1 People's History group meetings:

Fred: Her mother said that if we could get there, she might be able to get me a job. We had Eva then, our eldest. The labour money was twenty-eight shillings a week, and the train fare to Stockton was twelve and six. I said, 'We can't afford that. You can go on the train, I'll borrow a bike, and we'll save twelve and sixpence.' Twelve and sixpence was terrific, what you could get for it; and I didn't think no more of it. Borrowed a bike off a boy across the road called Freddie Kippick.

Dolly: You left on the Friday night, I left on the Sunday morning, and we practically met at the door.

Fred: I was about five minutes after.

Jane: Do you remember the journey?

Fred: Yes.

Jane: Was it raining?

Fred: No.

Jenny: You were lucky.

Fred: When would it be, in August? Must have been, because I remember picking Victoria plums by the roadside. The first night I slept somewhere in St Albans, I think it was; and the next night I spent in Doncaster racecourse. Just went off the road, like, and you were on the course. Just put a groundsheet down, and a blanket. I bought fish and chips for threepence, and a bottle of Tizer. And I started off with half a crown.

Dolly: I got there at lunchtime, and my mother was just dishing the lunch up, 4 o'clock.

Fred: I had a terrific ride.

Gladys: All that way on a bike?

Fred: Yes. Dick Turpin had nothing on me, love, by the time I got there.

The combination of Dolly's account with this interchange between her, Fred and their listeners conveys a different sense of the reminiscence process (the intersections and creative moments) than would have been possible with the first-person narrative of Dolly alone. It was that mix of telling and retelling, which was the work of her autobiography.

Talk in a group causes an individual later to write alone

It was a discussion between Lal and three other people in the Lee Centre which led her later, alone, to write about her life. When I met her in 1980, Lal, a woman in her seventies, was a member of the Centre's retired group. What was later to become the Now and Then Group began with a morning when she and two others met with me and talked on tape about their lives. She told me later about her decision, afterwards, to go to sit one evening at home and write. The following comes from my transcript of her retelling this to me:

Lal: Well, of course, the point was, we had that chat round the Centre, didn't we: and you were saying, 'Oh, you should write some of that down.' I thought to myself, 'Oh, that's a sweat.' But there was nothing on telly one night, and I thought to myself, 'I wonder if I could write some of it.'

Jane: There was a storm, wasn't there?

Lal: That's right. Course, storms never worry me. And I looked for some paper — I thought to myself, 'I'm not going to do it on my best writing paper', and I found some old Christmas cards, and I wrote it on the plain bits of the Christmas cards. Course, the more I thought about it, the more incidents came to mind, and I was scrabbling away there like mad, you know, as it came into my mind.

Lal's next comment recalls Frank Smith's idea of writing as a means to 'create worlds'; it also speaks of how the oral work of the earlier discussion influenced the way she wrote:

Jane: It's hard to keep up with your thoughts, isn't it?

Lal: Well, it sort of opened, opened one thing on top of the other. Funny, isn't it?

Jane: It is. Strange process. In a way you often write, to start with, just for yourself, don't you. But as you —

Lal: Well, I was writing as I talk. Just as I suppose I was telling you it …

And, just as reminiscence participants describe how other people's recollections stir their own in oral exchange, so Lal spoke of how her own written words prompted her to recall other details she had until then forgotten:

> You see, it wasn't till after I'd written that, I thought to myself, 'Oh yes, it was after I was doing my laundry that I had these spots come out all over my body.' Course, I was doing my own washing, but I wasn't airing it properly. That's how it was that I got that skin complaint.[3]

Listening to another group member's text being read aloud and discussion

Such writing, at home, can also following reading — in reminiscence as in literacy groups. During the fourth meeting of the Cottage Homes Making History Group in December 1992, Kirsty had read aloud for us an article published in Debenham Pensioners' Magazine in 1986, written by Florence Hawkes, one of the residents on the estate, whom I had interviewed a few weeks earlier. At my invitation, Florence attended the meeting, and sat listening with the other seven people there that day as Kirsty read. This is how the piece began:

> I would like you to come with me down 'Memory Lane' to the year 1925 — a span of fifty years when, as an apprentice of fourteen years of age, I

began my career in the workroom of the fashionable establishment Madame Paulette, at number 36 Berkeley Square. (Hawkes, 1993: 59)

Kirsty went on reading, and we went on listening, and relived with Florence her description of her working day all those years ago. At the end of the reading, I invited comments and questions to Florence, and tried to shape the talk that followed so that it focused both on her and on her text. She recalled extra details for us. Others in the group asked her questions. One man, who had worked as a tailor in the East End in the 1940s, compared conditions of his work then (and of his father before him) with those that Florence had described. Several people reflected on the notion of bespoke tailoring, on the declining use of fur in costume design, and on 'pick-pack' buttons, covered in the material of a customer's choice. We enjoyed imagining the other people whom Florence had described. The discussion was not taped: but it was a memorable occasion for all of us.

The first week back in January, Bertha Fried, a regular group member, brought in some writing that she had done. Bertha had not been interviewed on tape; her first contact with the Project was at the November open meeting. But inspired, she said, by Florence's writing, she had decided to sit down and write something of her own. This text, with some additions she made in a later draft, was included in the group's publication, as was an extract both from Florence's original text and from her taped interview with me (Mace, 1993).

In summary, so far: these intersections are examples, as I see it, of the creative moments when participants in reminiscence are offered the choice to move from oral exchange to the more public (and silent) medium of print. None of this is simple or unproblematic; and the issue of power remains. In the artificially created setting of an adult education group or oral history interview, the adult educator or interviewer deliberately sets out to dramatise and encourage this cross-fertilisation. This, of course, involves us in a considerable degree of agenda-setting and selection. What role does this mean for the other participants — the older people who choose to join in the activity and what do they see themselves doing when they do join in?

Students, Members, Sources or Volunteers?

It is important to re-state here what I said at the beginning. The participants in the reminiscence activities I have been describing are not defining themselves, first and foremost, as having difficulty with reading and writing. In contrast, the reminiscence work which Dorothy Atkinson describes was with older people with learning difficulties, most of whom, as she tells us, 'were unable to read well or fluently (if at all)', and who 'saw the written word as authoritative'. For them, the production of a written account of their oral recollections, she argues, had the kind of significance with which literacy education is familiar:

It is the very exclusion which makes a written account so necessary — for such an account has a sense of permanence (compared with oral accounts) and enables people with learning difficulties to communicate with others ...

'Reminiscence in itself is valuable', she concludes, 'but the written word — especially for people with limited access to or input into documented history — is potentially powerful' (Atkinson, 1994: 97, 103).

The primary purpose of the members of this group, however, was still not that of the usual adult literacy class, whose participants define themselves, and are referred to as 'learners' or 'students'. (Nor were they — or any of the people I have referred to in the three groups I have described — in the position of being 'sources' or 'informants', being interviewed for an oral history study, with the probability that some of the material they provide will eventually be shared with others via a television or radio programme or published book or paper.) The elderly person who agrees to participate in a reminiscence project, where the focus of the activity is the development and exchange of recollections between herself and others, is being invited, instead, to feel that she is a 'member of a group' working on a public enterprise.

As a result of a conversation with Sav Kyriacou in one of the contributors' meetings for this book, however, I have come to recognise that despite my efforts to persuade them of their group membership in the work, some of the elderly people I have worked with saw themselves as 'volunteers' with a project they see as mine, rather than theirs. In the 'Making History Project' for instance, one woman told my colleague on the project, watching her making a note of something she had just told her: 'What you're doing is picking our brains, writing it all down, and making it into a book'; later adding, after she had told a particular anecdote: 'I hope you won't put that bit in!' During or after individual interviews, too, interviewees often asked if they were being 'any use' to me. As they saw it, their recollections were for my benefit, rather than theirs. This idea persisted, I found, in group meetings, too. After the fourth meeting of the Making History Group, for example, one person asked: 'So who is going to publish this book?' (This was after we had spent two meetings discussing ways and means of raising funds for the Project to pay for the print costs of publishing their writing.) And later still, even after the Project had already published its 'home-made' anthology, in which 20 of the 22 pages were by other authors then me, a new member to the group asked me: 'What made you want to write this book?'

At the time, I found myself feeling frustrated with all these comments. How had I failed to convey a sense of collective ownership for this work? Why were participants taking such a passive view of their own place in the project, let alone the production of a publication? Looking back, I think now that, far from seeing themselves as passive, both interviewees and group members regarded themselves as *active volunteers*, giving me — and an eventual wider public — information, help and support: not the other way around. And in any case, as I will come back to later, not all the elderly people who spoke to us, or who attended the regular meetings of the group itself chose or were chosen to be authors in the written product of the project.

Authorship, with the responsibility and power that this entails for people with no experience of writing for publication, is a theme which has recurred for me both in the 'lines of intersection' approach to reminiscence and in the strand of adult literacy education practice described by other contributors to this book (Mace & Wolfe, 1990; Mace, 1992: 83–102). But the central paradox of authorship and community writing, whether in literacy or reminiscence groups, lies in the coexistence of distance and intimacy. The idea of ourselves as 'authors' is an idea about distance: any one of these groups are, first and foremost, about attempting to create closeness: or, in Stella Fitzpatrick's phrase, 'safe spaces' (see earlier, this volume, p. 3) — making possible a recognition of each individual's claim to others' interest. The key to the problem I faced with the Making History Group was that, unlike any other reminiscence group with which I have worked, it was set up with publication as one of its first purposes: for Cottage Homes wanted there to be a published result, as well as the affirmative (or educational) process of reminiscence that would produce it. In the end, I was the editor of that publication: but 16 other people were the contributors to it. So, in some sense, the Cottage Homes residents were right. But the issue it also raises for me is that of status. The reason for seeking to challenge and reverse a view that the project and its publication were mine alone was that this kind of work seeks, as does literacy education, to challenge the larger view of which it is part: namely, the feeling experienced by many people of their own insignificance, both in cultural and historical terms.

For many people, especially women, do not see themselves as legitimate subjects of *history*; they do not believe that they are either 'relevant' or 'interesting'; let alone important to anyone else's understanding of the times in which they lived.[4] In the same way, many people (again, especially women) do not see themselves as worthy to be *writers*, in the published sense. The work of literacy, community publishing and reminiscence is to challenge all these ideas. It is this commitment, I believe, which distinguishes reminiscence practice from oral history research. For as adult educators, we are primarily concerned with the learning which participants gain from the work; as Patricia Duffin reminds us, the reminiscence worker has 'to be seen to be giving something, not just taking ... memories' (Duffin, 1992: 7). One contribution we can give, with groups of this kind, is the opportunity to open up the debate about who is worthy of being an author or interesting to the cause of 'History'. In the setting of a group making its own agenda from multiple interests, this is by no means simple to achieve, however; and, as Joanna Bornat has suggested, it is in the work of a group where most of the 'real tension of reminiscence work with older people' resides (Bornat, 1989: 22). Every time I try to answer the question: What is reminiscence work *for*? these dilemmas of purpose and power keep taking me back to the same answer: It is not for making history more complete: it is the chance to do creative work in the present.

Rewordings and Deletions

So far, I have made some general points about reminiscence, about the relationship between talk and writing, about the power relationships between the reminiscence 'worker' and elderly participants, and about the literacy practices entailed in the process, referring to three projects I know most about. Part of my original question remains to be answered: What is the difference (and dilemmas) between oral and written narratives?

Who makes the changes to oral transcripts, in order to transform them into written texts? What kind of changes are seen to be necessary? The editorial work is sometimes shadowy; a combination of reminiscence worker/educator and interviewee/author. Both need to see the transcript — or at least that amount of the tape which the transcriber has managed to translate to paper. A next move made by many reminiscence workers (including me) is to offer a draft of what the text might look like if some of the repetitions and (usually all) the interviewer's questions are removed. The interviewee/author then offers their own editorial changes. Some (but in my experience, a minority) reading the transcript of their speech on paper, engage in writing new material, to be added to it; fewer still choose to rewrite the whole thing. (Of the 16 authors in this position in the Making History Project, for instance, two women sat down at long-unused typewriters and rewrote much of their texts; a third wrote an additional three pages about earlier work experiences which she felt were crucial to add to the narrative; the rest expressed satisfaction with the text as it stood, apart from minor amendments.)

The exercise of editorial control, however, while it entails apparently small decisions of detail, can make significant alterations to an author's meaning and purpose, in any publishing enterprise, and in community publishing it is often the most shadowy stage of the process. It is, therefore, this minority of participants who choose to rewrite their draft texts which interests me; and in this last section we shall look at a set of moves made by one woman and me from our original interview to the transcript of the interview tape, and the 'public' written text of her narrative. I am giving her the pseudonym 'Nora' because, although her final published text, as a stencilled booklet, was public and therefore quotable, I have not had her permission to quote, as I will be here, from the transcript of her interview with me.

Nora was the third of the 17 people I visited in their homes in Lambeth between January and March 1979. Her completed text was one of four that I typed, duplicated and printed, and of which we circulated and sold a total of 120 copies (including 20 sets lodged with Lambeth libraries). What follows is an account of what she first told me, how I then edited it and how she, in turn, added to and altered it before it became published. The very first words recorded on the tape of her interview with me were these:

> We used to live up in the top flat till 1940. Then we moved down here. I've sort of grown up here. What was I? Thirteen, when I came here.

In the next 40 minutes of our interview, Nora went on to tell me of the other places where she lived, and how she had gone on to work for over 40 years as an office worker with the General Nursing Council. She then introduced almost immediately what was to be one of the two main stories in our conversation: the night of the Zeppelin raid (in 1915). There followed, in the interview and transcript, some regret for the changes in the local neighbourhood and shops; some more reference to the Zeppelin raid, and then the account of an incident (her second story) which took place nearly 25 years later in the Second World War, when she and her brother were caught in an air raid. She talked then of an unexploded bomb which landed in her street, how everyone had had to be evacuated, and how she had defied the air raid warden and had walked down the street when she came home to get groceries. Finally, we talked about the 1951 Festival of Britain, a reiteration of Nora's feeling of regret at the loss of neighbourliness and shops, and a brief summary of her childhood years.

The first moments of Nora's life, then, actually only came up in the last moments of our interview; and in the transcript, this narrative of her childhood appears on the last page. What she said is in Quote A:

Quote A
Going back to my childhood, we lived at Clapham, and of course there was five of us in the family. My father died a fortnight before I was born. And my mother had the boarding house then, so kept us all. Well, there was a gap — there was the two girls and a boy, then a baby boy died, so there was a gap. And my younger brother and I were the two kids then. And of course the others being older, they had all their friends in and out. And we had quite a happy, oh, I had a happy home. We were never short of anything: I'm not going to say there weren't things we would have liked, but you couldn't get, you saved up for them — because my mother wouldn't have anything on hire purchase.

I sent Nora a copy of the transcript of our dialogue, and went to meet her a week later. She had read it, and wanted to add several things for precision. She also made other comments, as we talked, which I noted down. I undertook to do my own editing on the transcript, ensuring that these additions and comments were included, and later sent her the edited version to read. In my editing, I did two things which until recently I found myself doing consistently in reminiscence work since:

(a) deleted my questions to her; and
(b) changed the sequence of her recollections into a chronology of life history.

When we met again a few weeks later, she had been busy. She had got out her old typewriter, obtained a new ribbon, and had re-typed her own version of the text.

Nora and I, then, both made changes to her original talk with me to a written text for others. Through my editing, the last thing Nora had told me in the interview had become the first paragraph I put in her edited text (namely her summary of early family life, Quote A). This replaced what had actually been the first thing she had told me about in the interview — a reference to the flat in which we were both sitting ('What was I? Thirteen, when I came here'). The text, I reasoned then, would be read by others not sitting as I was with her, and would need a different introduction to the author and what she had to say. Now, 15 years after that interview, I am not so sure. As I suggested at the beginning of this chapter, reminiscence is always a present activity; and autobiographical writing, no less so. Why not begin the narrative with the author's present context?

Nora, in any case, accepted this re-ordering: but chose to amend the wording. I now want to compare what she wrote (and we published) with the paragraph transcribed from her original words. What she wrote is Quote B:

Quote B

I was born in June 1902. My father had died in May *leaving my mother with five children — the four older still at school.* Mother then took in boarders in order **to keep the home going and us all together. We were always encouraged to bring our friends home, and therefore had a happy home life**. We were never short of **essential** things: I cannot say there were not other things we would have liked, but you had to save up for them, because my mother would not have anything on hire purchase. *She was a wonderful mother, and taught us the value of things.*

The key changes Nora made amounted to:

— the *rewording* of four statements (bold type);
— the *addition* of two pieces of inforrnation (italic type);

— and the *deletion* of her original version of the number of brothers and sisters in the family: 'There was a gap — there was the two girls and a boy, then a baby boy died, so there was a gap. And my younger brother and I were the two kids then. And of course the others being older, they had ...'.

Nora was working to produce a text for a public readership; she was consciously thinking about the effect of the writing on others. So, for example, to give historical information for the reader, she added the date of her birth. The *change* in this first sentence, however, also had the effect of changing the relationship between her birth and her father's death — which, in the earlier version, was very direct ('a fortnight before I was born'). The *omission* of detail about her as a child, in relation to her brothers and sisters, removes another personal dimension — resonant, perhaps, with old emotions which Nora would rather keep private. She then altered the identity of the children who brought friends home from 'they' to 'we'. This alteration, the change to a passive voice, and the formal connective 'therefore', effectively hid her child self still further from the reader. The change is from 'they had all their friends in and out' to: 'we were always encouraged to bring our friends home'.

Did Nora feel she had portrayed herself as too vulnerable, excluded from her mother's greater freedom with the older children, or from their games? Had she decided she wanted to convey a longer time span than her very early years, to a time when perhaps she too *was* encouraged to have 'all her friends in and out'? Or did she simply want to write what she felt was a more elegant and formal sentence, with less interruption? Perhaps she wanted all three. I do not know: for, at the time, these were not the questions I was asking her.

Tags like 'Of course' and 'as I say', are common features of oral discourse, designed to include the listener in the speaker's knowledge and carry her along in the story's flow; as in: 'And *of course* the others being older, they had all their friends in and out.' In a written text when reader and writer are at a greater distance from each other than speaker and listener, it makes sense to leave it out, as Nora decided to do. But what of the change from 'And we had quite a happy, oh, I had a happy home' to 'and therefore (we) had a happy home life'? Is that hesitant 'oh' in her original voice a sigh of pleasure at recalled happiness? Is it a hesitation, as she remembers sorrow or other feelings which were also there? Or is it an adult's sympathy for her seven-month pregnant mother, suddenly widowed with five children, she herself not yet born? (The intonation of her voice on the tape, which I have listened to again recently, could be interpreted in any of these ways.) In any case, in removing the 'we had quite a happy, oh, I had a happy home' Nora also erased past and present emotion, favouring instead a more impersonal and unequivocal assertion for her reading public: an authorised version that she preferred to her original, more ambiguous one.

Nora's final change, from 'any' to 'essential' ('we were never short of any-thing/essential things') I see as a change to precision. It was a happy home life with everything 'essential' provided for them; but as children, they were short of things they wanted. This time the text gives a glimpse of something that was less vivid in the original interview: the recalled longing of a child for 'inessentials'.

Some of the changes which Nora made to other parts of my edit of her tran-script meant, as some of these did, the removal of her own presence in the text. They also took away some of the rhythm and buoyancy which had been in her original spoken version. Here, for example, is what she told me, first, about a cafe breakfast which she and others had enjoyed the morning after they had been turned out of their flats following the fall of an unexploded bomb, when the 'all clear' sirens had sounded. Her original words had been:

> We all went in there, and had breakfast, of bacon and egg, and rolls. I've never tasted bacon so good since. It was marvellous!

In her re-typed version, Nora changed this to:

> We went into the cafe and had breakfast: tea, bacon and egg, and bread and butter. It was a really grand meal and much appreciated by us all.

Her personal pleasure, voiced with enthusiasm, is gone: instead, Nora has cho-sen the more banal voice of a formal thank-you letter.

While there were losses, however, there were also gains in the transpositions and additions which Nora made to her transcript. In re-reading it, she had seen things she wanted to add, to explain things more fully to a readership she was now holding in her imagination. An important example, from the paragraph she wrote out, is the sentence she added as a tribute to her mother: 'She was a won-derful mother, and taught us the value of things.'

Nora and I both worked on her text: each in a different way, but both taking an active part in its shape, style and tone. Over the years since then, I have changed both of my own editorial habits. Sometimes, as with Dolly's book, I have left in some of my own questions in preparing texts for publication; and sometimes I have suggested that texts begin in the middle rather than at the sup-posed beginning of a life. The important idea that I still work with is that the final text should be one that satisfies the authors, whether I have regrets about some of their choices or not.

A Conclusion

It is important to add two other points to this discussion. First, that in all three of the groups I have described, more people participated in interviews and group meetings than appeared later in the public writing we produced; and second, that publishing was only one of the means used to share more wide some of the reflections which these had generated — each of the groups also prepared exhibitions of photographs and captions. Community publications which are made from reminiscence activity only ever give a partial account of the thinking and talking from which they grow.

I began this chapter by agreeing with Frank Smith that writing has no innate superiority over speech for purposes of communication, but that, in terms of creative expression, it has possibilities that speech does not. I have ended it by suggesting how forms of expression chosen in writing may often mask or deaden a directness or eloquence which the writer may possess in speech. As I have tried to show, however, the oral exchange in interview and group discussion plays a central part in inspiring and shaping subsequent writing by speakers: and as the author develops a sense of a believable reader or readers, her decisions in writing can sometimes add to and enhance, as well as censor or make bland an earlier, spoken account. Reminiscence work, where speech is the primary and writing the secondary medium, moves sometimes uneasily between the closeness and distance of these two forms. The reminiscence worker, in turn — especially if she is, like me, at home in the world of writing and reading — moves (also sometimes uneasily) between the roles of literacy educator, community development worker, editor and researcher. The talking and listening that goes on in a group of people giving attention to each other's ideas, reflections and stories can never be conveyed in any print page. Listeners (and interviewers) are also observers and viewers: hands, eyes, heads, bodies speak, as well the voice, rising and falling, hesitating or declaiming, recapping and retelling. For me, the pleasure of having someone tell me a story is hard to overstate. I love watching and listening as the tale unfolds; I enjoy knowing that it is a story and, because of that, richer than any formal or impersonal historical account could be; for, as Alessandro Portelli has expressed it, the oral accounts of the past 'tell us not just what people did, but what they wanted to do, what they believed they were doing, what they now think they did' (Portelli, 1981: 10).

None of this is possible for us to see or hear in writing. But what we can do, through writing and publishing, is 'explore and change the worlds of (our) ideas and experience'; and, via our printed words, leave for others another means to explore and change their own. From being members of the community of the original, close group, published writers can also become members of another, larger community: that of readers. In all the projects I have described, activities also included the reading of texts by writers beyond group members (extracts from novels, history books, reports and poetry), and that reading experience, then and throughout their earlier lives, also informed the choices made by Nora and others as to how they themselves chose to appear as authors. Reminiscence work then provides another arena where a choice to be read can be extended beyond the world of commercially published authors of literature and history; and in that sense, despite its dilemmas, it remains an important space for creative moments of literacy development, as well as oral exchange, to be experienced and enjoyed by older people.

Notes

1. These four events were: The European Society for Research on the Education of Adults (ESREA)'s seminar on 'Popular Adult Education and Social Mobilization in Europe', Sweden, August 1993; seminars on literacy and oral history at Lancaster and Sussex Universities (Autumn 1993); and Age Exchange's first European Conference on Reminiscence, London, November 1993.
2. *Write First Time* published from 1975. Its last issue appeared in 1985. During those ten years, the collective organised residential weekends for literacy students and conferences. A complete archive of its work is available for consultation at Ruskin College Library, Ruskin College, Walton Street, Oxford.
3. From an unpublished interview, 28 November 1980. Lal's finished text, incorporating both her written pieces and edited text from the transcribed tape, appeared in *Something to Say: A Study in Community Education* (edited by Jane Mace), published by the Lee Centre/Goldsmiths' College in 1981. (Now out of print.)
4. Invited to see themselves as interesting, in historical terms, older people have different ways of disqualifying themselves. For example, when I began talking to people in Waterloo about the S.E.1 People's History Project, several said they would not be relevant because they did not know the area well enough. I recall one woman even saying to me: 'I don't think I will be much help to you, dear, as I've only lived round here forty years.' In Mill Hill, talking to residents there about the Making History project, a number of people felt they wouldn't 'count' because they hadn't had the public jobs of the retail trade: those of sales assistants. People who had worked as office workers, cleaners and telephonists, for example, regularly voiced these doubts; one woman, a former seamstress, felt she might not be relevant as she had only worked on sewing machines; another said she had not come to the meetings until she did (in April) because she thought her work as a caterer in a store would 'not be of interest'.

References

Atkinson, D. (1994) I got put away: group-based reminiscence with people with learning difficulties. In J. Bornat (ed.) *Reminiscence Reviewed* (pp. 96–105). Milton Keynes: Open University Press.

Barton, D. (1991) The social nature of writing. In D. Barton and R. Ivanic (eds) *Writing in the Community* (pp. 1–14). London: Sage.

Bornat, J. (1989) Oral history as a social movement: reminiscence and older people. *Oral History Journal* 17 (2), 18–24.

— (1992) Communities of community publishing. *Oral History Journal* 20 (2), 23–31.

Brice Heath, S. (1983) *Ways with Words*. Cambridge: Cambridge University Press.

Davey, D. (1980) *A Sense of Adventure*. London: S.E.1 People's History Project.

Duffin, P. (1992) *Then and Now: A Training Pack for Reminiscence Work*. Manchester: Gatehouse Books.

Hawkes, F. (1993) Couture was beautiful. In J. Mace (ibid.) (pp. 54–61).

Lawrence, J. and Mace, J. (1987, repr. 1992) *Remembering in Groups: Ideas from*

Literacy and Reminiscence Work. London: Oral History Society.

Mace, J. (1992) *Talking about Literacy: Principles and Practice of Adult Literacy Education.* London: Routledge.

— (ed.) (1993) *'Call Yourself a Draper?' Memories of Life in the Trade.* London: Linen and Woollen Drapers' Cottage Homes.

Mace, J. and Wolfe, M. (1990) Identity, authorship and status: issues for Britain in International Literacy Year. *Adults Learning* 10, 264–26.

O'Rourke, R. and Mace, J. (1992) *Versions and Variety: Student Publishing in Adult Literacy Education.* London: Goldsmiths' College. (Available from Avanti Books, 8 Parsons Green, Bolton Rd, Stevenage, Herts SG1 4QG.)

Portelli, A. (1981) The peculiarities of oral history. *History Workshop Journal* 12, 96–108.

Salmon, P. (1992) Old age and storytelling. In K. Kimberley, M. Meek and J. Miller (eds) *New Readings — Contributions to an Understanding of Literacy* (pp. 216–23). London: A & C Black.

Smith, F. (1983) *Essays into Literacy.* London: Heinemann.

Steedman, C. (1992) Horsemen. In *Past Tenses: Essays on Writing, Autobiography and History* (pp. 171–8). London: Rivers Oram Press.

Street, B. (1993) *Cross-Cultural Approaches to Literacy.* Cambridge: Cambridge University Press.

8 Disappearing Language: Fragments and Fractures Between Speech and Writing

ROXY HARRIS

This chapter is not intended to be an academic review of the literature on language standardisation. Nor is it an attempt to give a detailed explanation of the processes involved in the transition from speech to writing. It aims, rather, to pose a number of questions relevant to writers and the writing process in Britain, with special reference to the London context: What are some of the facts of the linguistic description of the little studied language varieties, other than Standard English, found in British urban environments? How does it happen that children in their early years as writers show regular and consistent signs of these varieties in their writing and yet have these signs erased from their writng in all contexts by practices, of which classroom literacy practices, form an important part? What is the classroom discourse between teachers and pupils which contributes to this? Why are teachers' aims in this respect persistently unsuccessful with a significant minority of learners so that signs of these learners' natural spoken language is still visible when they attempt to write Standard English in primary, secondary, further and adult education settings? What are some of the classroom pedagogies which might begin the process of making these issues explicit and start to enable learners to gain control over the conscious manipulation of both their own language and written Standard English?

The chapter seeks to raise these questions in the context of contemporary 'moral panics' in Britain concerning literacy levels and by means of some auto-biographical perceptions gained over more than two decades of classroom teaching and in-service teacher training.

Introduction

The language for literacy and for written academic performance in Britain is

Standard English. Yet the majority of British people most of the time in their everyday lives do not consistently speak Standard English (henceforth SE):

> The English public school has had an enormous influence on the dissemi- nation of one variety of English — what I call a super dialect — that is Received Standard or BBC English or Public School English whatever you call it; and it is only spoken by 1 in 50 people in this country. (Burchfield, 1986)

People regularly use their own lexis in preference to that indicated in SE dic- tionaries, and their own grammatical patterns in preference to those of SE. However, the myth persists that there is really only one English and that when people write there should be no particular problem for them in making the tran- sition from naturally occurring speech patterns to writing in SE.

> A better approach to English teaching in schools would reject every tenet of the new orthodoxy. It would recognise English as a subject — no more and no less: the subject in which pupils learn to write SE correctly and thereby speak it well, and in which they become acquainted with some of the English literary heritage. As such it would contain a distinct body of mate- rial which teachers must teach and pupils must learn. English teaching would therefore be 'child-centred' only in the very limited sense that all good teaching is child-centred — that it engages the interest and efforts of the pupils. Improvement in pupils' powers of speaking and listening would be achieved by improving their literacy.

> The teacher would not hesitate to prescribe to the children on matters of grammatical correctness. He would recognise the superiority of SE and see it as his task to make his pupils write it well and thereby gain the ability to speak it fluently. (Marenbon, 1987: 253)

It is true that natural speakers of SE also have to make adjustments in moving from speech to writing. I would suggest, though, that the adjustments are far fewer than for those whose normal spoken language is not SE. I would further suggest that there has been an under-estimation in education of the subtle diffi- culties of adjustment for very many learners faced with these issues. This is part- ly because so many people, with a great deal of effort, more or less manage a reasonable degree of basic competence in written SE by the time they leave school — although difficulties are more severe than is often supposed. A major language performance survey in England and Wales (APU, 1988) found, for instance, that when assessed in relation to grammar and orthography 20% of 11- year-olds and almost 10% of 15-year-olds produced more than 7 SE grammati- cal errors in 20 lines of writing and more than 10 orthographic errors in the first 10 lines of writing.

In this discussion I want to suggest that many writers have problems in writing SE because they have not been able to fully work out for themselves the following relatively complex distinctions:

1. between the lexis of their speech and that of SE;
2. between the grammar of their speech and that of SE;
3. between the idioms associated with their speech and those expected in a SE written context; and
4. the fact that the SE spelling system is not phonically regular for anybody and that 'spelling like it sounds' is not an adequate strategy, particularly where the writer's phonological patterns do not match SE orthography.

Evidence of these difficulties in both young and adult writers will be analysed. The chapter will end by suggesting ways in which the English language, communication skills and literacy curriculum ought to change in order to assist these learners in gaining more explicit access to information about how different varieties of language operate and how they relate or do not relate to SE.

The discussion presented here will look at the question from the particular perspective of teaching and learning in London; as such it will attempt to draw on the linguistic starting point of two main groups of learner:

1. users of British varieties of English other than SE;
2. users of English-lexicon Caribbean Creole languages.

Often, even close observers of the issue appear well able to identify what students are doing *wrong* in their writing, but are faltering and uncertain about why it is happening; nor is any soundly based pedagogy offered towards the beginnings of a solution. One survey of the written English of nearly 500 students across seven FE colleges concluded:

> Almost all the students in the sample clearly had difficulty in their use of written English, although the nature, frequency and 'seriousness' of these difficulties varied considerably. Anyone glancing through these scripts could not fail but be struck by the errors in spelling and punctuation and to a much lesser extent in grammar. In most cases they are obvious and create an unfavourable impression and undoubtedly colour the reader's reaction to the piece of writing.

and, most tellingly,

> A comparison of the two pieces of writing produced by each student suggests very strongly that most students possess only one style, in the case of many *a style more suited to informal speech than to writing* [emphasis added] and do not know how to write factually, descriptively, persuasively

or, indeed, in any way other than informally and personally. A personal style was adopted when convention context or audience demanded the use of a more formal style. Many students found the writing of factual, descriptive and discussive pieces difficult. (Austin-Ward, 1988: 98)

As suggested earlier, part of the explanation for these perceived problems with students' writing lies in the complexities involved in students moving from the English of their naturally occurring speech to the written SE required for academic performance. Beyond this I am arguing that there has long been a gap in teaching methodology in the classroom and in the curriculum sufficient to deal with these phenomena; as a result a significant minority of learners are left with intractable problems when they attempt to write and no effective strategies to deal with them.

I want to suggest that many writers in educational settings engage in a silent and often unnoticed struggle with the problem of how to create fluent and accurately written SE in a variety of styles when their starting point is not SE. I want to further suggest that there are, in fact, significant groups of learners who are adversely affected by a pedagogy which ignores the linguistic properties of their natural varieties of language. Finally I want to suggest that formerly teachers took a prescriptive and punitive approach i.e. *there is 'proper' English and any other variety is wrong.* Latterly, teachers have tended to be more relaxed about manifestations of other varieties of English in written SE contexts; but in their anxiety not to be prescriptive have, in the end, ducked this issue and have engaged in practice of an uneasily hybrid nature in which SE writing is expected yet inaccurate SE writing is accepted.

My speculative proposition is that signs of difficulty with SE writing can take a variety of forms including:

1. students who although relatively fluent writers show obvious, multiple and regular signs of their speech forms in their SE writing;
2. students with occasional signs of (1) sufficient to give an unfavourable impression of their SE writing skills;
3. students who experience major problems with the writing process — one aspect of these problems being their difficulties in coping with the differences between their speech and the writing they are trying to do;
4. students who go to elaborate lengths to avoid writing or who produce much less writing and much more slowly than they are capable of.

Their problems are exacerbated when their teachers, including the present writer, are slow to understand the ways in which their spoken language and their writing interact.

The Teacher as a Slow Learner

Most forms of enquiry involve some kind of personal journey. The present study is no exception. As a teacher I did not arrive at my current perceptions overnight. At first, fresh from my own selective schooling followed by extensive higher education, I was puzzled when confronted with learners at secondary school level who found the acquisition of SE literacy difficult. Why did they have such difficulties? Didn't everybody acquire literacy skills smoothly and naturally apart from a few people who had suffered at the hands of reactionary, incompetent teachers and an education system biased against working-class learners? Teaching white working-class bottom-stream pupils in Scottish urban comprehensive schools I was amazed at the acute discomfort they suffered whenever they were asked to write anything down; and the extraordinary lengths they went to to avoid putting pen to paper. Often, it seemed to me, they put more effort into evading even small acts of writing than would have been involved in simply attempting the writing. I was frustrated when pupils who had demonstrated a clear understanding of what was being taught in their readily offered oral responses suddenly claimed not to be able to replicate these responses when requested to do so in written form. I was aware that when they spoke they spoke in Scottish forms of language which were radically different from the SE that I was requiring them to write. However, I failed to think through any implications of this unstated diglossic situation. Nor did I develop any kind of pedagogy which even began to address the issue.

Later on in the early 1970s in London I taught black working-class teenagers mainly born in the Caribbean. Again, as in the context quoted earlier, I noticed a strong allergic reaction to written tasks alongside intelligent oral responses to the same tasks. Similarly, when they spoke they used markedly Caribbean or London forms of language. But what leapt out for me was the fact that when they did write they reproduced many aspects of their Caribbean language when they were trying to write in SE. To many teachers it looked like an epidemic of 'chronic careless errors', such as missing 'esses' or 'ed's off the ends of words. To me it became clear that they were using the grammar of their, usually Jamaican, Creole language in a SE written context. My awareness of this reality was sharpened by the way in which the pupils' Jamaican Creole had strong similarities with the Sierra Leone Krio (Creole) language of my childhood. I was also aware though that teaching strategies needed to be developed to help the pupils to understand what was happening without undermining their confidence or disparaging their Creole language. The minefield opened up by this task detonated when I began, simultaneously, to teach older Jamaican students in adult literacy classes in the evening. In this context even stronger and starker examples of Jamaican Creole being unconsciously written, when SE was intended, presented themselves. When I insensitively pointed this out to one middle-aged working-class Jamaican man he rounded on me angrily: 'Nah English me talk?'

This reaction provided me with my first real insight into the phenomenon of writers in educational settings not being fully conscious of what variety of language they were actually producing on paper. In many subsequent years of experience with adult literacy students I was made aware of how important this issue was. It could show itself in the dilemmas caused to tutors acting as scribes when using the language experience approach with beginner-writers. What if the students' spoken language was not SE? (a question Wendy Moss discusses in her chapter). On the other hand, even with relatively confident and skilled writers in literacy classes or FE it became clear that their control over the variety of language used was not total. Many of these writers had implicitly learned to write in one particular dialect, SE, as a result of the literacy skills learned through schooling. I discovered in many classrooms that if I asked writers ranging from age 16 in FE classes through to older students in adult literacy classes to name the language they were using for literacy, very few knew that it was called SE. Their reactions indicated that they had never been required to explicitly consider this question. Invariably they would ask in a quizzical response: 'Is it grammatical English?' 'Is it proper English?' 'Is that the kind of English we are expected to write?' Another lesson here for teachers. If students did not precisely know which variety of written language they were attempting to reproduce, how then was a teacher to assist the minority of students who reproduced on paper a hybrid variety of language incorporating SE mixed with elements of whichever variety of spoken language was most natural to them? For such students this uncertainty becomes a persistent problem and a constant feature of their whole educational experience. It also presents a challenge for their teachers. Teacher colleagues would often feel that they had to 'do something' about it. Yet they found themselves paralysed by two considerations: first, an understandable desire not to interfere with or disparage their students' spoken language; and second, the impossibility of dealing with the issue in piecemeal fashion in a few minutes at an individual student's side when marking or discussing some written work already produced by the student in question. The Proposals for a Curriculum Response at the end of this chapter are an atttempt at charting a possible way forward.

Despite these teacher hesitations, learners constantly made it clear to me that they required explicit teacher intervention and assistance in connection with the writing process, at least with the final draft. The prime value they attached to the teacher was as someone willing to share with them as far as possible his or her technical understanding of how both their natural spoken language and SE worked. In doing this the teacher would be supplying insights which they felt they could not acquire unaided. One adult student, referring to teaching sessions

I had conducted with her class about the nature and origins of Caribbean Creole languages and the ways in which they compared and contrasted with SE, wrote:

> At the age of sixteen I came to England and attended a secondary school. My English teacher would constantly correct my grammar mistakes. After a while I developed a complex and started to hate reading and writing.
>
> I just couldn't understand why I was getting it wrong. I knew I spoke English. It was always drummed into me yet I kept getting it wrong on paper.
>
> My friends would laugh at me. They would say I really developed a complex.
>
> I decided to sort out my English by coming to English class at the Bookplace. I seemed to be making the same mistakes. I borrowed a book from the library on Patwa. By reading the book I couldn't identify my problem. There were a few phrases however in the book which I use and sometimes come out in my writing.
>
> After listening to Roxy Harris and his tapes I immediately identified my problems. I was speaking and writing Creole English. I was very interested to listen to what he had to say. I have never come across any written books about Creole English. In future I will be more aware when I am writing SE because I will know what my mistakes are and will practise, hopefully I should be able to get it right. (Richards, 1988: 8)

This troubled encounter between English-lexicon Caribbean Creoles and SE has been an underlying aspect of London classrooms for the last two or three decades. This conflict is now virtually invisible in schools as most black pupils of Caribbean descent are now British born; but it is still a conspicuous issue in further and adult education particularly with adults returning to learning. More precisely, in the 1990s in London a teacher would be unlikely to find many 14-year-olds presenting some of the Jamaican Creole influenced patterns in their writing demonstrated in the following extract of writing which a 14-year-old born in Jamaica handed in to me in the mid 1970's in a London school:

> I think England is one of the beautiful country I can see so for. When I wash in Jamaica I heir some of the people sed dat England is no good but when I come in England and see who it stay I would not believe wash they say no more ... I think they are puting the peples under pressure whit tax in the country. Dat is way so mush man and woman are live the countries ... I think they are makeing too mush rules in the countries and one more tine I do not like they mush do some tine to stop the bombing ...
>
> [I think England is one of the most beautiful countries I have seen so far. When I was in Jamaica I heard some of the people say that England is no

good but when I came into England and saw how it was I would not believe what they said any more ... I think they are putting the people under pressure with tax in the country. That is why so many men and women are leaving the countries ... I think they are making too many rules in the countries and one more thing I do not like they must do something to stop the bombing ...]

In the early to mid 1970s, I sought to devise a variety of responses to assist with the writing of pupils who had entered British secondary schools after a childhood in Caribbean countries, especially Jamaica. In one case the pupil concerned was potentially capable of being successful on his 'O' level English course but, according to his teacher, produced a mixture of Jamaican Creole and SE features in his writing. The teacher felt that she was at a loss for an effective strategy to help him. It soon became apparent that this pupil was a prolific writer of short stories. One day I queried him as to why he had written his stories so consistently but awkwardly in the style of American pulp crime fiction, and added: 'Why don't you write about what you know — for example about your childhood in Jamaica.' His answer stunned me. He stated that he couldn't write about Jamaican life and people because he didn't know how to represent Jamaican language in writing. Here was an interesting phenomenon. When he attempted to write SE, features of Jamaican Creole language appeared. On the other hand if he wanted to write down Jamaican language he couldn't, as he had never been shown how to do it.

We developed a collaborative working method. He decided to write about his childhood in Jamaica. In each piece of writing we agreed that he would attempt to write the narrative in SE and any dialogue in Jamaican Creole language. We would experiment with ways of writing down Jamaican speech, attempting to achieve some sort of consistency within a framework that satisfied him. Eventually the result was a sustained piece of writing published by the Inner London Education Authority's English Centre as *Jamaica Child* (1978) and later incorporated within the publication *Our Lives* (1979). More interestingly for our purposes here, there were other by-products. First of all his control over SE writing improved. Simultaneously, he had made great strides in learning how to write down his mother tongue. From a teaching angle, I had learned that the commonsense idea that the way to help students to write SE was to either forget about or eradicate their first variety of language was seriously flawed.

Many years later, when charged with the task of developing ways of improving the written SE performance of students of Caribbean descent in further and adult education in Inner London, I was faced with a major methodological problem. Despite fantasies to the contrary, the students in question did not receive their education in segregated conditions apartheid-style. On the whole they were deeply embedded in classroom contexts which were profoundly mixed on every possible axis — race, gender, ethnicity, nationality and language. Teachers reported that even though many students of Caribbean descent needed specific assistance with particular aspects of written SE, they refused to participate in teaching arrangements which in any way *picked them out* or differentiated them from their fellow students. Of course the students were inadvertently trying to teach myself and my fellow teachers another lesson — they were not either Caribbean or British in their language patterns; they were both. For those brought up in London this meant employing the speech patterns of Caribbean Creoles and London English in varying combinations. Many researchers have attempted to pin down this elusive reality and have coined terms to match; terms such as 'British Black English' (Sutcliffe, 1982), 'British Jamaican Creole' (Sutcliffe 1984), 'London Jamaican' (Sebba, 1986: 149, 1993) and 'Black London English' (Sebba, 1986: 149, 1993). Hewitt (1986: 104) described the situation in this way:

> Whatever the relationship of the creoles used by young blacks born in this country to the creoles of black British people born and raised in the Caribbean, it is apparent that *some* young blacks can employ both an indigenous dialect of English — London vernacular or Yorkshire, say and a dialect closely related to Jamaican creole which has been termed 'British Jamaican Creole' or, specifically in relation to London speech, 'London Jamaican'. Some can also employ another creole, e.g. the French-based creole of St Lucia, as well as the generational prestige 'British' or 'London' and an 'indigenous' dialect. It is also the case that the young black users of these dialects switch from one to another at certain times and in certain contexts

Hewitt, in fact, goes on to identify Creole forms in white adolescent speech. An appreciation of all these linguistic complexities as played out in classroom contexts led me to two further insights. In the first place, if students of Caribbean descent had London English as an important part of their linguistic repertoire, would not a similar pattern apply to students from other ethnic and linguistic backgrounds; for example, to those of Greek and Turkish Cypriot, Pakistani, Bangladeshi, Indian and West African descent? If this were the case then a second insight emerged — the linguistic model which formed the basis for the teaching of language and literacy skills in most London classrooms needed to change. This model implied that SE was normal, that SE writing should therefore naturally follow and that individual students who found SE writing difficult possessed an individual problem and constituted a dysfunctional element in an otherwise satisfactory system. The inadequacy of this approach was exposed when a white British student in a GCE English class in which I was working in an FE college in Inner London, produced the following written phrase:

Me and me mate was walking home.

When I presented the phrase on the board to the whole class as an example of a London English phrase and asked the students to translate it into an SE phrase, I was surprised at the amount of difficulty that my intended *simple* request caused them. They offered as their SE alternative examples as varied as:

My mate and me was walking home.
Me and my mate was walking home.
Me and my friend was walking home.
My friend and I was walking home.

The latter version proved to be a sticking point. As hard as they tried, the students could see nothing *wrong* with this version of the phrase. As far as they were concerned it was an accurate SE phrase. I experimented in this way across many other classrooms in London with the typical London mix of students using the same initial phrase and always with a similar result. Indeed it was very often the case that it was the students considered most foreign to Britain and to the English language who were most able to produce the accurate SE version. The fact that students found the auxiliary verb form 'was' more natural than 'were' in this context was itself entirely natural since it represents an extremely common grammatical pattern within London English so that:

SE	London English
I was	I was
You were	You was
He/She was	He/She was
We were	We was
You were	You was
They were	They was

Yet, in common with many teachers I had expected the students to look at written phrases and sentences through the same prism of natural SE use which characterised my own language patterns. Unhelpful banalities such as 'always proof-read your work' or 'read your work over to check for mistakes before handing it in' had come easily to my lips. Now, by contrast, a new model began to suggest itself as an alternative basis for classroom practice. SE speech was not the norm for most of the students, SE writing did not follow naturally from their speech and any problems they had with writing SE needed to be analysed and tackled explicitly. This emerging model also exploded the notion of classrooms in which the language of white students was deemed to be English and therefore unproblematic in relation to writing in the classroom in contrast to the language of black and *foreign* students.

Instead of this kind of classroom divisiveness the new emerging model suggested a three-pronged basis for promoting both unity and diversity in the classroom.

First the students, whatever their background, had in common the fact that in educational contexts they were all required to write in accurate SE. Second, very few of them had SE as their first and most natural variety of spoken language; they had one of the 184 different home languages identified in the ILEA Catalogue of Languages (ILEA, 1989), London English, or a Caribbean Creole. Finally, the overwhelming majority of the students had London English in common. They spoke it as a first variety of language, for some of the time or, at the very least, were exposed to it everyday of their lives as Londoners. The perspective offered by the new model, then, was needed to form the foundation of teachers' classroom strategies in dealing with students' written language. The long personal journey of slow learning described in this part of the chapter informs the Proposals for a Curriculum Response which appear in the final section of the chapter. In doing so it describes classroom factors which arose against a wider socio-political and politico-linguistic background in Britain.

Societal Interventions

Compulsory schooling was introduced in Britain in the 1870s. From then until now there has been a constant and recurring complaint that standards of English literacy and/or English use are low, inadequate and declining. It is my contention that embedded in these complaints is a persistent sense of disappointment that schools have not achieved enough success in their often unstated mission to instigate a substantial language shift in the overwhelming majority of the population. Schools everywhere in Britain have been charged with the task of taking in all five-year-olds and moving them away from the varieties of English which dominate their region in the direction of SE — particularly SE in its written form. Although schools are substantially successful in achieving this, their efforts are heavily criticised by influential sectors of British society such as employers, government and the media.

As long ago as 1921, a government enquiry into the teaching of English in England, quoted three major employers' criticisms of the language and literacy skills of school leavers:

> Thus, Messrs Vickers, Ltd., 'find great difficulty in obtaining junior clerks who can speak and write English clearly and correctly, especially those aged from 15 to 16 years.' Messrs. Lever Brothers, Ltd., say 'it is a great surprise and disappointment to us to find that our young employees are so hopelessly deficient in their command of English.' Boots' Pure Drug Co. say: 'Teaching of English in the present day schools produces a very limited command of the English language.' (Newbolt, 1921: 72)

Over 70 years later it seems that employers are still making similar complaints.

For example, under a newspaper headline screaming 'Bosses forced to teach recruits the "three R's" ' we find the following: (*Daily Mail*, 1991)

> MANY company training schemes are turning into little more than remedial classes for school-leavers who cannot read, write or add up properly.
>
> Firms say they are having to spend hours bringing recruits' basic skills up to an acceptable standard before they can actually teach them the job.
>
> In a survey of managers, more than half said they are so worried about falling standards that they are prepared to pay higher taxes to improve the education system.
>
> The survey of 690 bosses, ranging from chief executives to foremen, was conducted by the British Institute of Management to find out what they thought of their own training schemes
>
> But 90 per cent seized on the chance to point out the way Britain's schools are letting down the children who are the nation's future, saying that proficiency in the three R's is their top priority in selecting recruits.

This perspective is one that has been actively encouraged and promoted by government ministers. A recent Secretary of State for Education, for instance, claimed (*The Guardian*, 1991) that

> Our schools are turning out some people who are illiterate. We have too many school leavers who cannot spell, use the language grammatically or perform simple mental arithmetic.

and again:

> PRINCE Charles's recent widely reported remarks expressing his dismay at low standards and low levels of achievement in education strike a strong chord in all of us. He vividly expressed what is a source of frustration to thousands of parents around Britain. Why do we not have a reliable state education system where our primary children learn to read, write, and add up fluently at the most basic level ...

The latter reference was to an outburst by Prince Charles in 1989 in which he reportedly (*Daily Mail*, 1989) 'launched a fierce attack yesterday on poor English teaching in schools. ... He told business executives in London:

> All the people I have in my office, they can't speak English properly, they can't write English properly.

> All the letters sent from my office I have to correct myself and that is because English is taught so bloody badly. That is the problem.

Of course the press has played its own gleeful part in this debate on language and literacy teaching.

It is true that many of these views are tendentious and based on wrong information. However, insofar as many people do indeed find writing SE difficult, even after prolonged schooling, it is useful for educators to set aside their irritation and ask what elements of the writing process cause difficulties for students and others. As mentioned earlier, this chapter is intended to make the modest suggestion that at least part of the picture is related to difficulties experienced by many people in handling the transition from speech to writing. In Britain this means a conflict between different, usually regionally based varieties of spoken English and written SE. This is a problem with which many educators are uneasy and which they tend to smooth over and not face directly.

When school-leavers and adults seek further help with writing SE in adult education or further education settings it is important that the pedagogic techniques employed are not merely 'more of the same' but genuinely engage the learners in reflecting on the underlying reasons for their difficulties. This discussion seeks to establish that for many learners these underlying reasons are related to problems in handling the transition from speech to writing where more than one variety of language is involved. What then is the picture with regard to British varieties of English other than SE?

Hidden Language

Peter Trudgill has researched and written widely on varieties of English within Britain, and specifically on how the fact of these many varieties impacts on the education process. One definition he proposes is particularly useful for the present discussion; namely, the scrapping of the idea that SE in Britain is a language, with all other varieties of English being inferior deviating dialects. Trudgill (1975) suggests that SE itself is one dialect among many, albeit a dialect which is uniquely powerful:

> The term dialect ... means any variety which is grammatically different from any other, as well, perhaps, as having a different vocabulary or pronunciation ... One of the most important varieties of English is that dialect which is widely known as Standard English. Standard English is the dialect used by most speakers who would consider themselves to be 'educated'; it is normally used in writing and on radio and television; it is the form of English normally taught to foreign learners; and in many important respects, it is the language of British schools ... (Trudgill, 1975: 17)

Two major consequences of SE being the language of British schools are, first, that teachers are, in effect, engaged in the task of eradicating the presence in writing of other English dialects and, second, most know relatively little about the linguistic properties of any English dialects other than SE including the ones that their pupils and students speak around them daily. Not that teachers are to blame: since, according to Edwards (1993) there has been only one systematic study of grammar undertaken in the south east (of England). The pressures for participants in the education system to acquire SE, particularly in its written form, are enormous. Consequently, most people in Britain who have passed through a minimum 11 years of compulsory schooling have managed to erase from their writing most traces of their original English dialect or Caribbean Creole; even if they wanted to consciously write it down they have no idea of how to do so and have never been given the chance.

The key question thrown up by this erasure is not: how did London English or Caribbean Creoles slip through the SE defences? but rather: what made the learner's first variety of spoken language disappear so totally from the realm of writing? By what process did this occur? What does a teacher say to a learner to cause this disappearance? Apart from occasional flourishes by radical school teachers the only sustained visibility in writing of other English varieties of language has been offered by writers and publishers working in the adult literacy or adult education sectors as other chapters in this volume suggest.

To begin with it is useful to mention some of the features which sociolinguists have identified as being characteristic of urban British dialects, with special emphasis on those found in London English. Among the pronunciation patterns of London English identified by Trudgill (1990) are 'town' pronounced as 'tahn' (A), 'news' pronounced as 'noos' (B), 'milk' pronounced as 'mioolk' or 'miook' and 'fill' as 'fi-oo(l)' (C), 'mother' pronounced as 'muvver' (D), and 'thing' pronounced as 'fing' (E).

In looking at the question of the grammar of what they call non-SE, Cheshire *et al.* (1993: 64) report the findings of the Survey of British Dialect Grammar (1989) 'on those features of dialect grammar that are reported as occurring in most of the urban centres of the British Isles'. They were: 'them' as demonstrative adjective (F); 'should of' (G); absence of plural marking (H); 'what' as subjective relative pronoun (I); 'never' as past tense negator (J); 'there was' with plural 'notional' subject (K); 'there's' with plural 'notional' subject (L); adverbial 'quick' (adjectives with adverbial function) (M); 'ain't' (N); non-standard 'was' (O); prepositions (P); regularization of reflexive pronouns (Q); past tense 'done' (R). Edwards (1993) writing specifically of Southern British English adds multiple negation (S), personal and reflexive pronouns (T) and nouns of measurement (U).

In the sense that these observations have a predictive quality it is worth taking a look at some of the ways in which they occur in the writing of learners across the age range in educational settings in London. The linguistic patterns which follow are familiar, implicitly, to many teachers of English in schools or in adult and further education. However, my experience with teachers over many years in the context of in-service training has shown me that those who in some way recognise these patterns are usually uneasy about them and find it difficult to develop any kind of coherent or consistent pedagogy in relation to them. On the other hand, there are large numbers of teachers who appear to be relatively unaware of the ways in which the writing of their pupils and students directly reflects their spoken language. I have found, for example, that such teachers react with amazement when exposed to the fact that there is a distinctive London English which has its own pronunciation patterns, lexis and grammar. These considerations influenced my decision to collect such a wide range of written samples covering writers of different ages and from different sectors of the education system. I wanted to establish beyond doubt that these linguistic factors are an important feature of the writing of many learners and, as such, deserve closer attention and more sophisticated approaches from teachers. The emphasis in the samples on the writing of young children is intended to show the starting points of writers and therefore to illuminate the effects of schooling on the development of adult writers. For example, one phenomenon which has long intrigued me is the fact that there is an almost total absence of a developed literature employing London English. At an earlier period I remember being surprised that even an impressive oral history project recording the lives of working-class Londoners somehow did not get to grips with this language (People's Autobiography of Hackney, 1977). Of course, the writing samples selected here are only a fraction of what could have been chosen and are not subjected to any extended analysis. Nevertheless, they are offered as a contribution to the beginnings of a debate. They are broadly organised ranging from younger to older writers. One exception is Sample [42] which is placed at the end of the selection of London English writing samples at the end of a sequence of writing from older writers. This is deliberate as it represents an example of writing which bridges the linguistic categories of London English and Caribbean Creole and is produced by a 14-year-old of Caribbean descent most of whose contemporaries no longer exhibit overt features of their Caribbean language in their writing.

The samples were solicited from a small number of contacts in primary, secondary, further and adult education in London who were asked to supply examples of writing which seemed to indicate the occurrence of the writers' spoken language in their SE writing. The number of samples presented here is deliberately large for two main reasons. First, it was important to examine enough material to demonstrate the predictive quality of the work of the academic linguists already cited. Second, it was intended that the sceptical teachers mentioned earlier should be provided with many examples arising in different ways, so that they would be able to explore them at their leisure and would be able to relate them to examples identifiable in their own classrooms. It should also be possible for them to make their own observations on some of the phonological, lexical, idiomatic and grammatical patterns in the samples which have not been exhaustively analysed here. One other point is that the writers of the samples remain anonymous apart from an indication of their ages, or the stages they are at in the educational process. For the most part their gender, race, family linguistic background and other autobiographical information are deliberately omitted. In this chapter, the simple aim is to establish beyond doubt that such writing occurs in a widespread way in London, can be produced by writers of any age, gender or race and requires a specific pedagogic response.

[1]   Then we went to a difrent shop they did not have no jens [jeans]

[2]   On Saturday me and my mum and my brother and my dad went shoping … then just me my mum and my brother went back out again becase we was going to my old nushrys [nursery's] bazar.

[3]   On Saturday my Auntys and uncle came round my house for dinner. (K. aged 6/7)

[4]   We find a car wive [with] grnsu (guns) on it … aw no they cacht us. they wolt [walked] to the dunjoon. We hewd [held] aw [our] bref … wen we opoed awe iys we was in the diynjoon … we slept in the dungeon for friy [three] nights …we only had 10 pans [pounds] left. We fand 10,000 Pans on the strit Pavmot … we was wocen olog the rode … John basht into the wole … we got att [out] … they ran away they was nevu to bey sene a gen … Tony foth for a minit … James foth [thought] we can put a [all] are [our] money in the bank (J. aged 7)

[5]   Today my Brather Dont Fill very well …

[6]   On Sunday I went to hav somethink to eat and I had a roast dinner and then I had my arfders [afters].

[7]   My mum is gowin To get me sum huy [high] hiws [heels]

[8]   I went to see bootey and The beest and I went wiv my play senta (C. aged 6/7)

[9]   I went to a football mash with My bROTheR and they got bet (A. aged 6/7)

[10]   … and ther was two frens of min and wen I was upsters I was playing the compooter … me and my bravr froo snow balls at the peepoll (N. aged 6/7)

[11]   On Satarday when I stayed round my nans house

[12]   … and my mum said letse go down the curey shop I said yess sowe we went down the curey shop and I mist most of my pogram. (Je. aged 6/7)

[13]   on Sutday it wos my buf day [birthday] and aT my baffday I won a … (B. aged 6)

[14]   I went otr [out] wiv my mummy and naany and I susb [stuck] a big baballgam [bubblegum] in my maf [mouth]

[15]   I went to my noow [new] house (C. aged 6/7)

[16]   I went to my BRVSS [brother's] HAAS [house] (J.S. aged 6)

[17]   We raked up some Leves in the garden and there was so many Leves that we raked weel barows and weel barows of them.

[18]   On the hoilday I went skating

[19]   On the weekend I went to the park (K. aged 6/7)

[20]   On Sunday I went swiming with my nan and my sister and my mum and their was this silde.

[21]   On Satday I went to the marcet and went to the shops. and went home and dun sum home work

[22]   She stated to Larth [laugh] Then she dune it to me . Then I dune it to her. Then she dune it to me. Then I dune it to her …

[23]   my dads car got took a way and in the morning my dad was angre that his car had been took away

[24]   I saw sam and we playd to gever (A. aged 6/7)

[25]   She don't have children

[26]   the dragon stuck his hed out the door (J.J aged 7)

[27]   1989 I learnt to read and by then I wode of bin wrighting and walking [28] … 1987 I learnt to put my clovs on. (Ja. aged 9)

[29]   Yetserday ther was a rober nexs door and the plice came round my house and then they came round are house and they took my rige [ring] … and the plice cam round the hous and brot it back and I was happy and I sed Fag you very much … and I gave them a card and thay seD FacYou for the card (B. aged 7)

[30]   my dads car got took on a way and in the moning he had The Ravin ump his eys cam out (A. aged 7)

[31]   I was PLaying in the Prak wiv my mum and dad and I was playing football wiv my dad and my mum was sunbaving and my dog was laeing daon and thene we went home (Jy. aged 6/7)

[32]   I think I could of done a bit more writing in the project (R. aged 12)

[33]   There was no chairs and I had to sit on the floor … A man called mark matthews done a mime (T. aged 12)

[34]   thay fort he was Just A little nerd And that he dident know nothingk … he told her that he dident have no freinds … somethink in his body … he fort he was in love (D. aged 14)

[35]   There are many ways you could change things you don't like or things you think what is wrong (L. aged 14)

[36]   I still wasn't sure ... what I was going to do with them grades (H. student FE)

[37]   ... it must of been obvious that he was going to become supervisor ... It would of had an effect on anyone watching. If someone told me that it never I would personally think that they are lying ... I was waiting to see what Dan White had to say for his self ... Gay and lesbian people should come out from hiding and expose their selves to society (D. student FE)

[38]   the people who live in the places would have the right hump and they might pick on you if you was out having a meal ... they must of heated [hated] all English people (A. student FE)

[39]   It was like a race to see who could come out the plane first ... As soon as I came out the plane (K. student FE)

[40]   I realised I needed to attend regular for my work to improve (C. student FE)

[41]   We was thinking of going abroad to Pakistan and India ... The waiting lounge was nice, comfy and clean ... There was other passengers waiting ... My hand luggages felt like heavy logs tied to my shoulders ... Anyway we was then given a boarding card ... When it [the plane] went up I was sort of like sunk back in the seat ... I had heard from my friends that they had problems in customs but we was lucky! (S.Z. student FE)

[42]   My mum from Jamahicar and my dad from Barbados ... My mum never had that much friends around there ... my mum come over when she was fifteen ... my mum the oldest and my mum sista the youngest ... my sista use to live with gran from she was a baby ... my mums always preasuring me to do good in school ... [my gran] She 65 but she don't look it ... I once stole some money of my dad he found out he never hit me but I never don it again in my life (A. aged 14)

Commentary

Here there is space merely to direct the reader's attention to the fact of the existence in an extensive way of unconscious or unintentional features of London English in the writing of Londoners. This is marked in the writing of primary school children and much reduced but still detectable in writing produced at secondary schools, further education colleges and in adult education settings. Among the examples characteristic of the London English pronunciation patterns outlined earlier are:

(A) pans [4], fand [4], att [4], are money [4], maf [14], haas [16]
(B) bootey [8], noow [15], compooter [10]
(C) hewd [4], hiws [7]
(D) wive [4], wiv [8], [14], [31], bravr [10], BRVSS [16], to gever [24], clovs [28], sunbaving [31]
(E) bref [4], friy [4], foth [4], froo [10], buf day and baffday [13], Fag you and Fac You [29], fort [34].

As far as grammar is concerned the following are some of the features visible in the written samples:

(F) them grades [36]
(G) wode of bin [27], could of done [32], must of been and would of had [37], must of heated [38]
(I) things you think what is wrong [35]
(J) if someone told me that it never [37], he never hit me and I never don it [42]
(K) ther was two frens [10], there was so many Leves [17], there was no chairs [33], There was other passengers [39]
(M) I needed to attend regular [40], my mums always preasuring me to do good in school [42]
(O) we was going [2], we was wocen [4], if you was out [38], we was thinking [39], we was then given [39], we was lucky [39]
(P) round my house [3], round my nans house [11], down the curey shop [12], round are house and round the house [29] who could come out the plane [39], I came out the plane [39]
(Q) what Dan White had to say for his self ... expose their selves [37]
(R) I ... dun sum home work [21], she dune it [22], I dune it [22], A man ... done a mime [33], I never don it [42]
(S) they did not have no jens [1], he dident know nothingk [34], he dident have no freinds [34].

There are other features related to spoken London English which appear in the written samples and which should be noted. These include in the sphere of pronunciation, somethink [6] and somethink and nothingk [34]. As far as grammar is concerned there are, for instance, in relation to SE:

(i)   object pronoun used in subject position — me and my mum [2], me and my bravr [10]
(ii) regularisation of don't — my Brather don't fill very well [5], she don't look it [42], she don't have children [25]
(iii) verb form unmarked in context in which SE uses a past participle — they got bet [beat] [9], my dads car got took away [23], his car had been took away [23], got took on away [30].

(iv) London English verb form 'to lay down', cf. SE 'to lie down' — Laeing down [31].

Finally, there are idiomatic words and phrases specifically associated with London English speech. For example, arfders [afters] [6], on the hoilday [18], on the weekend [19], their was this slide [20], The Ravin ump [30], the right hump [37], comfy [39], I was sort of like sunk back in the seat [39].

Two additional points arise. First, [39] is taken from the writing of a student brought up in Britain in an Urdu, Gujerati and Panjabi speaking family from India and Pakistan. She encountered English for the first time only when she started school. It is relatively little remarked on that when people move into English they very often acquire the particular form of English native to the part of the country in which they happen to live, in this case London English and not SE as is often supposed. Secondly, as already mentioned, the overwhelming majority of young black people of Caribbean descent in Britain were born and brought up in Britain and not in the Caribbean. It is therefore unusual to find examples where their writing is solely and heavily influenced by Caribbean Creole languages. What is noticeable in some cases is SE writing heavily influenced by both London English and Caribbean Creoles as in [42]. Here there are several visible Caribbean language influences including repeated examples of the deleted copula (GG) 'my mum from Jamaicar, my dad from Barbados ... my mum the oldest, my mum sista youngest ... She 65'. Apart from this there are phrases characteristic of Caribbean idiomatic usage such as 'much friends' and 'from she was a baby'. Elsewhere in the same sample there are instances which could be the result of either Caribbean Creole or London English influences — 'my mum come over', 'she don't look it'. In addition there are features which are clearly related to London English — 'preasuring me to do good in school', 'stole some money of my dad', 'I never done it again'.

When describing some general characteristics of English-lexicon Caribbean Creoles, Roberts (1988) identified pronunciation patterns including the following: 'thing' pronounced as 'ting' (V); 'this' pronounced as 'dis' (W); 'him' pronounced as 'im' (X); 'ask' pronounced as 'hask' (Y); 'best' pronounced as 'bes', 'husband' pronounced as 'husban' final consonant clusters (Z). To this he added significant grammatical features: third-person singular 's' (AA); possessive 's' (BB); subject–verb agreement — one form for singular and plural (CC); pronoun inflexion (DD); plural of nouns (EE); demonstrative plural (FF); predicative adjective–subject + adjective (deleted copula) (GG); tense and aspect marked outside the verb (e.g. present and past tense) (HH).

A few samples of students' writing will suffice to illustrate the general point that just as with London English shown earlier, many writers are strongly influenced by Caribbean Creoles when they attempt to write SE.

[43] It's has if they don't care about me. They just send me away has if I am a little brown pastel ... My mother notice I not sleeping very well ... I can feel her cool soft hans stroking my hair has if I am a Tinmid (timid) dog. I feel much better when my mother talk to me. I slept away my bad feelings inside and leave it for the next day ... I wave good buy, has the plane took off ... (R. student FE)

[44] with God help and my family sorporting me ... After that me and my baby settle down in my flat ... To all single parent you must always remember that there is a light at the end of the tennel. (H. student Adult education)

[45] I went into the facklift ... when I reach in the wearhouse, I realize that the wearhouse was pack with other things ... As I go down I hear a noise ... Then I realize that the end of the forkblade brake some of the glass. One of the worker said ... In my mine I was thinking 'what is the best thing to do?' ... the sail manager is in charge ... In is voice he sound very please ... When he see the damage he shake is head ... (W. return to study student)

[46] ... within the space of tree weeks my job was in japadie ... I was tole that I would get my ordenary license back ... a person who has a heart attact is able to keep is HGV license but a diabetic loses is license. (D. Adult basic education student)

[47] I fine it difficulty in learning (W. Adult basic education student)

Commentary

Despite the earlier example of the presence of Caribbean Creole features in the SE writing of school children, this phenomenon is most noticeable in the writing of mature students in further and adult education. The very few instances cited earlier correspond in several ways with the comments made by Roberts with regard to pronunciation:

(V) tree weeks [46]
(X) in is voice [45], he shake is head [45], able to keep is HGV license [46], a diabetic loses is license [46]
(Y) It's has if they don't care [43], has if I am [43], has the plane took off [43]
(Z) cool soft hans [43], In my mine [45], I was tole [46], I fine it difficulty [47].

Finally, some of the grammatical matchings can be indicated:

(BB) with God help [44]
(EE) to all single parent [44], sail manager [45]
(GG) I not sleeping very well [43]

(HH) they just send me away , my mother notice , I feel much better , when my mother talk to me, I leave it for the next day, I wave good buy [43], me and my baby settle down [44], when I reach in the wearhouse, I realize, As I go down I hear, he sound very please, when he see the damage he shake his head [45].

Once again, to sum up this section of the chapter, the questions remain. What happens to people's natural spoken language when they attempt to write SE? How is this language radically erased from the writing of most people? What are the processes involved? What discourse transpires between teachers and writers to achieve this? At what cost to the writer?

A Proposal for a Curriculum Response

It is clear that many children begin their life as writers by reproducing, on paper, many of the aspects of their spoken language even though the target of their writing is SE. Equally clear is the fact that teachers manage to prevent most writers from continuing to do this to any major extent by the time they leave school. However, many teachers are frustrated in schools as well as in further and adult education contexts by a significant minority of writers who continue to find the writing of SE difficult. A further frustration experienced by teachers is the impossibility of sorting out these complexities in a few minutes at the shoulder of the individual writer in a classroom during the marking process or at the time when written work is being returned. Some teachers additionally express uneasiness about how to raise these questions with writers without undermining their confidence or appearing to be negative about their natural spoken language. Yet the issue is one that teachers cannot avoid in view of the countervailing societal pressures in this regard mentioned earlier in the chapter. Perera (1984, 1990) begins to address this issue but stops short of explicitly advocating that teachers should deal with it in a proactive way throughout the education process. Richmond (1986: 131) also grappled with the dilemma and concluded:

> In the primary school and the early years of secondary school we should not attempt to standardize the (usually very small) number of non-standard features that intervene unconsciously in some children's mainstream school writing.

In his view:

> At some point in the middle years of secondary school, if it is obvious that some pupils are continuing to produce non-standard features in their writing for which they will ultimately be penalized, teachers should point out to them what these features are, and what their standard equivalents are.

I do not believe that this is an adequate strategy for teachers committed to helping learners to gain power and control over the writing process. If teachers and linguists know the rules of the game why should these not be shared with those struggling to express themselves in written form? Knowledge of British urban dialects and Caribbean Creoles needs to be explored explicitly and shared, including an understanding of the ways in which these varieties of language are attacked and undermined in order to promote SE as the language of literacy and power. Not doing this as early and as continuously as possible does not avoid the problem, as direct testimony from adult learners confirms (Richards, 1988) and those working with adult writers emphasise elsewhere in this volume. This leads me to make four modest proposals for the curriculum which would apply to all writers whether children or adults. These proposals would be developed and adapted to suit the levels of proficiency and maturity of those developing their writing skills.

Naming language

Naming language explicitly is vital. My experience over many years in in-service training contexts with teachers in the school, further and adult education sectors was that they resisted the idea of naming SE as SE on the grounds that in some way this was being too prescriptive. Unfortunately, the coming of the National Curriculum, has yielded this ground to negative forces hostile to teachers and to the interests of the majority of learners with whom teachers are concerned, despite the efforts of the LINC project (Carter, 1990; Bain *et al.*, 1992). My argument in the earlier period was that even if SE was not named it was nevertheless assumed, because every school or college or adult education institution had English, comunication skills or literacy on its curriculum. Simply using terms like 'English' and 'literacy' without being specific, automatically excluded and problematised speakers of British urban dialects and Caribbean Creoles. So the foundation of any curriculum for writers should involve naming not only SE but also, for example, London English and Jamaican Creole. Naming them implies the next step which would involve, as an integral part of the writing process, a constant journey of exploring these language varieties and learning about how they work.

Accent/pronunciation/spelling, vocabulary and grammar

Accent/pronunciation/spelling, vocabulary and grammar as essential categories in the writing process need to be made explicit and shared with learner-writers together with their potential utility as tools for representing an infinite variety of spoken language on paper — not just SE.

Take, for instance, writers whose natural spoken language is London English. If these writers are attempting to write in SE they may need help in understanding that if they, for example, write 'free' where SE spelling requires 'three', this does not constitute a spelling error, but an attempt to spell words as the writers would say them with a typical London English pronunciation pattern. However, attempts to develop a pedagogy which clarifies this issue should not fall into the trap of problematising the pronunciation patterns associated with lower status language varieties. A useful corrective has been supplied by Steve Bell in his cartoon strip in the *Guardian* newspaper when he depicts the Queen as pronouncing the word 'trousers' as 'trizers' (Bell, 1993: 93). The important point here is that no one would suggest that the Queen is incapable of pronouncing the word as 'trizers' yet spelling it as 'trousers' in a SE written context. The same outlook, then, should apply to the pronunciation/spelling question when it concerns a writer whose starting point is London English or an English lexicon Caribbean Creole language. The overall lesson for the writer would be that for anybody writing SE, spelling words as you would pronounce them is a strategy likely to lead to error as much as success.

Another essential component in the suggested pedagogy for our notional learner-writers who are natural speakers of London English is the development of a sense of which vocabulary items are specifically part of London English vocabulary and which are integral to SE dictionary usage. In writing SE the writers need to achieve precision in placing the London English 'mate' as equivalent to SE 'friend', 'geezer' to 'man', 'skint' to 'penniless', 'grass' to 'informer' and so on. Earlier in the chapter we saw how 'blind' some London English speaking writers were to 'we was' as a London English grammatical usage. Similar patterns emerge when such writers consider London English's 'I done it' or 'she ain't got none'. Once again, the contention here is that it is of prime importance that there be developed between teachers and learner-writers a consistent, persistent and habitual practice of assisting writers to perceive the relationship between the writers' own spoken language and written SE. This on the basis that speaking a variety of language is not the same as knowing about it.

In a society where language use is stratified in the minds of large numbers of people into categories such as 'good–bad' or 'better–worse', the task is to create a practice which convinces learner-writers that there are multiple *de facto* pronunciation patterns, vocabularies and grammars, which in linguistic terms cannot usefully be stratified in this way.

Standard English

SE needs to be treated as a dialect which is not normal except in the context of writing in Britain and elsewhere in the former British empire. The processes by which it came to dominate or squeeze out so many other written varieties of language should be explored. Here a useful starting point could be offered by the section and chapter headings of the book of language teaching materials entitled *Language and Power* (Harris *et al.*, 1990):

Section A: The history of Standard English: the early history of English — English writing from the past — the history of English words — the history of English spelling.

Section B: Language in the World: Languages of the world — language families — alphabets and the beginning of writing — what languages have in common — names and naming — language power and identity.

Section C: Caribbean Creole languages: An outline history of the Caribbean — myths and facts about Caribbean Creole languages — the creation of Caribbean Creole languages — Creole languages of the world — Creole writing — Caribbean Creole language in Britain.

These materials, identified as an 'encouraging development' in critical language awareness (Bhatt & Martin-Jones, 1992: 290), were produced over a period of five years by the Afro-Caribbean Language and Literacy Project working in more than 20 further education colleges and adult education institute adult literacy schemes across inner London. As such they were the result of extensive discussions by lecturers and tutors in conferences and smaller working groups, and were based on a detailed analysis of some of the language issues which puzzled and undermined the confidence of the students they taught in classrooms on a daily basis. The Project itself had been given the task of improving the written SE performance of students of Caribbean descent. It came to understand that this could not be achieved without helping the students to understand why Caribbean Creole languages have historically had low status and SE high status, and the extent to which these relative positions of power have a political, military, economic and social rather than a linguistic basis.

The general position being suggested here is that when the speakers of low status languages approach the task of writing in a high status standardised language, it is essential that they have the opportunity to explore the specific historical development of both languages, as well as the nature of any historical and\or contemporary relationship between them.

Personal language history and current community and personal language use

Personal language history and current community and personal language use needs to be constantly on the agenda for both oral and written discussion and as the conscious backdrop to the writing process itself.

A start was made on this idea, in terms of classroom and curriculum practice, in the publication *My Personal Language History* (Richards, 1988), mentioned earlier. Writing a personal language history was the outcome of a curriculum intervention in a wide variety of multilingual further and adult education classrooms in London, and followed teaching input and oral work concerning the process of language standardisation in favour of SE, and the phenomenon of high status and low status in language. This work with students showed that a large number of writers were ignorant of the issues involved. Perhaps more importantly, a large number of writers were aware of some of the issues but interpreted them in a way that was detrimental to their conception of their own languages or undermined their self-confidence when writing in SE. Significantly, this approach was not developed as a tagged-on special part of the curriculum, but was, in many cases, built in as an integral part of the coursework leading to an external examination qualification.

These proposals are offered as a beginning. All are intended to be integral to the writing process and to classroom practice for young and adult writers, not to be one-off special phenomena. They are aimed at helping to create the conscious, confident, controlled writer in a society in which, as far as languages are concerned, *many are spoken, but few are chosen for writing.*

Acknowledgements

Thanks to the following teachers for their generous assistance in supplying many of the samples of writing used in this chapter: Maggie Fordham, Karen Giles, Pat Harris, Nikki Marriott, Jenny Savory.

References

Assessment of Performance Unit (1988), *Language for Learning*. (London: SEAC and The Central Office of Information, 1991).
Austin-Ward, B. (1988) The written English of FE students. *Journal of Further and Higher Education* 12 (3).
Bain, R., Fitzgerald, B., and Taylor, M. (1992) *Looking into Language*. London: Hodder and Stoughton.
Bell, S. (1993) *If ... Bottoms Out.* Mandarin.
Bhatt, A. and Martin-Jones, M. (1992) Whose resource? minority languages, bilingual learners and language awareness. In N. Fairclough (ed.) *Critical Language Awareness.* Harlow, Essex: Longman.
Burchfield, R. (1986) *The Story of English* prog. 1. BBC TV.
Carter, R. (ed.) (1990) *Knowledge About Language.* London: Hodder and Stoughton.
Cheshire, J., Edwards, V. and Whittle, P. (1993) Non-standard English and dialect levelling. In J. Milroy and L. Milroy (eds) *Real English.* Harlow, Essex: Longman.
Daily Mail 29 June 89.
Daily Mail 23 September 91.
Edwards, V. (1993) The grammar of Southern British English. In J. Milroy and L. Milroy (eds.) *Real English.* Harlow, Essex: Longman.

The Guardian 26 April 91.

The Guardian 13 June 91.

Harris, R., Schwab, I. and Whitman, L (eds) (1990) *Language and Power*. New York: Harcourt Brace Jovanovich.

Hewitt, R (1986) *White Talk Black Talk*. Cambridge: Cambridge University Press.

ILEA (1989) *Catalogue of Languages spoken by Inner London School Pupils*. London: ILEA Research and Statistics.

Marenbon, J. (1987) English our English: The new orthodoxy examined (Centre for Policy Studies) cited in T. Crowley (ed.) *Proper English?* London: Routledge (1991).

Newbolt, H. (1921) *The Teaching of English in England*. London: HMSO.

O'Connor, E. (1978) *Jamaica Child*. London: ILEA English Centre.

People's Autobiography of Hackney Group (1977) *Working Lives Volume Two: Hackney 1945–77*. London: Centerprise.

Perera, K. (1984) *Children's Writing and Reading*. Edinburgh: Blackwell.

— (1990) Grammatical differentiation between speech and writing in children aged 8 to 12. In R. Carter (ed.) *Knowledge about Language*. London: Hodder and Stoughton.

Richards, R. (1988) In R. Harris and F. Savitzky *My Personal Language History*. New Beacon Books.

Richmond, J. (1986) The language of black children and the language debate in schools. In D. Sutcliffe and A. Wong (eds) *The Language of the Black Experience*. Edinburgh: Blackwell.

Roberts, P. (1988) *West Indians and Their Language*. Cambridge: Cambridge University Press.

Sebba, M. (1986) London Jamaican and black London English. In D. Sutcliffe and A. Wong (eds) *The Language of the Black Experience*. Edinburgh: Blackwell.

— (1993) *London Jamaican*. Harlow, Essex: Longman.

Sutcliffe, D. (1982) *British Black English*. Edinburgh: Blackwell.

— (1984) In Trudgill, P (ed.) *Language in the British Isles*. Cambridge: Cambridge University Press.

Trudgill, P. (1975) *Accent, Dialect and the School*. London: Edward Arnold.

— (1990) *The Dialects of England*. Edinburgh: Blackwell.

9 Controlling or Empowering? Writing Through a Scribe in Adult Basic Education

WENDY MOSS

(1)

Navel String

When all my baby born
I collected the navel string
and send it home to Nigeria,
to my mother in law
for them to bury it at home.
It could be buried
next to a coconut tree or orange tree.
After that,
the tree belongs to the child. (Ngusi Thompson)

This writing is from a collection called *Every Birth it Comes Different* written by students at Hackney Reading Centre, in East London; it is a fascinating and moving collection about different experiences and practices of childbirth from all over the world. The group of women writers took two years to compile their book in meetings and in their classes. As they were all learner-readers and writers, they wrote by either by talking on tape, or by dictating to a scribe — a technique used in the teaching of reading called the 'Language Experience Approach'. They then spent a long time discussing their writing. Their pieces are not in Standard English, but the power of the writing is reflected in the comment by a midwife in the group who said:

> … These are stunning, these accounts; they stand alone. Don't make it into a sociological text. Leave it on its own. (Schwab & Stone, undated: 32).

One of the coordinators wrote about the value of the women exploring their different cultural experiences and having these published:

> We found that customs relating to burying the navel cord and placenta which were current in Africa were certainly known and practised by some of the older women in the Caribbean. ... Baby massage, a totally new idea to the white women was discovered to be commonplace among those from Africa, the West Indies and Cyprus.

> None of these things had been thought about much by individuals before. They were just things that they did and so the discovery, that these practices are culturally specific and have a history was interesting and new to all of us ...

> For many women, the process was one of affirmation and validation. Childbirth, which is a central experience in their lives, was seen as a subject for study, for research and for a book. (Schwab & Stone, undated: 32–3)

The language experience approach is commonly used in adult literacy teaching in Britain because it is an effective technique for providing readable and relevant texts for early readers. For some projects, of which Hackney Reading Centre was an example, it is used because it is a way of giving a voice in written form to the experiences, ideas, knowledge and culture of communities whose voice is rarely heard. Even groups who do not have the means to formally publish those texts may produce home-produced collections, typed and photocopied.

The key to language experience writing is that the text is produced as close to the 'writer's' original words as possible. For beginner-readers there are technical advantages to this — the words have special meaning to the writer and the structures reflect her own spoken language. Because these are familiar, she can form expectations about the text and read it fluently and quickly. It will be easier for her to read for meaning, and not simply decode words. This is now well recognised as key to effective reading.[1] The language experience Approach also directly shows the connection between spoken and written language and can produce powerful and original readings at the learners' own language levels.

More significant, perhaps, is the connection between language experience writing and a philosophy of adult literacy teaching which is committed to empowerment. Paulo Freire (1978) expresses this connection cogently: language, culture and identity are inextricably linked; people creating their own texts about their own experiences in their own words allows them to experience themselves as 'authentic' and affirmed in societies where control of writing is limited to the dominant class and culture. This Freire describes as part of 'cultural action for freedom'.

In this chapter I want to explore the *process* of writing through language experience and, in particular, the interaction between the scribe and the writer. In language experience writing, the tutor's role, as the scribe, is to free the learner from the mechanics of writing so she can express experiences, thoughts and ideas otherwise in advance of her reading and writing skills. It is important that the tutor acts as a 'facilitator', not as a 'corrector'. The tutor's aim is to ensure that the writer controls the process of composition and is the true author of the final text. As I will show in this chapter, this role is complex; it seems rare for a tutor to simply silently write down an unedited version of what the learner says. A tutor is likely, furthermore, to have a different educational, and probably class and cultural background to the learner. She must unpack much of her own educational history which has taught her that certain ways of writing are 'wrong' and invalid. She has to learn to listen and go with the learner-writer. At the same time, as a scribe, she does need to share some of her own writing skills in order that the learner has the repertoire she needs to express her meaning for another reader.

I found an example of a tutor whose own language replaced and effectively erased that of the student in *Opening Time*, published by The Gatehouse Project (Frost & Hoy, 1985). One of the authors, William, had been working with a tutor doing language experience writing. He wanted to write about his experience working on his uncle's farm in Jamaica. This is an extract from what he had originally said and wanted written:

(2)
When the pimento come,
he employ people
to help to reap it
and also the cane
and the coffee.
When it ripe you got to pick it
off the trees and pulp it.
You start reap
on Monday
and you finish Friday.
You cut the coffee
Friday evening.
Saturday morning
you go to the river
and you wash it
and spread it out
in the barbecue
and leave it get sun
and dry.

> So you got to have
> more than two hands
> to help to get it
> because sometime,
> coffee always come in rain,
> in the rainy season.

This is what his tutor wrote down:

> People of any age
> and both male and female
> work on the plantations
> in Jamaica.
> The owners of the plantations
> are not large corporations
> but small groups
> of self employed people.

The difference between the tutor's text's and William's is large, and we can only guess what motivated the tutor: a belief in the importance of 'good' standard written English; an idea that the final text needed to be entirely transparent to a British audience; a belief that a tutor's role is to *model* 'good' writing for a learner. There is little sense of the tutor/scribe valuing or recognising the depth of William's experience or his choice of language. William's words were finally published (as he wanted them) in *Just Lately I Realise* published by Gatehouse (1985).

Another example of a tutor/scribe erasing or distorting the author's language comes from a tape I made of a learner (Helen) and an inexperienced volunteer tutor (Jennifer) writing about a royal wedding they had just watched on television. This was the first time they had tried language experience writing; Jennifer had little or no training on how to use this approach or its purposes; very little of the final text was in Helen's original words and throughout the tape Jennifer queries and changes Helen's ideas for writing At this point in the tape they have just been writing about Sarah Ferguson's dress and the bouquet. They are discussing now whether to include the blessing of the rings.

(3)

Jennifer: Well then, now do you want to include there the blessing of the rings.

Helen: Oh yes. And then they blessed the rings and then they got married.

Jennifer: Well yes. How would you say that?

Helen: While they were getting married they blessed the rings.

Jennifer: Yes but how did it affect you, that is really what we want to know ...

Helen: (interrupts) It was very nice.

Jennifer: How did it affect you? Something you hadn't seen before?

Helen: Yes it was something I hadn't seen before.

Jennifer: Ah you were impressed with the blessing of the rings by the archbishop

Helen: That's right.

Jennifer wrote from this sequence: 'I was impressed by the blessing of the ring by the archbishop.' The word 'impressed' was not one that came easily to Helen and she stumbled over it when they read through the final text. When Jennifer later spoke to me about using the language experience approach, she said she felt her job was to 'put into more literary terms the conversational style'. As for Helen, unlike William, she told me she liked the final writing. When I suggested it might not exactly be her choice of words, she said: 'It's alright like Jennifer's doing it.' I can't see, however, how this experience could have helped Helen develop a greater sense of her own power in the world or in the value of her own voice.

These examples are good illustrations of the traditional prejudice against use of 'oral' styles and non-standard language in writing, which remains, as Roxy Harris' chapter argues, a dominant cultural preoccupation in our society. As many contributors to this book argue, however, the range of possibilities offered by these language choices are to be used and valued. I take as a given that the purposes of language experience writing in basic education are grounded in this view, and that the approach is underpinned by sound educational theory. For the remains of this chapter, I will look at the complexity of making it happen, and pick out some of the issues which need acknowledgement if learner-writers are to be genuine authors of their own texts.

One of the most important advantages of using the language experience Approach is that a learner-writer can watch her own spoken words become writing, and make direct connections between the spoken and written word. However, just how straightforward is it to transcribe oral speech verbatim? In 1986, I carried out some research in London and Lancaster to explore some of these issues.[2] I tape recorded four pairs of literacy students and tutors (one of whom was myself working with a student called Carol). I asked each pair to do a longish piece of writing using the language experience Approach. I also asked them to try out different kinds of writing tasks/styles — such as autobiography, description, giving your opinion. I wanted to see if the communicative task involved had an impact on how learners and tutors managed the process. I studied tapes and transcripts of these recordings and that of another tutor and learner which I had been loaned.[3]

Each tutor and student pair[4] went about the process in a different way. For example, Jane and Lee discussed a piece of writing from *Just Lately I Realise* (Gatehouse, 1985) . They talked about whether 'so called experts' always know best. Jane wrote some points down as they talked and tried to simultaneously turn it into a piece of writing, using Lee's words, but without communicating directly about what she was writing. She was not very happy with this when I spoke to her after, and wasn't sure the exercise had been useful. Later I will discuss why I think this was so.

Carol spent some time talking to Wendy (myself) about memories of her childhood. I wrote down notes. Afterwards I went back through the notes reminding Carol what she had said, and I produced a written text with Carol line by line from this second discussion. This approach was similar to that used by Sue and Margaret — they talked about Margaret's memories of everyday life in the 1930s, then Sue suggested they started writing. They had talked about a range of things and they decided to focus on 'Wash Day'. An extract from the tape and the final piece of writing appears in *Conversation with Strangers* (Shrapnel Gardner, 1985)

Jennifer and Helen (who I have already introduced) decided to write about a royal wedding. Helen talked and Jennifer, the tutor, took notes. Jennifer planned to write the piece herself after they finished (she was a relatively inexperienced volunteer tutor). I suggested they write the final piece together — negotiated line by line — which they tried.

Janet, Mary and Terry had a rich and energetic discussion about a television programme on child abuse they had all seen the day before. In a one-to-one session Terry then dictated her piece and Janet wrote, Janet saying very little. Janet read back what she had written afterwards.

Out of all the pairs, then, only Terry and Janet came close to the 'ideal' of language experience writing where the tutor intervenes little and the learner dictates. On all the other tapes, the tutor was fully involved in negotiating the text. When I examined the tapes in detail, I looked at how the finished text matched the oral discussions that they had, and at how the two people interacted as the tutor wrote.

Spoken and Written Language

In the last 10–15 years, linguists have become interested in comparing speech and writing. Wallace Chafe (1982) analyses spoken and written language and argues that many differences between them can be ascribed to the different situations in which they occur — one face to face and one at a distance. When people are in conversation, the speaker tries to involve personally the listener in what they are saying, so speech includes far more use of 'I's' and 'you's', collo-quial expressions, emphatic particles 'oh! wow!', 'you sees', 'you means', 'I thinks' etc. The emphasis in speech is on *involvement*. In writing, on the other hand, the emphasis is on the message or content, and writing has a more *detached* quality because it needs to be readable to someone in a different time and place. Writers have to be more explicit than in speech. I might say to a col-league, 'The meeting's on Tuesday', but write in a circular letter, 'The next staff meeting is on Tuesday 15th March', otherwise readers may not know which Tuesday, or which meeting, I am referring to. The need for writing to be more detached also results in differing language use — for example, avoidance of the 'involving' features of speech mentioned earlier, and more use of third person, latinate words and passives which give texts an 'objective' feel.

This distinction between speech and writing is far from being clear cut, how-ever. Other linguists[5] have more recently argued that while writing tends to be more 'detached' and message-focused, and speech more 'involving', we can choose to be more or less 'detached' or 'involving' in either, according to our purposes. There are a large number of written styles; some are more 'detached' and message-focused than others (compare a formal report and a love letter, for example). Not all are valued equally, though. Robin Lakoff (1982) points out that more *typically* written 'detached' styles are considered more authoritative in Western societies. She also suggests they are often accredited with moral and intellectual values there is no real evidence to support, e.g. respectability, sensi-tivity, clarity, intelligence and complexity of thought. Correspondingly, writing that includes 'oral' features, such as colloquialisms or non-standard language, is often perceived as *threatening* those values (such as the belief that children's comics are 'bad' for children).

However, more 'oral' writing is also more personally 'involving' and linked with closeness, authenticity and spontaneity. Some writers fully exploit these meanings by using non-standard varieties, and drawing on characteristics of everyday speech. This gives their writing a particular emotional and authentic power. In doing so, they can also implicitly challenge social values and the structures that support them. By writing in a non-standard language variety, writers can give a powerful and radical voice to particular communities and cul-tures. Some examples might be Alice Walker's novel *The Color Purple*, the poetry of Linton Kwesi Johnson (the London Jamaican poet) and the poetry of Robert Burns. The effect is powerful and immediate. In much the same way we might argue that William's and Ngusi's writing quoted earlier is moving and powerful exactly because it flouts the standard forms.

This discussion can help to explain why the use of the language experience Approach can be both controversial (because it is more 'oral' and therefore 'bad') and also so successful (because it is 'oral' it is more involving, authentic and reflects cultural voices usually excluded from print). The spoken *versus* written debate can also help us look at why the task of the scribe and learner is a tricky one. Although there may be no *absolute* differences between the two modes in themselves, there are a range of surface ones. Even very 'oral' writing is rarely an exact duplicate of speech, most people taped, then transcribed, find their apparently articulate talk full of disfluencies — stops and starts, fillers, pauses and repetitions. These may hardly be registered by a listener, as they are gone in an instant and all have a function in speech — time to think and respond, for example. However, they do register with a reader, and can make written texts confusing and hard to read. We also do not speak in sentences, but in what Chafe (1982) terms 'idea units', which may or may not have verbal connections between them. These kinds of differences caused Chafe to describe speech as having a 'fragmented' quality, and writing a more 'integrated' one. Writing, for example, will typically be more concise, be in complete sentences, and use main and sub-clauses with a wider range of logical connectors.

What, then, are some of the implications of this discussion for the learner-writer and tutor using the language experience Approach? We might expect a piece of writing written through the language experience approach to need some adjustment because of the fragmentation of speech; the tutor-scribe may want to iron out disfluencies (such as 'erms' and 'umms' and repetitions) and produce a more 'integrated' text, but we might still expect the writing to display 'typically oral' characteristics. These are some examples:

- use of non-standard English varieties; regional and 'colloquial' expressions: these automatically give writing a more personal feel — more standard is linked with more distant;
- use of 'ands' and 'buts' to link sentences rather than more complex links (despite, although, since etc.) or short sentences with no links and no sub-clauses (a device much used by novelists because it gives writing a sense of drama and immediacy);
- use of direct quotes I said '...' so she said '...' rather than indirect ones (e.g. 'She told me she was ill');
- mixture of present and past tense (William Labov (1972) has described how it is typical for oral story-tellers to break into the present tense at the crux of a story);
- repetition of phrases (allowable in speech because repetition is useful to make sure meaning is held in memory — a listener can't go back to look);
- use of 'I' and 'You', tags ('isn't it?', 'doesn't it?' etc.), fillers ('you know'), use of 'I think', 'I agree', use of expletives (oh no!) etc. (these are all typical of language between two people present in the same space,

where the emphasis is on personal involvement and where intonation can be used to full effect. Tags and fillers such as 'isn't it' and 'you know what I mean' give the speaker time to pause, and are also appeals for reassurance that the speaker is understood).

In the next section, I look at how the tutor-scribes in my study transcribed learners' spoken language; at whether they could unpack their expertise as writers enough to carry 'orality' into written form, but also draw on that expertise when required.

Tutors Translating Learners' Speech into Writing.

Apart from Jennifer and Helen whom I mentioned earlier, I found the learner-tutor pairs happy to include 'typically oral' features in their written texts. Here are some examples from other texts with the 'typically oral' features identified:

(5)
I was impressed with *this* book on building because the words were easy and there were diagrams (Lee and Jane) (use of first person, and 'this' instead of 'the').

One day when my *mum* pulled out Keith's trousers and threw them at me and *said*, 'Wear those', *I said* 'I'm not wearing boy's trousers'. *She said*, 'There's nothing else cleaner for you to put on' (Carol and Wendy) (use of 'mum' — colloquial; repetition for effect of 'I said' … 'she said'; use of direct quotes).

I think that child abuse is a terrible thing *and* there should be more places that people can go for help. *And* when the mother or father *takes it out* on the child there should be a punishment for them. *And I think* that small babies should not be hit but they should have more love (Terry and Janet) (repetition of 'and' … 'and' … to link sentences; use of 'I think', colloquial expression 'takes it out on').

Put the soap powder in, *put* the rubbing board in, *put* the *posher* in and posh it round for a *bit*, then we used to rub it on the board. *Oh*, it *were* hard work then (Margaret and Sue) (repetition of 'put', use of imperative, emphatic particle (oh), non-standard grammar ('were' instead of 'was').

Even though, as these examples illustrate, tutors were all happy to reproduce oral features in the written texts, they still didn't write down learners' words verbatim: they selected and edited. It was possible for me to use the tapes to check the circumstances in which they did this.

As expected, much editing seemed to be to concerned with cutting out the natural disfluencies of speech: fillers, tags and repetitions, as in this example from Carol's and my tape:

(6)

Carol:	Well they always knew who was in and who was out, you know. All the neighbours knew which neighbour was in and which neighbour was out and they used to come and knock at me mum's door, come in and have a cup of tea. Chat.
Wendy:	(writes) who was in and who was out. They used to come in a and knock at my mum's door and ermm come in and have a chat?
Carol:	yes
Wendy:	(reads while writing)and come in and have a chat.
Written text:	*All the neighbours knew who was in and who was out. They used to come in and knock at my mum's door and come in and have a chat.*

Here, I ironed out some of the disfluencies and repetitions in Carol's account and produced two complete 'integrated' sentences.

In this next example, the tutor, Sue, reinstated ellipsis (words missed out in speech as they are redundant, but which need reinstating in writing):

(7)

Sue:	What was the first thing you had to do
Margaret:	Oh we'd to light fire to heat water, you see.
Written text:	*First we had to light the fire to heat the water.*

Margaret here did not repeat 'The first thing we had to do was ...' as this was unnecessary. So Sue included the word 'First' when she wrote the text.

Ironing out these kinds of disfluencies seems to be appropriate and necessary for scribes to do. They are characteristics of spoken speech which do not reproduce well in writing. This kind of editing was also often necessary because the scribes were constructing texts across turns (as in Sue and Margaret (7)) so were making text out of interactive conversation. The meaning was constructed between the two people and the tutor was then writing it as one voice. I will discuss later some of the pros and cons of this, but in this situation tutors would have to write both parts of the conversation as one.

I was more ambivalent about situations where, when producing more 'integrated' writing , tutors not only adjusted for disfluency, but omitted phrases, and words and inserted linking words. Consider Extract (8) — on the left is what Lee said; on the right what Jane wrote down:

(8)

	Tape	**Written Text**
Lee:	Be honest, I don't hardly read	The books I read I don't

	because the books … I don't understand …	understand
Lee:	I got some books what I can read.	except a few easy books
Jane:	Like what?	and books I'm interested in.
Lee:	Like just kind of beginning books and the books I'm interested in.	

Lee's talk was fragmented, and Jane created an integrated sentence instead. It is actually, in structure, quite different from Lee's talk. She missed out or rearranged more typically oral features, e.g. she omitted 'be honest', the double negative 'don't hardly read'. She created instead a more typically written clause: 'The books I read I don't understand' (which actually alters Lee's sense). She then inserted 'except' in the text, creating a sub-clause, and could then omit 'I got some books what I can read' altogether. She also inserted 'few' in 'few easy books' (it is unclear why she changed 'beginning' to 'easy'). Under pressure, as she simultaneously tried to encourage Lee to talk and construct a text, she produced a sentence based on his meaning, but drawing considerably on her own writing experience. However, an alternative she could have chosen would have been both closer to Lee's original words and just as comprehensible to another reader: 'Be honest, I hardly read because I don't understand the books. (But) I got some books what I can read, like beginning books and books I'm interested in.'

This is quite a strong example, but all the tutors used their experience as writers to, quite subtly, create more concise, more integrated, 'typically written' sentences. In doing so they often lost or adjusted nuances of meaning, and diverged from learner's original words. We can perhaps argue that the resulting sentences are more fully formed and result in a more concise text that is easier to read; but what cannot be claimed, certainly in Jane and Lee's case, is that the final text is fully the student's work.

Nevertheless, these kinds of changes feel different to those cited at the beginning of the chapter where tutors seriously altered students words and meanings. Even in Jane's and Lee's case, Lee's essential meaning and much of his vocabulary is maintained, with some selection and reorganisation. (Jane might have found it easier to avoid a situation where she felt she had to do so much 'integrating' on her own initiative if she had explicitly checked the wording of the text with Lee as they went along.)

I found one result of the need to produce more integrated, more typically written text surprising. Although most of the final written texts feel 'oral', they contain surprisingly few non-standard features, given that all the learner-writers spoke in non-standard varieties. (Sue's and Margaret's text was an exception to this.) I was interested in analysing why and how this was happening. I suspect that because tutors tended to use their writing skills to produce more integrated texts, we simply (and probably unconsciously) edited out non-standard words and phrases in the process. For example in Extract (6), I changed 'me mum's' to 'my mum's'. In Extract (8), Jane selected out: 'I got some books what I can read.' This seems much more likely to happen when tutors are selecting from lengthy dialogue, and less likely to when a student is actually dictating to a tutor-scribe. But what I found in all the tapes was a kind of 'creeping standardisation'.

A final situation where I felt ambivalent about the tutor's role was where tutors offered a word that they felt more succinctly expressed the learner's meaning. This examples is from Jane's and Lee's tape:

(9)

Lee:	Some I say some people can learn from books but like me I'm better doing it myself kind of
Jane:	and when you say doing it yourself what do you mean? (pause) How can you do something yourself?
Lee:	Well, I can show, you know … When I'm doing something, people can see what I'm doing and they can see what type of person I am kind of
Jane:	Yeah
Lee:	But I ca- … You know, as I say, reading out a book, I can't you know. I'm not an expert reader
Jane:	Mmmm
Lee:	So I can show someone the way I work by showing you know by showing them.
Jane:	Yeah, so you prefer to do things *practically*.
Lee:	Practically, yeah.
Written text:	*Some people can learn from books, but like me, I do it better by myself. I'm not an expert in reading, so I can show people practically.*

Jane clearly has had some trouble following Lee here so she asks him what he means by 'do it better by myself'. She also seems not to follow what Lee means by 'showing someone'. By the end of the sequence though she has understood his meaning so offers the word 'practically' to make the meaning clearer . This is not Lee's word, though.

We can see from these examples that the transcription of a learner's own language in language experience writing is not a straightforward matter. Most of the scribes I researched edited and attempted to produce more integrated texts. There will always be circumstances when this is necessary in using the language experience approach, owing to the 'fragmented' quality of talk. However, I'd suggest that, when editing, tutors should be conscious of interference from their own experience of 'good' writing practice. It is easy, when integrating, to unconsciously edit out non-standard grammar, to 'not hear' text and to introduce words that are not the learner's. It is also easy to include obvious non-standard words or phrases, but unconsciously edit out other structures, such as 'I got some books what I can read'; which are equally part of a learner's language variety. If the purpose is to create a text for a beginner-reader, using our own words can cause particular problems, as these are harder to predict. Thus Helen had difficulty reading Jennifer's word 'impressed' in Extract (3).

A further point to note for transcribers is that, in some cases, learner-writers can say something informally in discussion and then 'formalise' their language when they know it is being written down. For example, this is how Carol first explained to me about clothes to wear on Sunday:

(10)

Carol: Well, my mum and dad — oh I can't remember how old we was — we came home from Sunday school and because you wore your Sunday best she said 'Change clothes.' And she's got out the boys trousers and ... 'I'm not wearing those trousers, they're boys'. She says 'Yes, you are'. I says, 'No I'm not'.

Wendy: Was this to go to Sunday School?

Carol: No after Sunday School. After we been. But like me mum says now, 'Look at you now: unisex.'

Carol then repeated the story for me to write. The parts in italics are the words I actually wrote down:

Carol: Every Sunday we used to go to Sunday School. We always wore our Sunday best. Oh yeah. *During the week and after Sunday school we used to come home and change into* old ... *what we called 'old clothes', One day when my mum pulled out* the boys ... one of them I can't think who it would have been ... *Keith's trousers* ... she threw them at me and said here you are, put these on. I'm not wearing them they're boys. Never forget it. She talks about it now *and she threw them at me and ... said 'Wear those'.*

Wendy: And you said (writes: *I said*)

Carol: *I'm not wearing boys trousers* (laughs) ... it was always like that at that time. When she threw the trousers at me, she said, 'There's nothing else cleaner to put on.' *She said, 'There's nothing else cleaner to put on.'*

In Carol's original oral version, there were many SE London features (such as 'how old we was', 'me mum', 'after we been', 'you wore your Sunday best') and the story was told in strings of clauses without spoken connection. She broke into continuous present tense at the crux of the story ('And she's got out the boys trousers') to mark the drama. When she told the story again for writing, Carol shifted into a more formal, more typically written style. She told the story consistently in the past tense, she referred to 'my mum' instead of 'she'. She added in 'she said' carefully and changed 'me' to 'my'. She also changed her original opening line 'Every Sunday we went to Sunday School' to 'During the week and after Sunday School, we used to come home' — a more complex sentence with a main and sub-clause — and changed her mother's words from 'Here you are, put those on' to 'Wear those'. Overall there are far fewer features of SE London English in the second account.

Carol was not a beginner-reader, and her reading experience may have given her more consciousness of written conventions than a beginner would have had. However, this example illustrates how tutors should not make the mistake of assuming students only use one code in speech. Linguists have noted that in many language communities, people speak more or less formally, and can shift closer and further from a standard variety. Student-writers may have views on which they prefer. Carol, for example, may use 'me mum' frequently when talking, but prefer 'my mum' in the text. I have certainly experienced beginner-readers and writers switching between non-standard and standard grammar in language experience writing.

Sue and Margaret usefully discussed Margaret's preferences when they re-ead their text. They talked about the writing that resulted from the following piece of dialogue:

(11)

Sue: … you can't think of a particular wash day?

Margaret: no well (that/it) depended on weather like.

Sue: All right. That's a good start. (Reads as writes): *It used to depend on* the *weather.*

They discussed whether Sue was right to include 'the' in the written text. They decided that they would because the definite article did appear in Margaret's speech but either as a glottal stop or in the contracted form 't'. The only way this could be reproduced in writing was in the fully spelt form 'the'.

I have raised several issues in transcribing speech to writing, and I don't have any straightforward guidelines to offer on the line between 'acceptable' and 'unacceptable' editing. However, perhaps the best route is for tutors to always err on the side of 'orality'. When learner and writer go over the text once its written they can make editing decisions together. And by showing she is willing to stick to the learner's words as close as possible, the tutor is showing that orality is acceptable in writing.

Given the risk of 'tutor-effect' in language experience writing, one obvious solution might seem to be to use tape-recording and trancribing — avoiding tutors unconsciously 'over-editing' without the learner (or tutor) being aware of it. This is one solution, especially for developing longer pieces of writing and, as Stella Fitzpatrick describes (this volume, pp. 1–22), can sometimes be used in combination with language experience work. However, there are two disadvantages to taping and transcribing in adult basic education classes. First transcribing a tape is enormously time-consuming (roughly 6–8 hours of transcribing for every 1 hour of tape). Second, the experience of reading back a verbatim transcript of speech is a disconcerting experience; and for literacy students can be distressing.[6]

Writer and Scribe in Dialogue

When listening to tutors and learners working together, I was also interested in their verbal interaction and what would motivate the tutor-scribe's contributions to the dialogue. I found that the tutors played a powerful role in the text's development through their oral interventions and I will argue later that there are strong reasons why they took on this role. Their ultimate aim was undoubtedly to support the learner-writers not to bulldoze them. Nevertheless it is worth identifying and critiquing the roles they took.

First, I found several examples, as in this extract from my work with Carol, of two people apparently talking at cross purposes:

(12)

Wendy: **have you got any ideas about where start.think a good place to start**

Carol: no, I haven't erm

Wendy: you started when you spoke saying (reading from notes): *There's ten of us in our family*

Carol: *seven boys and three girls* (reading notes)

Wendy: and **then you said I think I prefer it, to have seven boys**

Carol: *yes, which is what we have got, seven boys.*

Wendy: So we could save that bit till later and then say we've got ten in our family seven boys and three girls.

Carol: mmmm

Wendy: And then perhaps put in your nephews. And then say we used to live in this street. And then you could go back to you know talk about your street, and then **go to I prefer being with**

Carol: *In the family with seven boys.*

Wendy: And **then you could sort of talk about** all your erm all those funny things your mum said, and your trousers and the cricket out on the street and things like that

Carol: *I can pic- I can its all coming back to me — picture of when I was younger, you know. What we call the bomb site like. there where the old houses been pulled down.*

Wendy: Don't stop talking yet — I can't get it all in (writes notes on a separate piece of paper)

Carol: yes, what we called the bomb site (continues on theme of bomb site)

Wendy: Shall we start with … **how about starting with 'There was ten of us in our family**.

Carol: *That's right there were ten of us in our family.*

It seems in this extract that while I was trying to talk about what should go into the text (the parts in bold indicate that this is my purpose), Carol seemed more interested in confirming the accuracy of what I was saying. Leech (1983) describes this as a conflict of conversational goals. If we describe myself and Carol as operating in two different 'discourse fields'. I was in Discourse Field A — talking about the text, and Carol is in Discourse Field B — relating her memories.

The following is an even clearer example:

(13)

Wendy: (Writes) *seven boys and three girls*. we can change this after. Now where to go next. Do you want to speak about your street first.

Carol: er how we lived in New Cross

Wendy: Yeah

Carol: Okay then

Wendy: **We lived at New Cross?**

Carol: **sorry**

Wendy: We lived at New Cross (…)

Carol: in a three bedroomed house.

Why did Carol say 'sorry' in reply to my question? I wanted to know if she'd like me to write 'We lived at New Cross?' . Carol didn't seem to understand me. Her 'sorry' meant 'I don't understand'. On re-listening to the tape, I realised Carol was still operating in Discourse Field B and in that context my question didn't make sense (she and I didn't live at New Cross!). It could only have made sense if we had both shared a common conversational purpose of establishing what should be written down. As a result I wrote 'We lived at New Cross', even though I had no clear agreement from Carol that that was what she wanted to say.

I found it characteristic of all the tapes that tutor-scribe were more consistently operating in Discourse Field A than the learner-writers — that is, far more of our contributions were about eliciting text. Learners often didn't realise this (this was particularly true when writing was starting). I think this may happen in language experience writing because tutor-scribes are engaged in a double task: responding positively and with interest to the content of what learners are saying, *and* eliciting writing. This is quite a difficult conversational exercise for both parties and the purposes of the conversation can easily get confused. This confusion meant, however, that tutors were using the conversation as a warrant for writing without learners realising.

In the tapes, tutor-scribes interventions in Discourse Field A seemed overwhelmingly motivated by the need to shape and develop text. Extract (12) illustrates this, as does this example from Sue's and Margaret's tape:

(14)

Sue:	alright lets do wash day. OK, now then, you tell me what to do and it may be a bit long for us, but we'll have to keep it going. Let's see **if we can start with** ... well, let's make it your old house. You can think of just a particular wash day.
Margaret:	No, well (that/it) depended on the weather like
Sue:	all right, **that's a good start**. It used to depend on the weather. **Let's call it 'Wash Day'**. Try and follow it line by line as I write it and then we'll remember what you've said and we can read on to the next bit. Ok, it used to depend on the weather. Right. **we'd better say why**. Its obvious in a way that if it was wet ... What did you do?
Margaret:	We used to have dry (them) in front (of) fire. Then we'd to put lines up in houses.
Sue:	Right. **We may have to put this later on**. So if it was dry ... **Let's do if it was dry first**.

From Sue's contributions in bold, it can be seen how much she was operating in Discourse Field A and how much her purpose was in organising the text — in this case in a logical sequence that is also explicit for writing.

I found another example in Jennifer's and Helen's tape: (Jennifer has just written: *I thought the dress was very nice especially the train with the embroidery on it — the large 'A'*. This is what they said next.)

(15)

Helen:	and I thought it was very nice how the service was done.
Jennifer:	**You don't want to say anything more about the dress ...?**
Helen:	er
Jennifer:	Did you like the shape of it?
Helen:	I liked the shape of it. It fit her well at the waist.

Jennifer's desire to develop the theme of 'the dress' led her to ignore Helen's contribution about the service.

When I was examining the interventions made by tutors, I found it useful to draw on Discourse Analysis, an area of study in linguistics. This attempts to analyse how conversations are structured, and examines the rules for interpreting interventions. Labov & Fanshel (1977), Candlin & Lucas (1984) and Fuller (1985) have all considered the strategies used in non-directive counselling and therapy. They have been particularly interested in how counsellors use discoursal strategies to direct or structure the talk, but at the same time do so in a way that reduces the power relationship between the two participants. Generally the greater the power distance the more direct the more powerful participant can be, the lesser the power distance the more indirect. For example, teachers and children in school are in an open power relationship both because of the teacher's position and because of the power distance between adults and children. So it is allowable for a teacher to use a direct request such as 'Please, get your book out' or even a direct imperative 'Get your book out'. Where the power relationship is reduced, or where the speaker wants to de-emphasise that relationship, the speaker might phrase the request as a *question*: 'Would you like to get your book out?' (an indirect request). It will be harder for the other person to say 'no' than 'yes', and a reply of 'no' will be taken as significant, even confrontative. But by apparently providing her/him with an option, and phrasing it as a question, the speaker 'mitigates' the controllingness of the request.

In non-directive counselling, counsellors do exercise their power, but by using more indirect discoursal strategies such as indirect requests, simultaneously try to lessen the power distance between them and their clients. I found this work very useful in looking at how the tutor's contributions to the discourse in language experience writing.

Tutors often used discoursal strategies comparable to those used by counsellors . These are some examples of *indirect suggestions* (phrased as questions about learners' preferences) from the tapes:

Jennifer: Would you like to say anything about the Bouquet?
Wendy: Do you want to speak about your street first?

It is easier, conversationally, for the learner to say 'yes' rather than 'no', especially given the imbalance of power in the relationship.

Importantly, tutor-scribes often used a range of such strategies to elicit content when it was not obvious their purpose was to get material for writing. They asked from within Discourse Field A (constructing the text) — we know this because they used the responses for text — but they could just as easily be understood as operating in Discourse Field B (the discussion). And because learners would tend to agree rather than disagree with their indirect suggestions, questions and so on, tutors were subtly controlling text development. The following are some examples:

Asking questions

By asking questions at a particular point, the tutor can influence structure without directly saying 'I think this should go next' as in this example quoted earlier:

(16)

Sue:	Lets get back to this set pot thing. **What was the first thing you had to do?**
Margaret:	Oh we'd to light the fire to heat water, you see.
Sue:	Right
(Written text:	*First we'd to light the fire to heat the water*)

There isn't an overt agreement with Margaret that this should go into the text but Sue uses Margaret's response to her question and writes it down.

Reformulation

Another means of indirectly controlling content is by reformulating a point the learner has made: the tutor restates it in her own words. Candlin *et al.* (1985) have pointed that this will act as a question — 'Is this right?' (the tendency will be to reply positively).

In this example, from Janet's and Terry's tape, Janet offered a reformulation (in bold):

(17)

Janet:	Are you happy that you've made a point and you've said enough?
Terry:	Yes, it sounds just small, but yes, to the point. Yes
Janet:	Mmm … saying what you want to say.
Terry:	That I hate it (laughs). The whole thing you know.
Janet:	**You feel its something that … Its something you feel very strongly about.**
Terry:	Yes I do think its awful.

Janet then suggested (indirectly) that Terry ended with this reformulation:

Janet:	Do you want to put that at the end? **That you feel very strongly about it?**
Terry:	Yes, can do.
Janet:	So how shall I put it (as writes), **I** …
Terry:	I feel erm
Janet:	**very strongly?**

Terry:	Yes strongly about this ... erm ... this ... Is it issue?
Janet:	Issue, yes.
Terry:	Issue. (...)

Reminding the learner-writer of what was said earlier

Another strategy scribes use is that of reminding people of what they have said previously in the discussion. Labov & Fanshel (1977) note that in counselling this is a common strategy and acts as a 'request for confirmation'. The tendency is to agree. It also acts here as a way of influencing content — the confirmation is taken as a warrant for what to write next. The learner-writer may reply positively (That's what I said), but is she agreeing directly that she wants this in the text?

Take the following example

(18)

Wendy:	(looks at notes) **you talked about it being a dead end street in New Cross.**
Carol:	Mmm ... the school at the end of the road. Which we called 'the dead end street'.
Wendy:	Yes, right. (writes) *we called it the dead end street.* That's nice, dead end street.

Sentence completion

Tutor-scribes also used the strategy of offering the first part of a sentence, leaving the learner writer to complete it. The whole sentence would then go into the text. For example:

(19)

Wendy:	You said it was a dead end street **because it had** ...
Carol:	school at the end of the road.

Throughout the tapes then, tutors are using a variety of discoursal strategies which appeal to learners to supply wording appropriate for a 'literate' text. Although the strategies they use act conversationally to reduce the power distance between themselves and their learner-writers (apparently deferring to learners and giving them space in the interaction) tutors are still directing text development — often ambiguously. They are not simply acting as a 'channel' for the learner. How can this be resolved with the goal of language experience writing?

The Role of the Tutor-scribe: Controlling or Empowering?

In listening to the tapes, I was consistently struck by tutors' good intentions to reproduce the learner-writers words on paper. Almost all are a very far cry from the two examples I cited at the beginning of the article where the tutors seemed to understand their role as reproducing the students meaning only within the standard conventions of fluent 'good' written English. Nevertheless tutors were controlling and in the rest of this section I will discuss some of the factors that I believe contributed to this.

First, for the majority of the learners (all except Terry), and for two of the tutors (Jane and Jennifer), this was their first experience of language experience writing. I'd suggest that confusion of discourse fields is more likely to happen when this is a new activity. Sue Gardner helpfully drew attention to this after reading the first draft of this chapter. She remembered how new Margaret was to language experience work when they made their tape. She wrote:[7]

> ... if students become more experienced and adept at using the method, as they can and more able to direct it in ways they want, it doesn't eliminate the duality of action (she is telling a story, or conducting an argument, or trying to identify her thoughts and impressions: I am trying to do justice to all of that as a listener and a scribe ...), but it does enable the student to switch discourse fields as she goes and to join in the process of commentary, shaping and oral editing. My hunch would be that tapes with experienced students would show more Discourse Field A from students as well as scribes. People learn to intermesh the two purposes and not get lost in their primary purpose.

This would coincide with my own experience of scribing for more experienced language experience writers, and is perhaps confirmed by Terry's and Janet's tape. Terry was the only student who had previous experience of writing through a scribe (she had dictated exam answers to a teacher at school) and she quite clearly *dictated* much of her text to Janet. There seems much more commonness of purpose between tutor and learner in their tape.

Secondly, I believe that the particular communicative tasks some learners and tutors were engaged in contributed to the tutors taking a more controlling role, notably expressing an opinion and giving an explanation. Gunther Kress (1982) has looked at how children develop skills in the expository writing used in schools. He argues that early writers must learn different conventions of organisation and structuring for writing because they do it in isolation. He notes, however, that the organisation of *narrative* poses new writers fewer problems as the sequence of the events suggests a sequential linear structure, and the order of clauses and sentences is provided by the order of events in the world; a point that Katharine Perera (1984: 217) also makes:

> In a chronologically ordered text (which can loosely be called narrative) the sequence of events in time structures the material; in a non-chronological

ordered text, the relationships between the parts are not temporal but logical, e.g. comparison, contrast–similarity, whole–part, cause–effect, and so on.

If Kress and Perera are right, we would expect a learner to find narrative easier to structure, and dictate for writing, than writing which is structured non-chronologically. This seemed true of Carol and myself. I suggested she started by describing the context in which she grew up (where she lived as a child and what it was like). How was this information to be organised? Perhaps Carol was unsure. We started slowly with Carol hesitant. After a while, though, Carol began a story (about her brother's trousers) and started to dictate her text with more confidence.

When Margaret started to write about 'Wash Day', Sue suggested that they began with the first thing she had to do. Once that had become the first line of the text, the scene was set for a piece of writing which used the order tasks were carried out as a basis for organisation. However, even though there is a virtual chronological structure here, was Margaret clear that this was the structure? Giving an ordered explanation of how a complex task is performed is difficult, too, without receiving feedback from a listener. A writer has to be clear about sequence, and also continually make judgements about how much knowledge she should assume in the reader. Sue continually gave Margaret that feedback by asking her questions; simultaneously influencing the text's development. This was a useful role, but it meant Sue took a lot of control.

Another difficult transition from speech to writing is expressing a point of view as in Terry's (dictated) piece on 'child abuse' and Lee's on 'whether experts always know best'. The discussion that preceded Terry's writing relied a lot on the empathy of everyone with the horrors of child abuse, having seen the television programme, and points were made, added to or changed as the conversation moved from person to person. The structure was determined by the interplay of talk. Making this into a single developed expression of your own views, orally or in writing, and deciding on the *order* to put those views, is a learned skill. So it is likely a learner-writer 'dictating' will struggle more over structuring writing giving her views than she will over relating a story or an autobiographical experience. Although Terry became quite fluent in dictation once she decided on a theme to develop, she seemed, prior to that, to struggle from line to line, listing points disconnected to each other.

Given the contrast between expressing opinions and giving explanations in conversation and in writing, it is not surprising that learners might hesitate about where to start, how to sequence the text, and that tutors, with their greater experience of these styles, should be making more interventions. What then is the balance between learner-writers' control and valid intervention by the scribe? Obviously, taking the content of what the student is saying and re-wording it is neither helpful to the student's literacy development or empowering. The whole point of language experience writing is that it is in the learner-writer's own words and language. However, we are working with a myth if we pretend that tutor-scribes never intervene or have any influence over the writing which results. One advantage of the strategies I described earlier is that they have a double role: they are a way for the tutor to simultaneously show a warm interest and to help people be more explicit about and develop their ideas. By asking a question, a tutor can both affirm what someone is saying and encourage them to be clearer. The strategies tutors used were controlling but also validating.

To finish, I wouldd like to suggest some issues and guidelines to help us find boundaries between facilitation and disempowering control. I have already suggested earlier that tutors need to exercise care over 'integrating' texts for learners. I now raise some further points:

1. The tapes here suggest that the discussion *of the topic* needs to be clearly identified as discussion *for writing* to enable the learner to realise that this is the main motivation for the discussion. Only if the tutor and learner are both clear about the process of turning writing into text will the balance of control become more equal. Jane tried to hold a discussion and simply write down sentences, without pausing, looking back at the text or talking about this process with Lee. The result was a text quite far removed, I think, from Lee's control. It was edited afterwards, but on listening to the tape it is clear much of the learner-writer's meaning had not been recorded.

2. Tutors used many discoursal devices to encourage learners to talk and develop their ideas, and to elicit text they considered appropriate at a particular point. The strategies they used were 'power reducing' and generally enabling. However, the confusion of discourse fields meant their influence in text development was often disguised. Tutors could make this role clearer, particularly for new language experience writers by saying at the beginning, for example: 'I'll ask you some questions if you get stuck because it may help you work out what you want to say.'

3. If the writing is non-chronological, learner-writers may have particular problems in getting started, with ordering and with ending. It may be helpful to explain why it is difficult, and explicitly *discuss possible ways it could be ordered*. I could have said to Carol, 'Think of your strongest memory and start with that' or 'What's the most important thing you want your reader to know first?'. Sue might have said to Margaret: 'We could write it in the order you did things in the day. That would help us get everything in.'

4. It also seems important, when evaluating the role of the tutor, to consider the *purpose* of language experience writing. If its prime purpose is to produce a readable text for a beginner-reader, there is strong argument, for producing something which is as close to the learner's own words as possible, but also, as

Catherine Wallace (1988) notes, in complete sentences with elisions filled in. There may also be occasions when a tutor-scribe *can* usefully offer her expertise in literate styles to a student and 'model' these, particularly for more formal written styles, such as formal letters and essays. I discussed this recently with a London access student,[8] identifying as dyslexic, and planning to go into higher education. She regularly dictated her essays for friends to type. She was very clear that she did not want her tutor-scribe generally to intervene or to alter what she said, but if she was stuck for wording, she found it helpful if her transcriber could offer her a more 'essay-like' variation. However, she herself would ask for this — she was in control. It is important to note, too, that this writer found it hard not to accept her scribes 'suggestions' as she tended to assume her transcriber 'knew better'. So this 'modelling' role is one to be treated with caution and fully discussed with the writer.

5. It is very important I think to discuss with students, when appropriate, issues of *language awareness* and 'critical' language awareness. David Corson (1993) describes a range of activities on language and power for use in schools, that could be adapted for discussion with adults. In the context of language experience writing, it would be possible to read out two examples (say William's mentioned earlier) and talk to students about why one seems more powerful than the other. Consciousness of the power of oral writing and its effectiveness can help deal with doubts about whether this is 'real' writing. Over time this can be used to talk about whose language is valued in writing and introduce learner-writers to the idea of written conventions. It is also possible to discuss with students some of the skills of speech that are not repeatable in writing — exploring the skills of oral story-telling for example, and about the role of interaction, intonation and gesture that are lost in writing. Learner-writers are often conscious that something written is not as good as something spoken, but they are at a loss to know why. It is not because their oral skills are problematic, but because different skills are used in writing.

6. Finally, I would like to address the question of whether tutors in the tapes should simply have given students more time to think and kept quiet while scribing. This is an important issue relevant to any teaching which tries to give responsibility and self-directedness to learners. Encouraging self-directedness is undoubtedly most important in any form of education, and means tutors knowing when to withdraw and leave the learner in control. However, it surely does not necessarily mean either 'leaving the learner to get on with it' without support when appropriate. Most of us would find this very difficult. These tapes indicate the need for further exploring of how tutors can use a range of discoursal strategies in an 'enabling' role and still leave power and responsibility with the learner.

As far as I know, there are no detailed studies of tutor-learner discourse where the tutor is taking a facilitating role. Nor is, as far as I know, practice in useful and empowering interaction part of teacher training (though it is very much so in the training of counsellors). Looking back at this research after nearly eight years, it feels more than ever that both this research and this practice are important areas for us to explore further. Tutors need to be both self-critical and more confident to be sure that work such as that which I quoted right at the beginning continues and develops in adult literacy education.

Notes

1. See, for example, Catherine Wallace (1988).
2. See Moss (1986).
3. Part of the transcript of their tape, and their final written piece, is in Shrapnel Gardner (1985).
4. Most of the names I use here are fictitious, except for myself (Wendy) and Sue and Margaret (see Shrapnel Gardner (1985)).
5. Tannen, D. (1982, 1985) and Akinnaso (1982).
6. An example of this is described in O'Mahony (1992).
7. Private letter, May 1994.
8. Thanks to Chris Edwards for her comments here.

References

Akinnaso, F.N. (1982) On the differences between written and spoken language. *Language and Speech* 25, 97–125.

Chafe, W.L. (1982) Integration and involvement in speaking, writing and oral literature. In D. Tannen (ed.) *Spoken and Written Language: Exploring Orality and Literacy.* Norwood, NJ: Ablex.

Candlin, C.N. and Lucas, J. (1985) Modes of counselling in Family Planning. *Lancaster Papers in Linguistics.* Department of Linguistics and English Language, University of Lancaster.

Corson D. (1993) *Language, Minority Education and Gender, Linking Social Justice and Power.* Clevedon: Multilingual Matters.

Freire, P. (1978) *Cultural Action for Freedom.* Harmondsworth: Penguin.

Frost, G. and Hoy, C. (1985) *Opening Time: A Resource Pack.* Manchester: Gatehouse.

Fuller, A. (1985) Unpublished dissertation, Dept of Linguistics, Lancaster University.

Gatehouse (1985) *Just Lately I Realise: Writing from West Indian Lives.*

Hackney Reading Centre (1980) *Every Birth it Comes Different.* London: Hackney Reading Centre and Centerprise Publications.

Kress, G. (1982) *Learning to Write.* London: RKP.

Labov, W. (1972) *Language in the Inner City.* University of Pennsylvania Press.

Labov, W. and Fanshel, D. (1977) *Therapeutic Discourses.* Academic Press.

Lakoff, R.T. (1982) Some of my favorite writers are literate: The mingling of oral and literate strategies in written communication. In D. Tannen (ed.) *Spoken and Written Language: Exploring Orality and Literacy.* Norwood, NJ: Ablex.

Moss, W. (1986) From conversation to composition, language experience writing in adult basic education. Unpublished MA dissertation, Department of Linguistics, University of Lancaster.

O'Mahony, C. (1992) The Open Learning in Adult Basic Education Research Project. *RAPAL Bulletin* 18, 15–17.

Perera, K. (1994) *Children's Writing and Reading. Analysing Classroom Language.* Basil Blackwell.

Shrapnel Gardner, S. (1985) *Conversations with Strangers.* ALBSU/*Write First Time* Collective.

Schwab, I. and Stone, J. (undated) *Language, Writing and Publishing.* London: Hackney Reading Centre, City and East London College/ILEA Afro-Caribbean Language and Literacy Unit.

Tannen, D. (1982) The oral/literate continuum in discourse. In D. Tannen (ed.) *Spoken and Written Language: Exploring Orality and Literacy.* Norwoood, NJ: Ablex.

— (1985) Relative focus on involvement in oral and written discourse. In D.R. Olson, N. Torrance and A. Hildyard (eds) *Literacy, Language and Learning.* Cambridge: Cambridge University Press.

Wallace, C. (1988) *Learning to Read in a Multicultural Society. The Social Context of Second Language Literacy.* New York: Prentice Hall.

10 Oral History and Bilingual Publishing

SAV KYRIACOU

If English is not your first and most fluent language, how do you share your life experiences with others, not familiar with yours? Community publishing work in this country has been committed to ensuring that 'ordinary people's' life histories deserve as wide a readership as possible. It has also been committed to ensuring that the author has the choice of being read and understood in a language that feels their own. In this chapter, I will be picking out three main issues faced by community publishers working with ethnic communities whose first language is not English.

Using examples from eight oral history and publishing projects, I will describe some of the solutions we have explored in the work of the Ethnic Communities Oral History Project, for which I have been co-ordinator since 1987. The first languages of participants included Farsi, Greek, Polish and Bengali. The issues I will discuss are those of language choice; translations and transcripts; and the idea of having to be 'representative'.

Background

Probably the most important factor that has affected the work of the Ethnic Communities Oral History Project (ECOHP) has been that the way it was created directly affected the way it was to be managed. Mr Aftab, a member of the Hammersmith and Fulham Asian Association, was watching Alex Haley's *Roots* on television and thought to himself: 'What about *our* roots?' He approached his colleagues in the local Labour Party who agreed that it was important to chronicle the lives of the different ethnic community groups in the borough and put forward an item in their 1986 manifesto.

Labour won the following election and the borough archivist was placed in charge of putting together a report on the best way to achieve this. After several meetings with community leaders, local and oral historians, his report suggested a voluntary organisation, grant aided by the borough and managed by local people would provide the best basis for this kind of work. He recognised that if it was an arm of the local Archives, as was once mooted, it would be more difficult to involve local people as it would not seem to be their own. He felt that the Archives would have their own agenda which might not be that of the local ethnic communities. He also felt a voluntary organisation would be able to raise funds from charitable trusts and regional arts boards that wouldn't be available to the Archives.

An open meeting followed which attracted many people from local ethnic community groups and people from voluntary organisations that worked closely with those communities. They quickly constituted themselves into a group and applied for a grant from the local council. A grant for one salary and a small amount of running costs was secured. The job was advertised and interviews took place.

When starting the job I was torn between finding premises for the Project, money to equip the Project and to do some work. Luckily our grants officer found us the first two and it was now time for our first project.

I felt it was important to get a public profile for the Project as quickly as possible and within a month of starting, the Exploring Living Memory Festival was due to take place at County Hall. I had previously worked in a neighbouring borough and had recorded a few people from Hammersmith and Fulham. I contacted two of these, an African-Caribbean woman and a Polish woman, and asked whether I could use their tapes and some of their photos. They agreed and we put together an exhibition of photographs, text blocks and a short edited tape of their memories. The launch of the festival was a big event with mayors and assorted big-wigs attending. Members of the management committee and the contributors also attended. We even managed to get some local press coverage and it was only at this point that I felt the Project was really born.

From then on, the Project's funding (between 1987 and 1994) came from the London Borough of Hammersmith and Fulham, together with grants for specific projects and the extra costs of translation and community language typesetting raised from bodies like Age Concern and Greater London Arts.

Some of the issues the Project has faced have been common to other work described in this book: in particular, the tension between process and product, the importance of recognising the context of an individual's life story and the role that a group can play in supporting an individual.

Early on I realised that collecting the material was not enough; it needed a public face. By making the material accessible it became alive — it had a use. Collecting the material and putting it into an archive wasn't good enough. That way it would only find those people who were actively looking for it, researchers in the main. The real challenge was to get the material out in the public domain, out into the community. If we were going to use oral history to chronicle the lives of those who did not normally have access to telling their story, then we had to get that story out so people could read it.

When I say the collection of the material is not all important there is a danger that I seem to be denying the social and personal development that can be gained through the process of a reminiscence session or a life-story interview. I do not want to deny the importance of this: but as an organisation, the Ethnic Communities Oral History Project's primary aims were *to collect and make accessible oral history material.* This meant that the process of reminiscing was, for some time, a secondary consideration for us. There was never any doubt, to me, that this process could be of use to the contributor, but our priority was to avoid tokenism: we were always committed, first and foremost, to an education- al role — but the education was to be of the wider society (including their own communities), in their understanding of the experiences of those ethnic commu- nities that make up a vital part of it. Right from the start, the groups I was work- ing with made it clear to me that, for their involvement in the work to be worthwhile to them, they needed the promise of a visible product to be used in this way.

Authors of published social histories commonly quote extracts from inter- views within a structure they have chosen themselves of themes such as 'child- hood', 'emigration' and so on. This is a tempting, and sometimes appropriate solution to the question of how to organise a mass of interview material. However, it felt important for our work not to do this; and for our first publi- cation (ECOHP, 1988), about the experiences of Irish emigration, we made the decision to hold onto single life-stories as whole pieces. We had decided that the best format would be to keep to long pieces of text, i.e. what was basical- ly the transcript without the questions. This allowed the contributors' stories to unfold, in one piece. Rather than split the book up into themes such as Childhood in Ireland, Coming to Britain ... we kept it to Mary's Story and Gerard's Story. This gives a flow to the stories and recognises that they are important in themselves.

When the Project began, the chair of the management committee was an Irish man, a pensioner who was heavily involved with the Irish community and ran an Irish senior citizens group. We had a mutual friend with experience in oral histo- ry who was keen to produce a book of Irish reminiscences. Our chair was able to supply her with introductions to local Irish people who were interested in con- tributing their stories. Anne Lynch undertook the interviews and transcribed the tapes. Anne, Paddy, myself and the contributors edited the stories. Although Anne was keen to concentrate on the emigration process, all the interviews were undertaken as life histories covering childhood, youth, adult working life and so on. This is important as it gives a context to the reminiscences and shows that people's life-stories are important, not just a small part of their experiences which we may find interesting.

Another common theme in this publication is the role which a group can play in giving support to an individual's sense of pain in recalling past experiences.

There was one instance when a member of the Polish Reminiscence Group, which we ran, started to cry when recollecting going to her village square in Poland one morning and seeing some of her Jewish friends hung from gallows. This could have been a very difficult and uncomfortable moment in the reminiscence session. But I believe by having struck up some sort of relationship through the reminiscence group, I and the other members were able to console her. I suspect that if she had not felt supported by the people in the group she would not have said it in the first place. If this is true it has wider consequences to the collection of material. If a person interviews someone they have never met before they cannot get a full picture of their lives. There will be many things they may never get to hear, but I believe that by having some kind of relationship beforehand, you will get a more in-depth interview than you might otherwise. It may only be as little as a pre-meeting of an hour or so to explain why you are undertaking this work, to build up some trust and to get an idea of their experiences to help you decide on the questions you will ask them. Also, by knowing them better and having some knowledge of their experiences, you are less likely to make assumptions about them, which could lead to conflicts during the interview.

I will now look at some of the issues that have needed to be addressed by the Project and to describe how they have been raised and dealt with. I have attempted to place each project description under the most appropriate heading but some do cover more than one issue.

Language Choice

The Polish woman who originally appeared in our first exhibition was keen to help with the collection of Polish reminiscences for the project. She felt a Polish reminiscence group would be best as she didn't feel confident using recording equipment and she recognised that some people's English language skills wouldn't do their stories justice. Hammersmith and Fulham Age Concern were keen to support such a project and offered us a meeting room in their centre for a 12-week programme. This was more than ideal as it had full disabled access and facilities as well as being in the same building as the Polish Centre. The local Age Concern also have a monthly newspaper and they put a notice in it, publicising the first meeting of the group. Other local networks were also used to publicise it.

Previous to my experiences with this group I was determined that we would only record people in their mother-tongue. However, some of the people who met in the group told me that they found the idea insulting, commenting that they 'hadn't been learning English for forty years for nothing'. I, therefore, realised that I needed to change my tune, and instead began speaking of the Project as providing everyone with the *opportunity* to be recorded in their mother-tongue. It was to be their choice. The choice would also be there for their text to be published both in their mother-tongue and in English. The key issue was still the same: that the speaker would be using the language they chose to use, in the knowledge that any printed result would also be readable by the widest possible community.

The first thing the group did was to discuss — in both English and Polish — what the questions in the interviews would be. The experiences of war seemed to be very important for most of them and after the interviews it was clear why. Childhood and youth were other popular topics. It was only when the 12-week programme had finished that we realised — and so did they — that this was only part one. It was as if they felt their lives came in two parts — up to the end of the Second World War and then beyond. Each session worked in two parts. First a general discussion either on a particular theme or about their thoughts for the programme, this is where the questions for interviews were compiled. This would be followed by one member of the group being the subject of a life-story interview. One person would be interviewed by another, in the language of their choice. The other members of the group would act as audience to what really amounted to story-telling.

The group transcribed the Polish interviews and I transcribed the English ones. They then edited their own pieces and each other's and it was time to do the typesetting. All the members of the group said that having the Polish section of the book in Roman script would be fine because it is very common and we could do it on our Amstrad and get it converted into photosetting the same way as we would the English. To me, the Polish script only seemed to differ by a strike through the 'L' and a wobbly bit under the 'A', so I went along with them. We got the typesetting back and we were ready to do the layout. I got the group down to my office, cleared the big table, put out the layout sheets and unrolled the typesetting. They greedily grabbed hold of the rolls of Polish setting and started to read them. A few minutes later one of them started laughing and showed it to another. It was all I could do to stop them rolling around the floor like three-year-olds being tickled. When they eventually calmed down they told me that by not having a strike through one of the 'L's it changed the meaning of one of the sentences. Another member of the group looked at it and said that people would understand it in context. There was a fierce debate and it was decided to put a stroke in by hand. Of course, once this happened there was no stopping them and they were putting wobbly bits under 'A's and all sorts of strange marks all over the typesetting. We eventually laid it out and sent it to the printer. When we received copies of the book (ECOHP, 1988b) someone commented that it looked like there were hundreds of tiny dead flies stuck on the second half of the book. Ever since then I have been publicising the book as 'Can also be used as flypaper!'. The group were happy with the results and we haven't received any adverse comments about it from Polish readers. I suspect this is because Poles are used to seeing far worse quality, and quite often handwritten stuff, although locally things have improved greatly for Polish setting over the past two or three years.

A second experience, which brought my own bi-lingualism into play, reminded me of the complexity of issues raised by the question of language choice. I had my office at this time at the Greek Cypriot Association in Fulham. Thasis, a committee member and stalwart Greek Cypriot, said it was about time we documented the community's experiences (ECOHP, 1990). He interviewed some people in Greek while I held the microphone; the worker at the Association interviewed some others while I again held the microphone, and this time, for a change, I understood what was being said. I then interviewed my uncle who had lived in Fulham since the 1940s. He is actually a Greek and not Cypriot but we felt the contrast would be an interesting one.

I recorded him in Greek which was a bit of a struggle for me, and I think there is probably more of me talking English while he answered in Greek. I was also getting lost a bit while he was talking — it was not easy when all I knew was conversational Cypriot village-Greek and he was talking in the modernised mainland-Greek about the political machinations of the Greek Civil War. For instance, I had never heard the word 'Αλογο' before and I kept on getting lost when he was talking. It turns out to mean 'horse', but the Cypriot dialect (or at least that which my parents use — and which stopped developing in 1945 when they came to England) uses a word for 'horse' that derives from the Ancient Greek word 'Ιππος'. I felt very vulnerable not being able to understand the language very well and had to keep stopping and asking him to explain in broken English and basic Greek. The frustration I felt helped me to realise the problems faced by people from ethnic community groups, who are expected to recount their experiences to English-speaking interviewers. Still, he was very patient with his nephew, but it does raise the issues surrounding mother-tongue recording.

There have been many examples of community publishing having taken place where English-speaking interviewers have recorded people in their second or third language. Caroline Adams, editor and compiler of one such publication, recognised the problem this raises.

> Some readers will certainly feel that it is inappropriate for these stories to
> have been recorded by a white person. I have always felt that a Bangladeshi
> person would have done it better, and was only anxious to catch the stories
> before it was too late. (Adams, 1987: xv)

It is clear that some of the extracts from the interviews are fine and maybe,
like the Polish Group, they preferred to be recorded in English; but others read
awkwardly. My own view is that those people who have struggled with the language are being mis-represented as it is not their true voice that is being heard. If
these people were not given the choice of which language they wanted to be
interviewed in, one must assume that the editor was either unable or unwilling to
pass any of the control over to others. This is a great problem when someone has
the interest and is prepared to put in a great deal of time and energy into a
recording project. But ultimately, I feel, their energies should be channelled into
enabling others to carry out the interviews. There is also the issue of omission,
as those who are unable to speak English are not being recorded.

For this project I also recorded a second-generation Greek Cypriot. This was
something I had wanted to do for a while because I felt that the second genera-
tion was being ignored and yet the part they play in upholding the traditions of
the community can be quite phenomenal. Thasis transcribed the tapes and translated them.

The Greek Cypriot Association said they would put the launch on at a local
library. There were incredible amounts of people, food and drink. Thasis's contacts meant we had advertisements in the book which helped with the printing
costs and a donation of food and drink for the launch. The Association's Greek
school provided the Greek dancers and we had readings in both Greek and
English. This is something I have continually found: when you work with a
community organisation that has been going for a long time they can be very
well organised and will have many people that they can call on to help them.

Translations and Transcripts

Between oral narrative and written text, the transcriber plays an important
role, and their own preferences and style may either be in harmony or at odds
with the interviewee for whom they are working.

As Roxy Harris argues elsewhere in this book, the issue of what constitutes
'proper English' can be critical for adults who are least confident with their own
writing skills. One person with whom we worked was William, a student at
Hammersmith Neighbourhood Literacy Scheme, with whom I had done some
work in the past. One of the workers there said she had a student who would
benefit a great deal from getting their story down using oral history methods.

We recorded William and I transcribed the tape, word for word as usual. William wanted it to read like a written piece (I suppose one of his aims of going to the literacy scheme was to learn to write grammatically). With his tutor they sat together and went over the piece amending and editing. One of the other tutors at the scheme was disappointed with these changes because he had hoped it could be published the way it was spoken — to keep the colour of the language. Ultimately this had to be William's choice and he had not been keen on the original, which he felt had made him appear stupid. When this tutor read the final piece, however, he was mollified because he felt: 'It still *sounded* like William':

> I came on my own, I came on a ship called Begona. The journey was OK. I stopped in Spain for three days, Tenerife for one day. We finished up landing in Southampton after 16 days of travelling. It was OK, your belly was full all the time, you could eat and leave food. (ECOHP, 1989a)

As the last sentence of this extract shows I think, standardising English need not mean losing the colour of the language. The important factor here is keeping the control of the material with the contributor.

A second issue, related to that of transcribing oral narrative, is — in the medium of film — that of subtitling. Simi, a student on a video course, had come to us with an idea and needed help in getting some money together. She was local and wanted to use the reminiscences of Somali sailors to produce a documentary film (ECOHP, 1992). With the help of the local Horn of Africa Group, we were able to put her in touch with some Somali sailors, and we then helped her to raise the funds for the production costs of making the film. We then encountered an unexpected language problem. Simi had recorded the interviews in English. The result, on film, was that some of them proved difficult to understand to the untrained ear. On the other hand, every Somali we showed it to appeared to have no difficulties at all. It was partly the fault of the medium that Simi used that she felt it had to be in English. Her concern was that it needed to be understood by the wider community; she wanted to disseminate the information. Also, although our Project later published a video of her film, this was above all her project for her college course, and our usual policy that a mother-tongue interviewer should be available did not apply. Again this brings up a similar problem which faced Caroline Adams when recording Sylhetti seamen in English, but complicated further by the medium of film. I believe that when asked later, one of the contributors felt he would have preferred to have used his mother-tongue.

One of the people at the Video and AV Unit suggested that Simi put English sub-titles on to get over the problem of what was basically a strong accent, allied to a slightly imperfect sound recording. Simi felt this was insulting and it would make people lazy by encouraging them to read it rather than listen to it. I agreed with her at the time; now, however, although I still agree with her sentiments, I feel we should have sub-titled the whole thing — the lyrics of the songs (which could have been translated), the reminiscences and the narration. This would have helped the hard of hearing and I feel it is something people should be doing on community videos as a matter of course.

Punctuation is the only means we have, in writing, for conveying the pauses and intonations of speech. Not everyone is confident as a transcriber, with enough feel for both speech and writing to use punctuation well. We had an experience which showed me the difference this can make. Stephen Bourne phoned me one day and said he had been given my number by a friend of his in Hammersmith and Fulham's Press Office. He went on to explain that he had recorded his Aunt Esther a few times and that he was editing the tapes into a story (Bourne & Bruce, 1991). He said Esther was 80 years old and had been born in Fulham to a Guyanese father and Scottish mother. This caught my imagination as I expected that a Black woman born in London 80 years ago would have an interesting perspective on growing up in a predominantly white, working-class area of London between the wars. He told me a few anecdotes that she had come out with as well as a basic synopsis of her life-story.

I arranged to meet him in Soho a few days later where he promised me an edited piece and some photographs that I could show my committee. This is an extract from it:

> There weren't many Black people living in Fulham in those days. My dad had only two Black friends who visited him. My godfather, Mr Greenidge, and old Mr Fammi. He was Egyptian. He was a great, tall bloke. All the kids used to talk to him: 'Hi, Mr Fammi!' He must have been about one hundred years old. Nobody knew exactly how old he really was, he was so old. He earned a living by working as a film extra in Paul Robeson's films, like *Sanders of the River* and *King Solomon's Mines*. I don't know when he died. I never saw the goings of him. (Bourne & Bruce, 1991: 6)

I felt the story read beautifully and was funny and charming. I took it to my committee and they jumped at the chance to publish it as it was local, oral history and she had an ethnic community background. I was surprised at how well it read and wondered how much was Stephen putting his own stamp on it. I asked him for copies of the tapes and was relieved when I listened to them as they were almost word for word. I noticed that more than anything it was the punctuation that made it read so easily. Stephen is a writer and I think this helped him in the transcription process.

Mr Aftab from the Asian Association suggested that I make preliminary enquiries into the possibilities of producing an Asian book (ECOHP, 1993). He said that he and his organisation would be happy to help. I contacted two other organisations, only one replied and so I popped down to see the Bangladeshi Association for Culture and Education. I told them about the project and they said it was definitely something they would like to support. I went back to Mr Aftab and asked him what his ideas were. He was quite adamant that it had to be a book that included the whole Indian sub-continent. I was expecting a Pakistani book in Urdu and English or a Bangladeshi book in Bengali and English. A book covering the whole of the Indian sub-continent would have to be produced in about six languages! I didn't want to have the Bangladeshi pieces only available to English and Bengali speakers and so on, because I feel that if people are expected to buy a book they should have everything that is in it available to them.

Anyway, we got on with the recordings. I recorded Mr Aftab in English using questions that he and I, with the help of some others, had devised. He then recorded someone else. His wife recorded some women from a group she ran at the Asian Association. A young woman member of the Association recorded her father and Syed Husain from the Bangladeshi Association recorded two of their members. With all these people involved we were able to, at least, cover the bases — Indians, Pakistanis, Bangladeshis, East African Asians, Muslims, Hindus, Sikhs, men, women and ages spanning 50 years. The volunteers put a great deal of work into transcribing the material and editing it with the contributors. It was then translated into English, put together and this became the book. It was then handed back to the translators to translate the material that did not originate in their mother-tongue into their own language.

We never had the money to pay the going rate for translations so we had to rely on part favours. This meant that some stories were translated faster than others. Some of the translators found it difficult making time for what was a great deal of work. The Panjabi translator was waiting for the Urdu translator to finish his work so he could read it aloud to him, which would allow him to write it down in Panjabi script. Apparently, the oral language is the same. It got to the point where some people were getting frustrated waiting for the book to come out as they had finished their work much earlier. I decided to ask around and people were quite happy to see it come out in two volumes. Volume one would include English, Bengali and Urdu as they were the first completed and volume two, Panjabi, Hindi and Gujerati. This divide makes some sense as volume one covers the Muslim community and as Asian community book shops are often based on a particular religion this would help sales.

Having to be 'Representative'

The third issue I want to explore is that of 'representativeness'. The Project had always recognised that none of the work we did could possibly represent the experiences of a 'whole' ethnic community: oral history by its nature is subjective and therefore cannot be representative. What the Project did do was publish books giving an account from the explicit perspective of an ethnic identity.

I was made to think particularly acutely about this issue when a friend of mine approached me with the idea of an Iranian Project (ECOHP, 1989b). I said I would ask the committee. They said it sounded a good idea and suggested I liaise with the local Iranian Association. I visited the Association, told them what the proposal was and they said they would be happy to help. I went back to my friend and told her the good news. She said she wouldn't work with the Iranian Association. I asked her why and she said she would prefer to work with the London-wide association to which she belongs to. She said that they were more representative and there would be no problem in concentrating on people living in our borough. Basically, I accepted this. Yes it would have been nice to involve the local association in the work but it was clear I was going to lose an excellent and committed volunteer if I did so. I eventually found out that the two association were run by (and served, I think) two different political factions.

This made me think about representation. It is fairly obvious that you cannot represent an ethnic community by having six or seven life-stories in a book. The Irish book had no recent migrants, the Polish book had no Polish-Jews and the Iranian book was to be concerned with one political faction. I realised that none of our work could be representative and we have never really attempted to be. What we have tried to do is provide a publication of life-stories with common themes, that others will read and learn from or find similarities with their own experiences. We are not saying that our Asian book, for instance, gives a full story of why, where and how Asians settled in this country but the following quote from it can tell you a great deal:

> In those days I was living in Shepherds Bush, I left Earls Court in 1966. The reason I moved to that place was because the landlord was a Pakistani and I thought that now I could have more freedom. By that time I was thinking I was going to bring my family as well, so it was better to bring my family to where there were other Pakistani families; in Shepherds Bush there were about five or six families at that time. There were a lot of single Asian people but very few families in London at that time. (ECOHP, 1993)

Through one person's experience we have found out a great deal. This is the point of our work, not to represent everyone but to publish stories that may be typical or untypical, remarkable or unremarkable, but will provide first-hand experiences for people to read and understand the situations that others find themselves in.

All the interviews for the Iranian book were undertaken in Farsi. They were then transcribed and edited by the volunteer and the contributors. Only then was it translated. This saved a lot of work but meant that I couldn't read the material until the project had basically finished, but I was provided with summaries along the way. When I did get to read the material there were a couple of minor things that I felt didn't belong; these were basically opinions that were not based on personal experience. I discussed this with the volunteer and we came to a happy compromise.

My committee looked at the proofs and some people were worried that perhaps some of the material was too forthright and strong. I felt then and still feel now that as a subjective piece, which all oral history is, it cannot be *too* forthright. They did put the blame for their plight squarely on the shoulders of the Muslim fundamentalist revolution and the stories were quite clear about what they had to face (in one case torture) and why they left the country as refugees. Some people on the committee wanted the stories toned down and edited further, while others were totally against this. One rather astute member realised what the problem was and suggested we print a rider in all our books stating that the opinions expressed in the book are those of the contributors and are not necessarily shared by the Project. Everybody was happy with this.

Just before the launch, we received a call on the day from someone from the local Iranian Association saying that he had had an invitation sent to him from someone else, that he was interested in the book but that he wasn't sure if he should come to the launch as he hadn't been invited directly. I said that I would send him a copy of the book and that maybe he shouldn't come to the launch as the people there might not appreciate his presence (I was told by our volunteer not to invite him). Later that day I received a call from someone purporting to be from the British Refugee Council (BRC) saying that it would put its full weight behind discrediting the book and that he was going to inform Hammersmith and Fulham Council that we were refusing to work with one of their funded groups. I told him that we had the full cooperation of many people at BRC and that he must know full well that there is tension between the factions which often leads to situations where they will not work with each other. I told our volunteer of the phone call and she said he was just trying it on. We heard nothing about it again.

Conclusion

I feel the main reasons for the success of the Project has been its willingness to hand over control of the work to the local community. It has been run by a voluntary management committee made up of local people; it has encouraged volunteers from ethnic community groups to take a full and active role in project work and it has given each community the support and resources to complete their own work in their own way.

The bi-lingual nature of the Project is now such an integral part of our work that we no longer consider it as an obstacle we feel we need to surmount; it has become the starting point of all our work. For instance, when we began our Chinese Project (ECOHP, 1994) we knew the book would be published in English and Chinese and the original budgets and funding targets were set accordingly. It is also important to have volunteers who can carry out mother-tongue recording. Our original volunteer for the Chinese project didn't have the language skills to undertake that work but she had great contacts, motivational skills and a good knowledge of funding authorities. She was able to get many people involved who had a range of skills useful to the Chinese project and was able to raise the majority of the money needed.

In community publishing, as I have tried to show, mother-tongue recording and bi-lingual publishing is not only a matter of respect for the people who are giving their life-stories, but an important means of empowerment. For many it is the only opportunity to break down the wall of frustration built by a host community, often unable or unwilling to listen.

References

Adams, C. (1987) *Across Seven Seas and Thirteen Rivers — Life Stories of Pioneer Sylhetti Settlers in Britain*. London: THAP Books.

Bourne, S. and Bruce, E. (1991) *The Sun Shone on Our Side of the Street — Aunt Esther's Story*. London: ECOHP.

Ethnic Communities Oral History Project (1988a) *The Irish in Exile — Stories of Emigration*. London: ECOHP.

— (1988b) *Passport to Exile — The Polish Way to London*. London: ECOHP.

— (1989a) *The Motherland Calls — African-Caribbean Experiences*. London: ECOHP.

— (1989b) *In Exile — Iranian Recollections*. London: ECOHP.

— (1990) *Xeni — Greek Cypriots in London*. London: ECOHP.

— (1992) *The Somali Sailors* (Video). London: ECOHP.

— (1993) *Asian Voices — Life-stories from the Indian Sub-continent*. London: ECOHP.

— (1994) *Such a Long Story! — Chinese Voices in Britain*. London: ECOHP.

11 Improving on the Blank Page

SEAN TAYLOR

Young Poets

Write as you will
In whatever style you like.
Too much blood has run under the bridge
To go on believing one road is right.
In poetry everything is permitted.
With only this condition of course:
You have to improve on the blank page.
Nicanor Parra (1968: 113)

I often use this poem as a starting point when I am working on writing with a group of students. I like the freedom it offers to writers. I like the doubleness suggested by the word 'improve'. And I like the way that the 'condition' is inevitably met by putting pen to paper. Because everything is permitted, everything is an improvement on the blank page.

It reminds me of advice my Dad used to give me about exams: 'It's not that you start with 100 percent and then gradually lose marks for mistakes, you start with no percent and you get marks for what you manage to get down.'

This idea of 'improving on the blank page' is a simple and positive way to think of writing. But having said that it is simple, I think there are concepts at work in it which are thought-provoking.

The idea of 'improvement' has a slipperiness which needs to be addressed by people trying to help others develop confidence as writers. And the notion of a 'blank page' is also complicated. How often do people have a truly 'blank page' in front of them? Most writing follows an instruction or serves a purpose which effectively maps out the page from the start. Even given an empty page without a defined function, how often do writers see it as empty of external conventions and demands? A page may look blank to someone who doesn't have to write on it, but for the one who does, it is scrawled with the invisible ink of expectations.

Jane Mace opens her chapter in this book with a quotation from Frank Smith which points out that writing and speech have different sorts of powers and potentials. I agree with that statement. Writing can be a bit like spoken language dressed up in a bow-tie and dinner jacket. It can go some places, and bring influence to bear in some places where speech cannot.

Nora, who Jane Mace describes re-writing a piece of oral reminiscence, is clearly someone who wanted to 'dress up' her language in its more formal and powerful guise when turning speech into writing.

This seems to be a recurrent issue for reminiscence facilitators and others encouraging people to write, who, while respecting the desire to revise work during transcription, may regret the loss of vitality and immediacy that this results in.

It seems inevitable that people should enjoy using the powers of speech when speaking, and that they should wish to adopt powerful written conventions when transcribing and re-drafting. Those conventions are impressive. They are 'what you are supposed to write'.

I want to suggest though that confident writers (as most reminiscence facilitators and literacy teachers are) see that the living, chaotic and colourful powers of off-the-cuff speech can work on paper. Let's face it — that's poetry!

If you are confident about the different ways in which language is powerful then you use those powers whenever it suits you. You feel unconstrained by the grids and expectations of what you should be writing, and free to write what and how you choose.

For Nora such confidence might mean being able to write about the past in a way that combines the undoubted powers of historical narrative with the undoubted powers of her own voice. For other people it might mean being able to write a job application that is forceful because it combines excellent formal writing skills with evidence of humour and charisma; or being able to take down phone messages for the first time by inventing a special short-hand; or finding pleasure in writing a personal diary after realising it wouldn't be necessary to use full sentences.

If, as Nicanor Parra's poem suggests, a blank page offers writers this chance to 'do everything', then how can that be taught? Does the idea that 'everything' is permitted sit comfortably with the idea of teaching anyhow? And is there actually a value in encouraging developing writers to 'write as they will'?

I want to explore these questions, looking first at the concept of 'improvement', and then at the types of blank page that teachers offer their students. I will be drawing on my experience as a literacy teacher in adult education, and a writing development worker in East London. And I will be writing with reference to three groups of people I have worked with for whom writing is challenging: adults looking to develop confidence around reading and writing, adults who have chosen creative writing as a way to develop their literacy skills and young people in schools given the opportunity to extend their writing skills within creative writing groups.

I am going to argue that improvement as a writer is very much bound up with the power of writing, and that it involves becoming a confident and independent user of that power, as well as a skilled technician.

And I will end by describing my own experience of writing this chapter, and considering what sort of confidence and independence it brought out in me.

Impressive Writing

In *Tristes Tropiques*, Claude Lévi-Strauss (1976: 388) gives an account of the time he spent among the Nambikwara people of Brazil. They had no written language and were very impressed by Lévi-Strauss's ability to write. A chief among them took advantage of this by announcing that since he had met Lévi-Strauss, he himself had learnt to write. He proceeded to demonstrate his skills in front of a large gathering of his people. In fact he had not learnt to write. He was drawing long squiggly lines across the page.

I have heard many different interpretations of what 'improving your writing' means. There is a tradition among educationalists going back to the last century that developing writing skills goes hand in hand with developing a sense of morality and responsibility. As Harvey Graff (1991: 262) says of the 'school builders' of early 19th century Canada: 'Literacy's place was not always as a skill or technology ... It was the best medium for tutelage in values and morality.' And since morals and values were strictly defined as right or wrong, so were writing skills.

Employers, as Roxy Harris pointed out in Chapter 8, have voiced complaints about their employees' literacy abilities within a particular view of 'standards'. Within this view, 'writing improvement' tends to be seen in terms of mechanical tasks: 'Her writing has improved enough for her to fill in her own time sheet.'

Governments and sponsors of literacy work often see improvement as something which puts paid to negatives, rather than something positively liberating. The attitude may be that until people improve their writing, they are a burden and a hindrance to society. Or it may be that 'we simply shouldn't have a problem around literacy here in the Western World'.

And people who are actually studying writing will often say something like: 'If I improve enough I'll be able to send postcards back from holiday like everyone else does.'

I notice in all these definitions of improvement something comparable to the way in which Lévi-Strauss's chief could be said to have improved. I mean the notion of improvement as being able to 'perform' as a writer — to demonstrate the necessary skills, write neatly, sign your name in the right place, spell 'accommodation'.

This is writing led by other people's expectations. Such writing may have a 'meaning' similar to that which the squiggly lines had to Lévi-Strauss's chief. Linguistically and expressively they meant nothing. In terms of reputation they meant a great deal.

Several times a student I have been teaching has used the expression: 'My spelling is not very impressive.'

Excellent spelling is impressive. And for centuries some skilled spellers have deliberately made others feel unimpressive because their spelling was not excellent. But if the need to improve one's writing is seen in terms of needing to become 'impressive' then that is only ever improvement relative to other people's perception. A logical conclusion of learning to spell in order to be impressive is to end up able to spell words without knowing their meaning.

What about seeing improvement in terms of becoming more 'expressive'? That sounds like cutting your own path, instead of running headlong after someone else. The fact that people see writing as something which makes an impression demonstrates just how much it is a medium bound up with power.

My definition of 'improvement' as a writer is rooted in this understanding of writing as a powerful thing. I see 'improvement' as a process whereby learners empower themselves through writing. Not the hollow empowerment afforded by squiggly lines or impressive spelling, but the empowerment of feeling unconstrained by expectations of one's writing. The empowerment of feeling able to 'perform' if needs be, but free to do a whole lot more than that.

Developing new writing skills does not affect anyone in the same way. It is commonly, and naively, believed that learning the technical skills of writing will inevitably improve a person's quality of life: 'It opens new possibilities'; 'puts you in touch with yourself', and 'enriches your life'. Exclamations like these are commonly heard.

As those who learn and teach writing know, the technical skills *change* a person's life. But you can't predict much more than that.

Literacy students rarely come to classes because their want of reading and writing skills has gravely incapacitated them (though this is the popular myth). Most literacy students come because they want to broaden their lives that are already rich with struggle and achievement. 'Improving' can sometimes nullify qualities that were a source of pride. For example, having exceptional oral or memory skills or being highly adept at covering up literacy needs (and proud of it too).

David Barton and Sarah Padmore researched people's writing patterns in Lancaster and found one woman whose writing caused friction in her marriage. They also found someone who felt that 'excessive personal writing' had contributed to a mental breakdown. Another woman, who a few years before developing new writing skills 'was apparently unconcerned by her difficulty', subsequently gave up writing a shopping list 'because she might drop it, and someone might discover it' (Barton & Padmore, 1991: 58).

Similarly, it is pointed out by the National Writing Project that a lot of children go into primary school saying they can write, but 'after a short time many of these will have decided that they cannot write'. They had thought of pages of their own marks as writing, until they were shown 'proper writing' and were taught that it is not something you play with (National Writing Project, 1989: 15).

It may be inevitable that developing a skill involves jumping hurdles and coming up against disillusionment. But these examples of set-backs caused by acquiring writing skills demonstrate that 'improvement' can sometimes be two steps forward and one step back (or even one step forward and two steps back).

The fact is that technical writing skills alone are by no means certain to create a *confident* writer.

Writing For Your Own Reasons

One of the hardest things to develop when learning writing (and one of the clearest signs of improvement as a writer) is the confidence to write for your own reasons. Many students spend months and months writing in response to assignments and exercises, but lack the confidence to initiate a composition of their own, and to write feeling in control of its tone, its direction and its purpose. This difficulty can be attributed to the whole range of obstacles that literacy students are facing up to: finding writing physically tiring; losing the flow of thought because of concentrating on spelling and other technicalities; feeling anxious because once something is written it is there permanently for others to see, etc.

The danger is that until people do write for themselves they will only know these negative associations. Ask children what 'good' writing is, and many will say it has to be long, neat and without too many mistakes. Ask adults the same question and there are plenty who will answer the same.

Writing, when perceived in this way, is an enemy rather than an ally. Its potential is seen much more in terms of its laboriousness and its riskiness than its fruitfulness. And in risky situations people often edit and censor themselves. I think it is this syndrome which accounts for the recurrent question improving writers ask: 'What am I supposed to write?' So how can people encouraging others to write best respond to this question?

As Stella Fitzpatrick, Helen Sunderland and Judy Wallis all point out in this book, they can first of all be a source of confidence and support. This means students must feel teachers are able to give them the help they need around the technicalities of writing. They also need to set students writing tasks that both build their confidence as a 'performer' *and* their confidence in writing for themselves.

Realising that a student is daunted, teachers often respond by taking away much of the risk and responsibility that made it hard to start. They give students pieces of work which they *are* 'supposed to write' in a certain way.

At one level this involves teachers putting words into students' mouths. At another level it involves 'framing' students' work for them. And at another level still, teachers obliquely tell students what to do, leading to what Robert Westall (1979: 11) has called 'pasteurised writing' — students writing what they think the teacher wants. One way or another, this dilutes the students' sense of writing for themselves. It takes us back to our chief's squiggly lines, and the realm of 'impressive spelling'. The function of the writing for the student is to satisfy someone else's challenge. They have missed out on both risks and rewards.

For the kind of improvement I have described to occur, teachers need to be doing more than building and tuning mechanical skills and rehearsing for the formal demands society makes of writers. They also need to help students feel unoppressed by neatness, accuracy, formality, fluency (or creativity for that matter).

I see this process as something no teacher can actually impart. It is in the realm of the emotions, and it is down to the students themselves. But I do see a way to help students towards such confidence in the idea of *the blank page*.

A situation where you are not sure what you are supposed to write because you are not, in fact, 'supposed' to write anything, frees up the writer's sense of what writing is for. It leads irresistibly to risk-taking, experimentation and, yes, mistakes.

The honesty and exploration involved in filling a blank page may ultimately make it less daunting than a piece of 'frame-filling'. 'Squiggly lines' and 'pasteurised writing' may seem easier to execute, but it depends what you mean by easy. That sort of writing often has the feel of a thank you letter written for a present that was not much liked; or of an essay cobbled together in an exam when the question was not understood. It is performing, but not expressing.

On the page gridded by expectations, any mark is a potential error. On the blank page, any mark is a success. And when you're feeling successful, all the inhibiting technicalities of writing that I have listed, suddenly reveal their positive alter-egos. It is physically tiring, yes, but because it is your physical process you have complete control over the pace that you work at and the way your text appears. You lose your flow of thought, yes, but writing is different to speech — one of its powers is the freedom the writer has to hesitate, rethink, revise and change tack. You are concerned that once something is written it is there permanently for others to see, yet that can be used for your own advantage when you *want* a permanent or public record, and you know you can choose when a piece of writing becomes such.

What I am taking about here is not a free-for-all whereby teachers scatter pieces of paper and say 'just write'. Students rightly want to be shown how to do some things and eased into others. I *am* talking about balancing the teacher's intervention and the learner's freedom — so that students develop the agility to move confidently between the many different voices, demands and potentials of writing. And so that they get to know its rewards as well as they know its pitfalls.

Breakthrough to Control

I want to describe three moments when I think that balance was reached — when students of mine in a classroom setting nevertheless knew they had a 'blank page'.

Steven

Steven is a 27-year-old man with learning difficulties. He is a warm man, but quiet with people. He moves slowly and speaks in broken, unfinished sentences. In many ways he is denied control over his life.

Steven was a regular at a group called 'The Chat Show Writers' that I set up a couple of years ago as a weekly writers group for adults with learning difficulties. We met to write and to share writing, and after the first year had enough material to publish a small book called *Cheese and Chips are Related to the Moon* (Willoughby, 1992).

One week in the group we were discussing different feelings, and we came to *boredom*. Everyone started writing about boredom. After a while Steven looked up at me and said: 'How do you spell tointless?' I looked a bit perplexed and asked him did he mean 'pointless'? He was adamant that the word he wanted was 'tointless', and looked at me as though I was a bit daft for being uncomfortable with the word. I spelt it out. He carried on writing. Shortly after, he looked up and asked: 'How do you spell shointless?' Again I looked quizzical. But he was quite sure of the word he wanted. I wrote it down for him. Then he looked up and said 'Fointless'. This time I didn't ask any questions.

The final poem felt like a breakthrough for Steven:

> Boredom is pointless
> Boredom is tointless
> Boredom is shointless
> Boredom is fointless. (Steven Willoughby, 1992)

Given his difficulties around spoken language, and the way his life is, in so many ways, mapped out by other people, it felt like he had found an uncommon freedom in his writing. More than that, he swept right through my hesitant, rule-bound expectations.

And the poem was exciting not just for the control and freedom that Steven found in it, but for the fact that he turned up the next week with another poem written in a similar style:

The city

> The city is my country
> The city is my continent
> The city is my founding
> The city is my abounding
> The city is my housing
> The city is my truth
> The city is my economy
> The city is my community
> The city is my mechanism
> The city is my England
> The city is my subject
> The city is my reforms
> The city is my outcome. (Steven Willoughby, 1992)

I like this poem. Steven wrote it on his own at home, and while it retains the sense of freedom that his boredom poem found, it is adventurous with language in new ways.

From that week on Steven continued to break whatever rules, expectations (and words) he wanted to. But he didn't just do it in one way. He did it where he felt it was appropriate. This dexterity suggests a sense of control. I am pretty sure he feels poetry offers him a blank page.

Val

I met Val on a day workshop that I was leading in Eastbourne one summer. She was part of a group of 12 students with whom I worked on poetry. Some of them were from literacy classes, some were involved in other classes, some were literacy tutors at the Adult Education Institute. I don't think Val was from a literacy class. She may have been a tutor. I don't know.

The theme of the day workshop was 'Unlocking Poetry'. To start with, we all wrote down something that we found daunting about poetry, which when combined, turned out to be a good poem. Then we looked at some poems that challenged our fears and assumptions about poetry: short poems, funny poems, approachable poems expressing strong feeling in simple language. We did a range of different exercises as a group and in pairs.

After lunch we came to what I saw as the main exercise of the day. I had brought with me a bag of about 20 different keys, and I asked everyone to pick one and write about it — imagining what it was the key to. I gave people about half an hour to do this.

There were some interesting ideas: 'the key to knowledge', 'the key to fortune', 'the key to a secret garden', 'the key to my heart'. Of everyone, Val chose one of the most straightforward images. 'It's the key to a drawer', she said.

I remember more about the writing process than the finished work. Val started crying while she was writing her poem. She explained why. She was writing about her husband's death and the new relationship she had started, which was beginning to take away some of the pain. Val carried on writing through her own determination and the support of the group. She then wrote a second poem following on from the first and, though it was difficult to do, read both poems onto a tape with the rest of the group at the end of the day. It gave her a strong sense of achievement.

The page in front of her had not been totally blank in as much as I had offered a theme, but the build up to the exercise had been intended to free students from grids of expectations, pasteurising pressures or formal rules. And it did.

These were her two poems:

Key to the deep drawer

This is the key
to the deep drawer in the chest.
A key rusting, long out of use.
Fallen by the wayside —
could have been lost for good.
I spied it.

Dare I pick it up?
And finally turn the key
and pull open the drawer?
Pull open the drawer?
It's too daring for me.
Slide it open,
slowly, gently, not too far —
to reveal its inner-most secrets.

Gone, lost forever

Gone, lost forever.
No goodbye, only tears.
Pain is the key.
Reach out and beyond it.
Feel again.
Begin again.
Leave death and pain behind.
Begin again.
Live again.

In writing, Val unlocked emotions that she had not unlocked in her life. She left some pain behind. And she did it for herself, without asking: 'What am I supposed to write?'

The group had arrived with apprehension about the technicalities of writing poetry. By the end of the afternoon they realised that far from being rulebound and restrictive, poetry is open to anything. And, thanks to Val, they also had a resonating sense of the deep therapeutic potential of writing.

At the end of that day I asked one man in the group if he had ever written poetry before. His response was: 'Well I realise now that I probably have.'

Thomas Buxton infant school

My third story comes from work I did in the 1992 Autumn Term at Thomas Buxton Infants School in Tower Hamlets. I worked with two groups of eight 6- and 7-year-olds. Their class's theme for the term was 'Toys and Games' and I was asked to encourage some writing around this theme.

So we wrote about rhymes that go with games, about boys' games and girls' games, about cheating, about wet playtime, about magic toys, and so on. Because these children still found writing very laborious we alternated between writing as individuals and writing as a whole group, when I would act as the scribe.

This group writing proved very fruitful, freeing up on the flow of words and enabling a lively exchange of thoughts. I played quite a big role in the final shape of the group poems we wrote. I often felt like a juggler — trying not to lose all the words and phrases tossed about, and doing my best to keep them all in the air while the children decided which they wanted to keep, and which they wanted to ditch.

The poem 'Hopscotch With Words' was written in this way.

Hopscotch with words

We can write a poem full of different words.
Short words like
cat,
dog,
was,
car.

Long words like
helicopter,
butterfly,
shortcut,
caterpillar.

Words beginning with 'Z' like
zebra,
zip,
zoo,
zap.

Silly words like
boing, boing,
goo goo,
teeny weeny,
cuckoo.

Nice words like
Hello.
What's your name?
My name is Roger.
Do you have any sisters and brothers?

Angry words like
Go out!
You are silly!

I will hit!
Shut up you!

Sad words like
No one is my friend.
My Mum hit me.
He cried.
I will miss you so much, goodbye.

We can even make up words like
wohwohwoh,
baba-bula,
balabalabala,
chucka-chuck-chuck.

Because we can play hopscotch with words.
We can play hide-and-seek with words.
We can play on-it with words.
(Maryam, Abu Arif, Shumon, Asma, Shahela and Akik, 1992)

Our starting point was a discussion about what sorts of words you could put into a poem. I said: 'For example do you think you can use very short words in poems?' They said: 'We can write a poem full of different words ...' Then it took off.

I intervened a little, suggesting, I think, the 'Words beginning with Z' bit. But apart from that, each category of words was their own choice and all of the 'different' words were theirs.

We enjoyed it. It was writing but it was playing. We were 'working' but using words like 'wohwohwoh'. The freedom of the poem was the children's own creation. They took an initial thought and ran riot down the page with it.

The poem in many ways exemplifies, for me, the potential of creative writing work in schools. It is liberating, expressive, cheeky, clever and a whole lot of other things that writing is unlikely to be for the children who wrote it. All the signs are that they find most writing restricting, complicated and something of a chore.

'Hopscotch with Words' was not writing as an error-detector or an enduring record of partial failure. It was about doing whatever we wanted, and it was fun. I wonder how often children, or anyone else for that matter, see people writing and finding pleasure in it?

In each of these three example, the end result was dependent on a sort of willfulness and energy in the writers, which tugged the writing emphatically into a shape that was 'right' for them.

That implies, in them, an awakening to the sense that writing is on their side. They felt free to use writing on their own terms.

That is improvement, in my book. It is writing as something that enhances your sense of control. It is making writing a space in which you can organise your thoughts with care, in which you can get things off your chest, in which you can be precise and exact in your choice of words, in which you can make concrete thoughts and information that were unrecorded, in which you can take imaginative risks, in which you can enjoy the music of language, and in which you can share what you have to say.

I don't want to pretend that the sort of work I describing is the cure-all for insecurities around writing.

It does not always work out. Steven from the Chat Show Writers was a regular for a year and then left just when I thought he was finding some real freedom in his writing. I still don't know whether there were external factors, or whether it was that very freedom which made him quit.

Similarly in my reading and writing evening classes, letting people have a go at more expressive forms of writing has sometimes been counter-productive. In one evening class, partly inspired by writing the first draft of this chapter, I decided to take a half-term break from the rather prescriptive work we had been doing on letter writing, and I gave people a chance to try their hand at creative writing.

The next week, after half term, at least five members of the class disappeared — never to return. People always drop out at the first half term of the year; but I did get the feeling that the shock of being given freedom to write in their own style was enough to convince some of 'the disappeared' that the class was not for them.

Writing What You Are Supposed To

That does not deter me. For most people the biggest steps forward as writers are those which signal new control over and freedom in their writing. As an improving writer myself, I know. In fact I would like to offer this chapter as an example. It certainly feels like an improvement on the last academic essay I wrote when I was finishing at university back in 1987.

I wrote the first draft of what you are now reading after having attended a short course on writing development at Goldsmiths' College in 1992. The reason I put pen to paper was quite simple, and quite personal: I wanted to make some sense of thoughts I had had about writing. I did not write this chapter for publication. I did not write it because a teacher asked me to. I did not write to earn money. I did not write it to influence other people.

Although I have not done any academic writing since I left university, I have written constantly, for a whole lot of reasons, and in a great range of styles: journalism, copy-writing for publishers, performance poetry, short stories, writing for children. It was with some delight that I turned my back on academic writing six years ago. I enjoy other forms of writing a lot more. What both pleases me personally and, I feel, reinforces my argument in this chapter, is that I have felt a very liberating control over, and freedom in writing it.

Because I am writing from experience and feeling, rather than formal research, and because I don't want to 'impress' anyone by parroting some kind of traditional academic written style, I have felt able to write as I wish. I have also felt skilled enough as a writer to use a style which is influenced by types of writing I enjoy, and by *my self*.

Quite unlike the last time I write an essay six years ago, I started writing this piece with a sense of having a blank page. And I had confidence in my ability to shape something on that blank page which would be an improvement on blankness, and an improvement in myself. In many ways I approached it with the same attitude that Steven, Val and my group at Thomas Buxton Infants approached their poems. We have written as we choose, rather than as we suppose we are supposed.

The notion of writing 'what you are supposed to' says a lot about the way that writing has power in the first place.

Our very first attempts at shaping letters involve moving a pen in a particular direction and following a pattern that is defined by convention and explained by an expert practitioner. From then on much of the way that we are taught to write involves shaping work according to external conventions.

In conventional 'comprehension' exercises at school we are told to give answers in full sentences based on the words in the question: 'How many fish does a North Sea trawler catch in an hour?' 'A North Sea trawler catches ten thousand fish in an hour.' We are taught to structure essays, to give our stories beginnings, middles and ends, to fill in forms with capital letters with black ballpoint pens, to put the date on the right in a formal letter.

To be adept at this type of writing is to be able to walk out from the dazzling glare of writing as an intimidating power. But to be adept at making your own rules and making your own shapes with writing, and to be able to make something of a blank page — that is to start shining yourself.

References

Barton, D. and Padmore, S. (1991) Roles, networks, and values in everyday writing. In D. Barton and R. Ivanic (eds) *Writing in the Community*. London: Sage.

Graff, H. (1991) *The Legacies of Literacy, Continuities and Contradictions in Western Culture and Society.* Bloomington, IN: Indiana University.

Lévi-Strauss, C. (1976) *Tristes Tropiques.* Harmondsworth: Penguin.

Maryam, Abu Arif, Shumon, Asma, Shahela and Akik (1992) *Cockadoodledoo.* London: Eastside Books.

National Writing Project (1989) *Becoming a Writer.* Thomas Nelson.

Parra, N. (1968) *Poems and Antipoems.* London: Jonathan Cape.

Westall, R. (1979) The author in the classroom. *The Use of English* 31 (1).

Willoughby, S. (1992) *Cheese and Chips are Related to the Moon.* London: Eastside Books.

Index

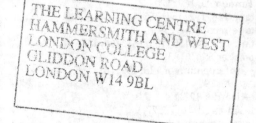